Introducing
Culture

Introducing Culture

Fourth Edition

Ernest L. Schusky
Southern Illinois University, Edwardsville

T. Patrick Culbert
University of Arizona, Tucson

PRENTICE-HALL, INC.
Englewood Cliffs, New Jersey   07632

Library of Congress Cataloging-in-Publication Data

Schusky, Ernest Lester (date)
   Introducing culture.

   Includes index.
      1. Anthropology.   I. Culbert, T. Patrick.   II. Title.
GN25.S35   1987   306   86-21251
ISBN 0-13-477449-3

Editorial/production supervision and
   interior design: Laura Cleveland
Cover design: Diane Saxe
Manufacturing buyer: Harry P. Baisley

Printed in the United States of America

10   9   8   7   6   5   4   3   2   1

ISBN   0-13-477449-3   01

Prentice-Hall International (UK) Limited, *London*
Prentice-Hall of Australia Pty. Limited, *Sydney*
Prentice-Hall Canada Inc., *Toronto*
Prentice-Hall Hispanoamericana, S.A., *Mexico*
Prentice-Hall of India Private Limited, *New Delhi*
Prentice-Hall of Japan, Inc., *Tokyo*
Prentice-Hall of Southeast Asia Pte. Ltd., *Singapore*
Editora Prentice-Hall do Brasil, Ltda., *Rio de Janeiro*

Contents

Note to Instructors

We have experienced major changes in teaching anthropology during our life-times. When we were undergraduate students in the 1950s, Kroeber's *Anthropology* was the commonly used text. It was not designed to attract any more than a handful of students destined for graduate school. By 1960, however, the discipline gained widespread fame and students overflowed introductory sections of anthropology. Introductory texts were issued by every major publisher; yet, most of them kept to the Kroeber tradition of attempting to publish everything that was known in anthro-pology. We aimed at a different goal in 1967 when the first edition of this work was published. We felt that a solid text was one that contained only the basics, and instructors would elaborate on basic principles according to their own experience and interest.

By the late 1970s, enrollments in the liberal arts had declined and anthropol-ogy faced far fewer students. We are convinced that a short, basic text is even more important now. So we address the student, striving to avoid professional jargon, limiting discussion to the essential elements, and still rely on the skill of instructors to make anthropology come alive. Instructors are free to elaborate and add details in whatever ways best meet their own preparation.

We believe the text has met a wide variety of needs since it has been adopted by instructors in junior colleges as well as in the most prestigious universities. It has also been translated into Korean and Japanese as further evidence of its providing the basics to a most varied student population. This was certainly our goal in writng *Introducing Culture*—to initiate students everywhere into the mysteries of anthro-pology. But, as in any rite of passage, it is the living, human guide who must im-press upon the initiates the importance of the basics and how to make use of them. Thus, we dedicate this book to the instructors of anthropology who pass along our culture from one generation to the next.

Introduction

A tiny, sparsely furred creature throws down a nearly shapeless stone chopper, shoulders a haunch of young gazelle, and stands upright in the warmth of an African sunset more than two million years ago. It is late and he is tired, and for a moment he has lost the edge of his customary caution; he does not see the crouching lioness attracted by the cries of the gazelle and the smell of blood. Later, the spring floods tumble the hunter's bones into a deep pool, where they are covered by accumulating sediments.

In the soft night of the Guatemalan jungle in the late ninth century A.D., an aged priest watches the eclipse that his crumbling books had told him would come. He no longer fears, for no evil is left for the once dreaded event to bring. His people have already been reduced to a bickering handful who care no longer for the temples and ceremonies of his youth and have long since ceased to listen to his warnings about the disfavor of the gods.

In the slums of Los Angeles, an American Indian packs his meager belongings by the light of a bare electric bulb and hurries to the bus that will return him to the reservation. There the company of relatives and friends and the brightness of the endless high plains may one day cure him of the illness and injury of the city.

These events are the facts of anthropology. Only an anthropologist would be foolhardy enough to try to weave them together into some coherent fabric that might have meaning for us and tell us something about the human condition as it has been, is, and will be. Space and time are anthropological playgrounds. They contain more than three million years of human and prehuman behavior and have only the ends of the earth as their spatial limit.

The gallery of anthropologists in popular literature contains some very strange characters: Indiana Jones pursues archaeological treasures like a demented Boy Scout; the physical anthropologist fondles skulls like Hamlet's gravedigger; the young cultural anthropologist tracks the Lost Tribe, which, when it is discovered, proves to have a language of only six words and customs that would shock a fan of X-rated movies. Dripping with romance and more than a little mad, these anthropological stereotypes reflect the idea that anthropology deals with the far off and exotic—the stuff of nightmares and bad late-night movies. Even with some basis in fact, this garbled message misses the very important point that anthropology also deals with urban blacks, middle-class suburbanites, and the wino culture of flophouses and dark alleyways. Anthropology is about people and what they do and think.

But wait. Anthropology is not the only discipline that deals with people; half the subjects in a college catalogue are concerned in some way with human beings and behavior. What makes anthropology different?

One difference is the foolhardy breadth of topics that anthropologists will tackle. A sociologist who was asked to account for the societal organization of a band of mammoth hunters from Europe of 200,000 B.C. would be horrified, and a marketing specialist who was asked how the use of native stone money on the island of Yap might affect buying habits in a new Sears outlet would scratch his head in puzzlement.

With this relentlessly eclectic bent, anthropology seeks understanding by comparing one culture with another. It strives to learn how cultures separated in time and space differ, but at the same time it must be alert to the common threads that unite them and make them similar. Nobody needs to be told that people differ in what they do and in the things they value. *Yuppies* and *good ole' boys* are terms from our own culture that conjure up stereotyped images that are far from accurate. But they have their origin in variations of life styles and value systems that are definable and real. To pretend that such differences do not exist gets us nowhere, for successful social interaction must be based on an understanding of reality. As we move to interaction on a worldwide scale, the cultural differences become greater and the problems of interaction more intense. Third World nations, OPEC oil chiefs, and the CIA are parts of different cultural systems and do not share the same views of how the world should be. Yet such things as food and energy supplies are parts of global systems that demand interaction among different cultural groups. Anthropological knowledge is certainly not the only kind of knowledge necessary to appreciate the problems of the world today, but it is a kind of knowledge that we avoid at our own peril.

If understanding cultural differences can be useful, research into culturally similar situations is also enlightening. Having more people than food, for example, is a recurring problem that has affected our species many times throughout its history. We now face desperate food shortages in several parts of Africa; within the next century or two there is a good chance that there will be a worldwide food crisis. It would be naive to suggest that knowing about earlier food shortages would by itself provide the answers. We have never been at this point before; we have never had such a range of technological resources for producing and distributing food; but we have never faced the possibility of shortage on a global scale. Nevertheless, to conclude that we have nothing to gain from knowing about earlier food crises would be equally naive. At the least, we might hope to avoid some of the more outlandish mistakes of the past. "Let them eat cake," was not a good answer.

Another example. Social problems occur throughout the modern world when rural populations pour into urban areas, where many of them find squalor and misery instead of the bright lights, city pleasures, and easy money they expected. Cities have existed for more than 5,000 years, and they seem always to have been an irresistible attraction for rural folk, with the accompanying development of slums. If modern urban problems are of concern to us, it seems only sensible to know something about cities themselves, a knowledge that we can gain only by comparing multiple examples through time and space.

Finally, anthropology views cultures as integrated *wholes*. Everything in a culture relates to everything else in an intricate and exceedingly complex manner. Understanding comes not from looking at all of the segments separately but from seeing how things interact. An agricultural system, for example, is most closely connected to the subsistence (food-getting) and economic aspects of a culture. But, for real understanding, one must know about land ownership, which may involve investigating inheritance and family structure; the value system and the attitudes that a culture has toward farming; and perhaps the religious system, which may impose restrictions on crops grown, scheduling, and the techniques used.

Anthropology, then, is broad in scope and comparative, and it studies cultures as wholes. Like almost every discipline in these days of information inflation, it has accumulated such a vast store of facts, methods, and theories that no single anthropologist can hope to know it all in depth. The problem is solved by the division of the field into four specialized subdisciplines.

1. *Physical anthropology*, sometimes called *biological anthropology*, is the study of the development of the human body through the processes of evolution, and of the biological variation that exists among human populations in the world today. Closely allied to the biological sciences and focusing on evolution as its major concept, physical anthropology stands somewhat apart from the other branches of anthropology in that it focuses on both biology and culture.

2. *Archaeology* has traditionally been defined as the study of cultures of the past. Archaeologists use *material culture*—the *things* that people manufactured and used—to reconstruct ancient ways of life and to see how cultures changed and adapted to their environments. Recently, archaeologists have also begun to study the material culture in the world today, even analyzing the garbage of modern American cities. Given this trend, archaeology might be redefined as the analysis of material culture as a key to human behavior.

3. *Anthropological linguistics* is the study of languages, especially unwritten languages. The origin and structure of language and how language relates to other parts of culture are matters of concern to anthropological linguists.

4. *Social (or cultural) anthropology* and *ethnology* study the cultures of people living in the world today. Although anthropologists are known for studying small and remote cultures very different from our own, they are equally interested in the cultures of the great nation-states. Social anthropology differs from ethnology in that the former seeks to develop generalizations about culture, and the latter describes and analyzes the origins and nature of specific cultures and the historical ties between them.

The Concept of Culture

Every discipline has at least one key concept upon which it depends. Society is such a concept for sociology; and personality, for psychology. For anthropology, the essential concept is *culture*. It might seem sensible to expect that such a critical concept at the heart of a discipline would have a very precise definition upon which all practitioners agreed. However, experts tend to become so enchanted with their key concepts that they define them over and over again, each time in a slightly different way, without ever coming to an agreement. As you will see in Chapter 5, different concepts of culture lead researchers into a variety of profitable paths.

We will start here with a very old definition proposed in 1871 by Edward B. Tylor, one of the first anthropologists. Tylor said that "culture is that complex whole which includes knowledge, belief, art, morals, law, custom, and any other capabilities and habits acquired by man as a member of society." Tylor's definition emphasizes that culture is learned, that it is shared with other members of society, and that it makes an interrelated whole. For our purposes, we also need to note that culture is accumulated and diverse and that it constantly changes.

As we come naked and squalling into the world, we do so without culture. But we have a very important capacity to *learn* culture that has been built into our species by the process of evolution, and we have a need for culture for our very survival. The process of *enculturation*, being taught a culture, begins instantly. The way a newborn baby is held and washed is a part of the infant's culture, and even these first simple experiences in the world outside the womb have their effect on development. After this, the impact of culture upon us never ceases until we lose consciousness for the final time. The agencies that teach us culture are legion. Parents and family are obviously critical in the earliest years of life, but playmates, friends and enemies, and, for the societies of today, schools, books, and television, all play important roles. *Which* culture is acquired is part of the lottery of circumstances, and there is no inborn predisposition to any one variety of culture. A United States infant transferred at the moment of birth to a Chinese family would learn the sayings of Chairman Mao as well as any Chinese child; the child would have no greater ability to acquire the elements of American culture than would any person who was born in China, were he or she to return here at some later date.

In addition to being learned, culture is *shared*. However much we may prize our individuality, most of the things that we do are patterned after the actions of the groups of which we are members. The number of groups that each of us participates in is large, and the groups are of very different sizes. Consider a teenage street-corner gang. It is possible to speak of the culture of one particular gang (much as one might speak of the culture of people on a tiny Pacific atoll) because each gang has a few customs that are its own and different from those of surrounding and competing gangs. There are other features that are common to all street-corner gangs, so there is a larger cultural system of street-corner gangs, in general. Finally, members of such gangs in the United States, however vigorously they may reject the establishment, are still Americans and share with their compatriots a far greater percentage of American culture than they ever manage to reject. The Super Bowl, the disposable can, and McDonald's are our heritage. We may not be directly involved with all of them, but they cry America to the corners of the world.

Third, culture is a *whole* or system, the parts of which are interrelated in complex and often surprising ways. Take, as an example, that particularly American obsession, the automobile. It is a machine designed to carry us from one place to another with greater speed than the horse and buggy. Is that all that automobiles are? Of course not. Automobiles are status. A mammoth luxury car, a sports car that can do 150 (if there were a place to do it), a low rider than can jump two feet straight up—these give messages about their owners. Automobiles are part of the dating-mating game. Acquiring a car can change an American's sex life: acquiring the right car, the ads hint, can change it beyond one's wildest dreams. Automobiles are also part of American values of freedom and independence. In many large American cities, public transportation is cheaper, quicker and safer. But in a bus you're not—free. Automobiles are America. We aren't going to give them up very fast.

Fourth, culture is *cumulative*. Knowledge is stored and passed on from one generation to the next, with new knowledge being added more rapidly than old knowledge is being lost. The storage place of culture has changed and expanded over time. Before the invention of writing, culture was stored completely within human minds. With writing, and particularly with the invention of the printing press, some culture could be stored in books and documents where, even if no single person remembered it, it was still available. With the computer revolution, increasingly greater amounts of knowledge are being stored in machines, which can even be instructed to sort out particular kinds of information and print it for our edification. We must not, however, let our minds drift too far toward the science fiction world in which the Great Computer—untouched by human hands for generations—has taken over the world and does everything from choosing our clothes in the morning to summoning deviants for reprogramming. Remember that a vast amount of basic knowledge is still stored almost entirely within human brains. No book can teach a child to walk or speak, nor can any written instructions tell how to interact with playmates. As in the days of Stone Age hunters and gatherers, the crucial first steps in acquiring culture still take place by the age-old formula of personal interaction within basic social groups.

Fifth, culture is *diverse*. Humans solve the basic problems of life by cultural means, but there is never just one solution. Instead, we find many solutions in various cultures. Furthermore, culture elaborates far beyond fulfilling needs to create the wondrous tapestry of cultural variety around the world.

Consider, for example, the cultural complex surrounding food. Biological need dictates only that we eat a sufficient amount of appropriately nutritious food. Certainly, culture helps us to get this job done in ways ranging from the tools and cooperative patterns of primitive hunters to the vast agricultural enterprises of modern America. Yet, the food production-consumption complex goes far beyond the simple process of filling stomachs. Culture defines what foods are considered palatable in ways that bear little relation to nutritional value. Many kinds of grubs and worms are considerably more nutritious than junk foods; but nobody in our culture would consider stopping at a wormy, rotten log for an after-school snack. There is also a complex series of rules about how to get food into the mouth. Fingers are fine for fried chicken in most American eating contexts, but not for meatballs. Children may eat sugar-coated cereals with great enjoyment, but an adult will often apologize with a humorous remark if he or she wants to eat them. The point is probably clear by now that culture does not stop at the simple point of fulfilling biological needs.

A final important property is that culture is *constantly changing*. We are particularly aware of this property because the modern world has undergone a period of unusually rapid change. Much of the change in twentieth-century America has been the result of an escalating technology that has brought us beyond the wildest imagining of past generations. A college audience of the 1940s would have doubted the suggestion that a man would walk on the moon in their lifetimes. They would have jeered the idea that not only would there be a moonwalk but that average Americans would sit in their living rooms and watch it. But social change has been rapid as well. Any college professor antique enough to remember the 1960s can assure you that students of today think and act differently. Some kinds of change swing back and forth with no obvious direction. Skirts go up and down; beards go in and out of fashion; attitudes toward sex alternate from repressive to tolerant. Other changes are more directional: we will never again return to days of doing laundry by hand or riding in buggies. Some change is the result of local invention within a culture. Other change reaches a culture by the process of *diffusion*, spreading from another culture. Almost everyone has read pieces that trace the roots of "typically American" culture and point out that we eat foods introduced at points all over the world and wear clothes that have their eventual origins on several different continents. Any single culture, then, is an amalgam of factors from an immense number of sources and vastly different ages. And this amalgam is constantly in flux.

We are creatures made *for* culture and *by* culture. We can no more escape culture than we can escape our lungs or our blood, because culture is as much a part of us as our bodies. With the aid of culture, our species has filled and changed the earth. That is what makes us human.

2

The Processes of Evolution

Human beings are animals. We breathe, eat and digest, and reproduce—the same life processes common to all animals. In a biological laboratory, rats, monkeys, and humans seem very much the same.

However, biological understanding is not enough: by itself, it can never tell us what human beings are. Stripped to our physical equipment—the naked human body—we are not an impressive animal. We are tropical creatures, nearly hairless and sensitive to cold. We are not fast and have neither claws nor sharp teeth to defend ourselves. We need a lot of food but have almost no physical equipment to help us get it. In the purely physical sense, our species seems a poor bet for survival.

But we have survived—survived and multiplied and filled the earth. Some day we will have a colony living on the moon, a place with neither air nor water and with temperatures that turn gases into solids. How can we have done all these things? Part of the answer is physical. In spite of its limitations, our physical equipment has some important potentials. We have excellent vision and hands that can manipulate objects with a precision unmatched by any other animal. Most importantly, we have a large brain with an almost infinite number of neural connections.

We have used this physical equipment to create culture, the key to our survival and success. If we live in the Arctic, we supply the warmth our tropical bodies need by clothing, shelter, and artifical heat. If a million people want to live in a desert that supplies natural food for only a few hundred, we find water to grow food and make up deficits by transporting supplies from distant places. Inhabitants of our eventual moon colony will bring their own food and oxygen and then create an artificial earth environment to supply necessities. With culture, we can overcome our natural limitations.

It was not always thus. Our distant ancestors were just animals, faced with the limits of their physical equipment. They had no culture and lacked the physical capacity to use it. This chapter tells the story of how our bodies changed to make culture—and humanness—possible. This is the story of human evolution.

The Idea of Evolution

Charles Darwin was a pioneer on an intellectual frontier. He found the natives hostile. When *On the Origin of Species* was published in 1859, it carefully documented Darwin's idea that species gradually changed to fit their environments. The only mention of humans was the cautious sentence in the conclusion that "light will be thrown on the origin of man and his history." Caution was of no use; nobody missed the message. Darwin was suggesting that we had evolved. Our ancestors had been some horrid kind of lower animal.

The storm broke immediately. Darwin was denounced from pulpits and derided in newspapers; cartoons pictured him as an ape. A few scientists came to his defense, but the public reaction was overwhelmingly negative. The theology of Divine Creation was at issue. Although Darwin wrote of a biological process and left untouched the question of whether a Creator was behind the process, the long, slow changes he implied could not be reconciled with the very literal interpretation of the Book of Genesis accepted by Christians at that time.

The debate has not ceased, but the balance of opinion has swung to Darwin's side. Scientists were not long in accepting the idea of evolution, and the public slowly followed. Eventually, the majority of organized religious groups concluded that the interpretation of a Divine Creator working through the process of evolution was theologically acceptable. The fact, however, that several state legislatures have in recent years passed laws restricting the teaching of evolution shows that the debate is still not settled to everyone's satisfaction.

The Process of Evolution

Darwin's major contribution to the scientific world was the concept of *natural selection*. Any naturalist can observe that most species produce far more offspring than have any hope for survival. It is just as well, for some species, adapting to the fact that only a tiny fraction of their young will reach maturity, reproduce extravagantly. An oyster, who can do nothing but spout its eggs into the water and hope, produces eight billion eggs each year. Imagine the results if half the oyster eggs reached maturity.

If most young do not survive, Darwin reasoned, those that do may have some characteristic that gives them a slight advantage over others. If that characteristic is passed on, it will increase with the passage of time. A butterfly that flutters better will produce more offspring, and better fluttering will become common.

In Darwin's day, the discussion of natural selection focused on survival—who lived and who died. This is important, certainly, for a creature that dies before reproductive age can make no contribution to later generations. But it is not the whole story, for among survivors some may reproduce more than others and have offspring that also survive and reproduce better. Natural selection is actually a biological numbers game. The characteristics favored will be those that permit higher reproduction generation after generation.

In some cases, it is easy to see how natural selection might work. For humans, the ability to use culture, an ability closely linked to intelligence, has been the key to success. Therefore, in the long span of human development, individuals genetically blessed with superior intelligence would have had a better chance to avoid early death, produce more children, and bring a higher number of them to reproduce in their turn. It is easy to imagine the disadvantage that might have faced one of our less gifted ancestors who fumbled dim-wittedly through a pile of tools looking for a weapon while a lion stalked him. A similar disadvantage faced the amorously inept, who were left sad and single while their more clever companions ran off laughing with the only available mates. (Meanwhile, the brightest of the lot had left the day before with two mates.) Inevitably, this continual sorting of the more intelligent from the less intelligent would lead to changes in the brain and to an ever greater ability to benefit from culture.

It is important to remember, however, that traits are advantageous or adaptive in terms of specific environments and not in any sense of abstract goodness. A characteristic that may be highly beneficial in one environment might prove to be a deadly disadvantage if the environment changed. In general, characteristics that are highly specialized for a single limited environment are very dangerous in the long run because they limit possibilities of responding to changes. Consider everybody's fuzzy favorite, the koala bear. Koalas eat almost nothing but eucalyptus leaves and soon perish in sadness if their supply is cut off. In their native Australia there are lots of eucalyptus trees, and few competitors share the koalas' enthusiasm for eating them. But what would happen if the climate changed and the eucalyptus died? Human evolution has taken the opposite approach; most human characteristics are useful in a wide range of environments. Our dependence on culture as a means of survival increases flexibility still more. So far, our generalized approach to adaptation has worked, and it is not just chance that there are more humans than koala bears.

In summary, several factors are necessary for evolutionary change that involves natural selection. There must be variation and differential reproduction so that some individuals produce more surviving offspring than others. In addition, the characteristics that provide a reproductive edge must be inherited.

Darwin was never to discover how inheritance works. That it does work is obvious—the results can be observed by anyone. We expect children to resemble their parents; we know that stock breeders can create cattle with desirable characteristics by carefully selecting animals for breeding; and if a cat gave birth to puppies rather than kittens it would be a national sensation.

But how and why does this happen? Actually, the experiments that made it clear were conducted during Darwin's lifetime. Gregor Mendel, an obscure monk, did research with garden peas in the monastery at Brno, Czechoslovakia, in the 1850s and 1860s. He proved that the characteristics of plants are inherited in mathematically precise ways that can be accounted for if inheritance is controlled by independent particles that are passed on unchanged from parent to descendent generation. His work was brilliant—a masterpiece of scientific logic and controlled experiment. But, when Mendel presented his results in a lecture and then in print, they were greeted by total silence. Nobody had understood; there was not even an opponent to call attention to the research with vociferous criticism.

It was not until 1900, when three researchers independently rediscovered Mendel's paper and recognized the importance of the principles he had spelled out, that the science of genetics had its start. A few years later, the locus of Mendel's particles was demonstrated to be on *chromosomes,* tiny threadlike bodies that occur in every living cell and that can be seen under a microscope when appropriately stained. In all cells except sex cells, chromosomes occur in pairs. In the process of cell division that produces sex cells, only one of each pair of chromosomes goes into each cell. That means that when the egg and sperm come together in fertilization to form the first cell of an embryo, the new cell will have a full set of chromosomes, half from each parent. The number of chromosome pairs differs from one kind of creature to another; in humans, there are 23 pairs (Figure 1). Further scientific detective work revealed that the particles of inheritance, called *genes,* act like segments of the chromosome, rather like beads on a string.

By the 1950s, geneticists had discovered that a chemical substance called deoxyribonucleic acid (DNA) was a critical part of chromosome composition and that DNA had the remarkable ability to produce exact copies of itself. The race to explain the chemical nature of inheritance was under way. In the 1950s, the brilliant insight of F. H. C. Crick and James D. Watson resulted in the famous model of the double helix structure of DNA that solved the mystery. The DNA helix resembles a spiral ladder, with the uprights composed of sugars and phosphates and the rungs composed of four organic bases: adenine, thymine, cytosine, and guanine. For structural reasons, each rung must always consist of a pair of these bases, among which adenine always pairs with thymine, and cytosine always pairs with guanine (Figure 2). DNA replicates by dividing at the hydrogen bands between the base pairs (like a zipper unzipping) and then picking up the complementary base from material within the cell nucleus. Because of the base pairing, there is small chance for error and the finished copies come out exactly like the original. Genes are segments of the DNA molecule, and the genetic instructions they contain are determined by the order of the base pairs within the segment.

The way in which genes contribute to the formation of physical characteristics as we see them or can test for them is very complex. The final result is determined by an interplay of genetic makeup plus environment. Genes provide a starting point—a set of tendencies or potentials that can then be modified by environmental circumstances during development. A few characteristics are determined primarily by the genes alone. Human blood types—the well-known O, A, B, and AB—are an

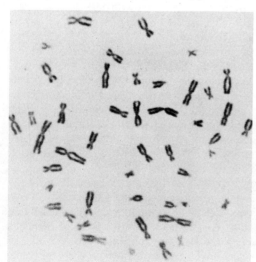

FIGURE 1   Human Chromosomes

With appropriate techniques of staining and high magnification, it is possible to photograph chromosomes within the nucleus of a human cell. (Courtesy of NIH)

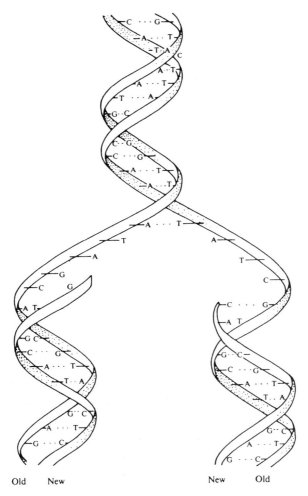

FIGURE 2   Model of DNA

This model shows the helical structure of DNA and demonstrates the process by which a molecule of DNA duplicates itself. (Courtesy of Prentice-Hall, Inc.)

example. The types are controlled by three variants (*alleles*) of a single gene that are inherited exactly the way Mendel's rules predict, and almost no factor in the environment can affect the actions of the genes.

Other characteristics are strongly influenced by environment. Take body form and weight as an example. Some people inherit a genetic tendency to gain weight that must relate to the way their genes affect their biochemistry. But such individuals are not doomed to obesity, for if they work hard enough at it they can maintain normal weight. Similarly, tendencies to suffer from certain diseases are inherited, but coming from a family in which a certain type of cancer is common does not mean that one will get the disease; it only means that statistical chances are higher than average. The relative role of heredity and environment in creating physical features—the nature versus nurture question—is a fascinating and little understood subject with real potential for making significant practical contributions to life and well-being.

The precision of inheritance creates a mystery in understanding evolution. If the genetic prescription for physical characteristics is passed on exactly from generation to generation, where does a totally new characteristic—the kind of characteristic that might enable a fish to live on land—come from?

Any naturalist recognizes that strange things appear in nature—a single plant with heart-shaped leaves in a field of plants with round leaves, a two-headed snake, a human with six fingers and toes. Darwin knew of such things and how important they were, but did not know their origin. "Not in one case out of a hundred can we pretend to assign any reason why this or that part differs, more or less, from the same part in the parents," he remarked.

The answer to such anomalies lies in a process called *mutation*. A mutation is a change in a gene that takes place during the process of cell division. When a mutation occurs, the changed gene operates differently and the physical characteristics it affects will be different. It now seems that mutations are mistakes in the duplication of DNA molecules, probably changes in the order of the nucleotide pairs that are the rungs of the DNA ladder. Once the change has occurred, the mutated form is copied as faithfully as the previous form had been and will continue to appear.

Discovering mutations was like finding a key piece in a jigsaw puzzle that fits several sections together. Mutations explained change. They provided the raw material from which natural selection could create wonderful new creatures. But they also provide the monsters that lurk in the remote parts of starships in science fiction novels. It is a mistake to envision nature as *intentionally* providing mutations for any purpose, either good or evil. Mutations are random chemical events, and their effects can be good, bad, or neutral. Since the bodies of creatures are carefully balanced mechanisms, most mutations probably have unfavorable, often deadly, results. Such unfavorable mutations are usually lost quickly because they kill their possessors or make them less likely to reproduce successfully. Neutral or favorable mutations, on the other hand, may be preserved and passed on to future generations if they appear in sex cells.

The situation is actually much more complex than the preceding paragraph suggests, because most genes do not act alone, but in combination with other genes. A mutation, then, may have little effect in combination with the genes with which it first appears, but be very important when it comes into combination with a different set of genes. Since a very large number of genes are represented in the human species, new combinations of genes that might have startling effects together (either good or bad) occur continually when *recombination* of genes occurs as new individuals are conceived.

The total collection of genes in a species (or in some breeding population of the species) is called the *gene pool*. For a widespread, numerous species such as humans, the gene pool contains a great amount of genetic variety. This genetic variety is important for survival, for if there are changes in the environment in which a species lives, the presence of variety will increase the chances that some individuals may carry genes that will be just what the species needs in its new environment. As a very practical example, it is likely that some humans in the world today are carriers of rare genes that are more resistant to the damaging effects of one or another kind of pollutant than "normal" genes. If pollution levels continue to rise, such genes might offer the possibility for the evolution of a more pollutant-resistant species in the future.

Mutation and natural selection are not quite the whole story. There is another evolutionary process that has nothing to do with natural selection or with a characteristic giving a reproductive advantage. Consider the example of a few survivors of a shipwreck (both males and females) that reach a desert island. Suppose they are never rescued, but live there for hundreds of years, intermarrying and eventually creating a large population. Suppose also that one of the initial shipwreck survivors had a very rare mutation that was neutral—neither better nor worse than other forms of the gene. If the descendants of that individual were numerous and became a large segment of the island's population, the frequency of the rare mutation would be much higher on the island than in populations elsewhere. Why? Not because the mutation was advantageous, but by the *sheer chance* that the individual that had it was a member of a small group cast away on a desert island. If an individual living in a city had the same mutation and the same number of descendants, they would be only a tiny fraction of the city's population and the new gene would still be rare.

This kind of evolutionary change by random chance is called *genetic drift*. It can be important only in small, isolated populations. But, in the past, when there were fewer human beings in the world, it was not uncommon for populations to be small and semi-isolated. The gene pools of such populations must often have come to differ somewhat through evolutionary processes. If the populations had remained separate from each other, as is the case for smaller, less mobile animals, they might eventually have become separate species.

Humans, however, do not stay isolated for long: they move, meet new populations, and interbreed. When this happens, *gene flow,* the movement of genes from one populaton to another, takes place. This alters gene frequencies, allows mutations to spread, and permits new combinations of genes to come together. Gene flow is most obvious when large-scale migrations take place, as when the Mongols descended upon Europe and, among other things, changed the genetic composition of European populations. But gene flow takes place more commonly, and perhaps more importantly, when one or a few individuals move to a neighboring valley and intermarry or interbreed.

We now have the information necessary for a precise definition of evolution. *Evolution is a change in gene frequency in a population over time.* What counts is the genes. A population that—with no change in genes—increases in size over time because it is getting more food *has not* evolved. A population of moths that has more dark individuals because the genes for dark color have become more common *has* evolved. Similarly, a population that undergoes the large number of genetic changes necessary to make a fish into an amphibian has evolved. Relatively small changes like the color of moths are referred to as *microevolution* while the large changes that create whole new species or even larger biological units are called *macroevolution*. Whether microevolution and macroevolution follow exactly the same course is a highly debated question that will be considered in the next section.

New Models of Evolution

This hard-won scientific information can be put together into a logical story of how evolution works. As a species reproduces, mutation adds new bits and pieces; to put it more elegantly, it increases genetic variety. If there are small, isolated populations of the species, genetic drift can occur, increasing variety still further. Natural selection acts upon the variety: a few of the new bits may help their possessors reproduce more and the species will change a little.

While the environment is stable, species become better adapted to their *ecological niches*, their way of living in some particular part of the environment. When the environment changes, species will change. Some species, whose genetic variety includes characteristics that are suited for new niches, will adapt; other species may become extinct.

The process is slow and gradual. Bit by bit, minute changes add up; very slowly what has been one species becomes another. Macroevolution, the major changes to whole new species, is nothing more than the accumulation of the little changes of microevolution. The interweaving of all the processes of evolution into this picture of slow, stately change—called *phyletic gradualism*—was agreed upon by specialists in evolution in the mid-1930s. They were satisfied with it and a period of unusual peace descended upon evolutionary theory.

But peace is no more natural in science than in politics, and mutterings began to disturb the tranquillity in the 1970s. The mutterings challenged the gradualists' conclusion that macroevolution came from adding lots of microevolution together.

Gradualism, the objections went, is quite acceptable as a means of perfecting species that already have a decent adaptation to an ecological niche. The gradual transformation of already adequate anteaters to ones with sharper eyes and more accurate tongues could well be the result of tiny mutations and slow selection. But could more drastic changes—the transformation of a fish to a land-dwelling creature or the change from an ape-like animal that swung by its hands to a human ancestor that walked on two feet—take place as the gradualists claimed? The new theorists doubted it. If a species changed very gradually from one way of life to another, it would become less fit for its old life long before it fitted the new. It would be doomed to spend a long time in a never-never land between two ecological niches, not well suited to either. That is not a good prescription for survival in a competitive world.

Topologists, who specialize in making pictures of very difficult mathematical problems, devised a useful way of looking at the problem. They pictured successful ecological niches as a series of upward-sloping ridges in an "evolutionary landscape." Adaptation consisted of getting to the top of a ridge so that a species already on a ridge and surviving in that particular niche could inch its way slowly upward to a better adaptation.

But to go from one ridge, say one that represented eating insects in the treetops, to another, perhaps eating lizards on the ground, would demand passing through a valley between the two ridges. And the valleys were areas of the evolutionary landscape that did not offer a viable way of life. They were lethal and a species that lingered long in their chilling shadows was doomed to extinction.

The proposed alternative to gradualism was that evolution had followed a pathway of "punctuated equilibria." Long periods of little or no change (equilibria)

during which species were perfected for particular niches were punctuated by periods of very rapid change in which new species or even larger units suddenly burst
forth. Trudging up ridges had alternated with mad dashes through lethal valleys. In
this manner, the transformations would leave creatures in an unacceptable halfway
condition for such short periods that they might survive the experience.

The proponents of punctuated equilibria marshaled the fossil record as evidence. They pointed out that most new species seem to appear very suddenly in a
geological time frame, leaving almost no evidence for the long set of intermediate
forms that one would predict from a gradualist model.

So far so good. But what genetic explanation might account for such rapid
changes? Recent research on the action of genes provided a possible answer. Genes,
it seems, do not all act alike. Some, called *structural genes,* are devoted to everyday
routines making, for example, a single protein with a very limited function within
the body. Mutations of such genes are likely to have relatively small effects. Another kind of genes, *regulator genes,* directs the activity of whole series of structural genes, sending out messages that turn genetic action on or off. A mutation in a
regulator gene might have secondary effects in a whole series of different places
within the body.

In other words, a regulator gene mutation might transform a creature suddenly
and dramatically, exactly the kind of rapid change needed for the new model of
evolution. The result might be what geneticists have sometimes called a "hopeful
monster," a wildly aberrant specimen whose survival depends on having a peculiar
combination of characteristics that fit some newly available way of life.

Genetic drift might be especially important in this kind of rapid evolution, for
major changes would have a greater chance of surviving and becoming common in
small, isolated populations. The idea is not that most drastic changes would succeed
in creating new species. Most hopeful monsters would prove to be hopeless and
would perish. Here and there, however, just the right new characteristics might
come together with the right environment to produce something new and special.

The debate about evolution goes on, but the case for the sudden emergence of
new species is gathering adherents. The result may be a new evolutionary synthesis
that makes room for far less gradual changes than the old. Whatever the final conclusion, evolutionary processes will still be at work. Mutation will still supply new
possibilities and will still be subject to the screen of natural selection.

The Evidence of Evolution

The case for the mechanisms by which evolution works, despite the remaining
arguments, is logical and satisfying. But did evolution really happen? How can we
be sure?

The evidence of evolution is all around us. We can see it in the layers of rock
in the Grand Canyon, in the cages of zoos, and in the halls of hospitals. It flies
through the air at night and swims in the seas. Evolution can be made to happen in
the laboratory and it has been observed and recorded by naturalists within the last
century.

To actually see evolution happen rather than simply infer it from the remains
of long-dead animals, one must turn to creatures that live and die so fast that they

pass through many generations within a human lifetime. Bacteria are like that and in a biological laboratory one can make bacteria evolve.

The recipe is simple. Take a colony of bacteria. Submit it to a dose of antibiotic. Occasionally, the process does not kill quite all of the bacteria. There may be a few survivors that happen to have a stronger resistance than usual to the antibiotic. When the survivors have grown into a new colony, repeat the process with a touch more antibiotic. If the experiment does well, you will, after a few repetitions, have a colony of bacteria resistant to any reasonable dose of the antibiotic used. The resistance will be passed on to future generations of that colony; that is, it is genetic. And you will have created a genetic change over time—evolution, in other words.

This process is not confined to the laboratory. Antibiotic-resistant bacteria also appear in hospitals where they have been known to cause disease outbreaks in nurseries of new-born infants. This is why pharmaceutical laboratories must continually develop new varieties of antibiotics to deal with the new varieties of bacteria that they have stimulated.

This may seem artificial and human-directed—evolution on command, almost. Let us turn to another, somewhat more natural, case—protective coloration in moths. Two hundred years ago, most moths in Europe were light gray. A few dark-colored specimens were curiosities avidly sought by moth collectors. The reason dark moths were so rare is that they stood out very obviously when they rested on the light gray tree trunks (Figure 3) and were as avidly collected by birds as by moth collectors.

Then came the Industrial Revolution and with it factories, smoke stacks, and pollution. Tree trunks were darkened by soot. Light gray moths began to be betrayed by their color and dark ones became harder to see. Within a century, the light-colored moths had become the rare collectors' items while the dark varieties, which also proved to be more resistant to pollution, thrived. There are good statistics to document the change; humans had recorded an instance of evolution.

These are little changes, however, not the impressive macroevolution that sends mammals into the air as bats and brings fish onto land as amphibians. Such major modifications take millions of years and we will never actually see them happen.

For such great leaps in evolution, we must turn to other kinds of evidence and to inference. The variety of animals in the world around us is testimony of the past. It points to relationships among animals that have become very different in habits and outward form. Darwin said it as well as anyone.

> What can be more curious than that the hand of a man, formed for grasping, that of a mole for digging, the leg of the horse, and the wing of the bat, should all be constructed on the same pattern and should include the same bones, in the same relative positions.'' (*On the Origin of Species*, p. 434)

The inference that all these creatures must have had a common ancestor from which they changed in adapting to different ways of life is certainly logical and appealing. For confirmation of the inference, however, one must turn to the fossil record.

Fossils are the preserved remains of ancient animals; mostly teeth and bones, the hard parts of the body. They are rare because the overwhelming majority of

FIGURE 3   Peppered Moths

This photograph makes it easy to appreciate the value of coloration in avoiding detection by predators. The light peppered moths stand out sharply against the dark background while the darker examples of the same species are nearly invisible. (Courtesy of the American Museum of Natural History)

living things of the past have disappeared without trace, their molecules dispersed back into the universe. But even the tiny fraction of creatures whose remains were subject to the freak circumstances that produce fossils tell us important things.

Fossils prove that there were kinds of animals in the past that are no longer alive. A quick look at a giant dinosaur skeleton can convince even the biologically naive that there is no animal like that today. More importantly, fossils demonstrate evolutionary change; they show ancient species that differ from modern relatives, sometimes whole series of species changing from the past into the present. In the next chapter, the fossil record of human development will be explored. It is by no means the best fossil record available for a species, but it convincingly shows the direction of change in the formation of our species.

Summary

It is amazing how little scientists knew about the processes of nature in the days when Charles Darwin scandalized the Western world. We have come a long way since then, and science can now describe events that range from happenings within molecules that take only microseconds to the way mountains form and climates change over millions of years. All of the scientific breakthroughs of the last century point inexorably toward evolution as the process that accounts for the variety of living things in the world.

DNA has been demonstrated to be the basis of heredity. Its precise mechanism of replication results in continuity in inherited features except for the rare instances in which mutations provide the chinks in the solid wall of heredity through which new things creep in. The genetic variety that results is the playground for such mechanisms of evolution as genetic drift and natural selection. Natural selection in its varied forms dictates which species will adapt to their environments and which will pay the price of not adapting—extinction. Since, in the long run, environments inevitably change, changes in living species are equally inevitable. Whether such changes follow the slow, stately path suggested by gradualism or the helter-skelter sudden transformations of punctuated equilibria (or a bit of both) may be bitterly argued by specialists, but they are not arguing over whether evolution takes place, they are simply asking how fast and by what patterns it happens.

The Origin of the Human Species

Life on our planet must have begun with some very simple, microscopic form. The way in which this remarkable event occurred is still not clear, but it seems certain to have happened in water, where the chemical elements necessary for life had become concentrated. In the chemical catastrophe that generated the first living substance, our own beginnings lie. The course that led to our present form was long and involved, passing through a series of forms of increasing size and complexity. For countless eons, life was confined to water until bacteria, plants, and insects slowly invaded the land. Eventually, through the chance concatenation of exactly the right circumstances, our first fish-derived ancestor emerged shivering and unwilling upon the land looking for more water. Throughout this sequence, the blind but relentless process of evolution continued to shape us and all other existing creatures, as well as the far more numerous ones that failed the test of survival and yielded to the ultimate indignity of extinction.

Primates

The story that traces life from sea to land then into the multiple niches that exist there for a great variety of living things is a fascinating one, but far too detailed for our purposes. One key point for us in that story is the emergence of the biological *class* of animals that are called *mammals*. Mammals have a number of features that distinguish them from the reptiles from which they developed. They are warm blooded; that is, they have a system of temperature control that keeps the body at a constant temperature. Mammals have a set of teeth of different shapes that serve different functions such as cutting, gouging, and grinding. Young mammals spend their earliest days of development shielded within the mother's body and are then born alive, rather than hatching from eggs. In addition, after birth they are nourished by milk provided by the mother's mammary glands. The enforced association between mother and infant provides an opportunity for learning that does not exist for those kinds of creatures that are hatched from eggs long after their parents have departed from the scene. Young mammals play—something that amphibians and reptiles never do—which provides additional learning opportunities.

The foregoing list leaves little doubt that we are mammals. There are, of course, a great many other kinds of mammals, most of which developed after the great extinction of dinosaurs and other reptiles about 65 million years ago that opened opportunities for the few small mammals that were already in existence. One of the groups of mammals that resulted was a biological *order* called *Primates* which includes monkeys, apes, humans, and some smaller creatures familiar only to ardent zoo-goers. Primates share a number of behavioral features that have played important roles in their evolutionary development. Most primates are arboreal; that is, they spend their lives in and among trees. Their tree-climbing and tree-dwelling habits impose needs that are reflected in primate anatomy. Although diet varies from species to species, many primates are largely vegetarian. But they can eat and digest meat, and some species vary their diets of leaves, shoots, and fruits by eating insects, birds' eggs, and even small animals. Primates are hand-feeders, depending on their hands both to collect food and to get it into their mouths. Perhaps the most important feature of their behavior is that primates are social animals. Their genetics, habits, and even their survival are geared to living in groups. Although human beings have come to have a way of life very different from that of typical primates, the basic primate adaptation provided prehumans with capabilities that allowed them to become culture-builders.

The anatomical features that separate primates from other kinds of animals relate clearly to the way primates behave.

1. The primate habits of climbing trees by grasping with the hands and feet and eating with the hands are closely tied to anatomical features of the limbs.
    A. The clavicle (collar bone), which has been lost in many four-footed mammals, is well developed in primates to serve as a strut to hold the highly mobile shoulder joint to the side of the body.
    B. The shoulder joint permits great mobility.
    C. The two bones of each forearm (and the leg in many primates) can rotate so that the outer bone moves over the inner bone, making it possible for primates to turn the forearm and hand in any direction.
    D. Primates have prehensile hands and feet; that is, hands and feet capable of grasping. To make this possible, the thumb (or big toe) can be turned to nearly oppose the other digits. Humans have lost the ability to grasp with their feet, but this is a relatively recent development related to the fact that we stand erect and support the entire weight of the body with our feet.
    E. The fingers and toes of primates are equipped with flat nails and touch-sensitive pads rather than with claws.
2. Primate arboreal life puts a premium on the development of good vision, resulting in a complex of features that affect the eyes, face, and brain.
    A. The eyes of most primates are located toward the front of the face and look forward rather than to the sides, as do the eyes of most mammals. Most primates have stereoscopic vision; that is, the eyes focus together to transmit a single image, with depth perception, to the brain. Depth perception is a critical capability for movement high in the trees; a primate that is not sure of the location of the branch it is leaping for has a very low survival value.
    B. The snout of primates is less pronounced than that of most mammals. Reduction of the snout is made possible by the fact that primates use their hands for many tasks that other animals perform with their teeth.

    C. With highly developed vision, primates depend less on the sense of small than many other mammals.

3. The social emphasis in primate life has had an impact upon patterns of reproduction and infant care.

    A. Normally, only a single primate infant is born at one time.

    B. Primates have a long gestation period associated with an efficient system of nourishment for the fetus.

    C. Primates have a relatively long period of postnatal growth related to careful maternal care and protection of infants. This provides more time for learning the skills necessary for their strongly developed social life.

4. These patterns have affected the evolution of the brain. Relative to most mammals, primates have highly developed areas in the brain related to vision and hand-eye coordination, as well as a genetic predisposition to social living.

Zoologists divide the primates into two suborders. The suborder *Prosimii* includes lorises, lemurs, and tarsiers, the living species of which are small tree-dwelling creatures lacking some of the more advanced primate characteristics. Members of this suborder are far removed from our ancestry and need not be further discussed here.

The suborder *Anthropoidea* includes monkeys, apes, and humans. Monkeys are divided into two groups, New World monkeys and Old World monkeys. The New World monkeys, who live in the forested tropical regions of Central and South America, seem to have diverged from the course of human development as long ago as 35 million years. The lack of any apes native to North or South America suggests that, in this hemisphere, evolution never passed the stage of monkeys. The Old World monkeys inhabit various tropical parts of Africa, Asia, and the large islands off the coast of Asia. They show a number of characteristics that relate them to humans and apes, although the relationship is clearly a distant one.

If all primates are our kin, our closest cousins in terms of anatomy, size, and habits are the apes. If we bear a striking, although perhaps not flattering, resemblance to apes, it would be comforting to think that the similarity is only skin deep. It isn't. The musculature, skeleton, and internal organs show the same close relationship.

Morphology (physical form), however, is not a sure clue to genetic similarities because it is strongly affected by environment and adaptation. An even more stunning proof of our close relationship to apes has come from recent research in molecular biology. New techniques at the molecular level allow interspecies comparison of proteins, which directly reflect genetic activity, and even the structure of DNA molecules. The results are undeniable. Our DNA and its products are extremely close to those of apes, especially the chimpanzee and gorilla. It has been estimated that 99 percent of the genetic material in humans and chimpanzees is identical—a very close relationship indeed. These results put to rest once and for all occasional earlier suggestions that humans might not have descended from apes, but perhaps derived independently from some kind of monkey or even a tarsier.

There are five kinds of living apes: the gibbon, siamang, and orangutan, who live in Southeast Asia and the nearby large islands of Borneo and Sumatra, and gorillas and chimpanzees from Africa. Gibbons and siamangs are small apes, only a fraction of human size (15 to 20 pounds) and with anatomical features adapted to hanging, reaching, and rapid and agile movements high in the trees. The "great apes"—orangutan, gorilla, and chimpanzee—approach or exceed the size of humans and provide the closest anatomical parallels for comparison with our species.

How Are Humans Different?

Despite their close relationship, modern humans differ from apes in a number of physical features that indicate the separate paths followed by human (*hominid*) and ape (*pongid*) evolution. The differences fall into four sets of features: (1) a number of varied characteristics related to posture and locomotion, (2) characteristics of the hands, (3) a set of features tied to the size and complexity of the brain, and (4) differences in the face and teeth.

Humans and modern apes are all descended from early apes that used their arms and hands a lot to climb, to hang from branches, and to reach for food. The extensive use of arms and hands separated apes from monkeys, because monkeys usually walk along the top of branches rather than hanging below them. The descendants of the early apes diverged a good deal to reach the species of today. Gibbons and siamangs have become even more specialized arm-swingers, aerial acrobats who swing through the trees at dizzying speed. (They also fall a lot; a study of a sample of wild gibbons showed that 30 percent of them had suffered broken bones).

The great apes have become too large for such antics. The orangutan has remained arboreal but climbs cautiously, spreading its weight between different branches by hanging on with both feet and hands. It is capable of bending both arms and legs at angles that would make a gymnast green with envy. Chimpanzees and gorillas spend much time on the ground. They are *knuckle-walkers* who bear their weight on the soles of the feet and the knuckles of closed fists. We, of course, have given up hands and arms entirely as a means of locomotion and walk erect.

Standing habitually on two feet is, given our ancestry, a downright unnatural thing to do. Our ancestral body was not designed for such a silly (for a primate) activity, and to make it work took a major structural re-engineering of the body that extends all the way from the bottom of the feet to the base of the skull.

To start at the bottom, the human foot has changed drastically from other primate feet. To understand the change most vividly, pick up a pencil from the floor with your hand, then with your foot. Watch your fingers and the toes in the process. The human foot isn't prehensile any more. The toes are too short and not flexible enough and the big toe has come up in line with the other toes so that it is no longer opposable to them (Figure 4). Fine for walking on, but no good for grasping. The heel has been enlarged and pushed backward (compare it to the heel of the hand) so that it can bear the weight of the whole body and serve as a lever to lift it off the ground when we step. Interestingly, the foot of the gorilla, the heaviest of the apes and the one that spends the most time on the ground, has undergone similar changes.

With the emphasis on lower limbs for locomotion, the human leg has become much longer in relation to arm length than the legs of the great apes. In addition, there have been large changes in the human pelvis and hip joints. Our pelvis is short and broad in comparison to those of apes, and the leg joins the pelvis at a different angle (Figure 5). The broader human pelvis provides a greater surface for the attach-

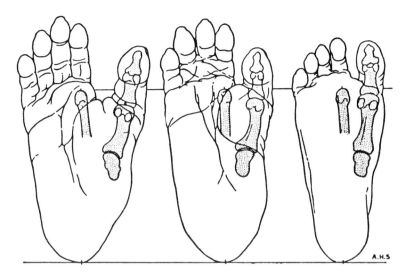

FIGURE 4   Feet of Human and Apes

The feet and partial skeletons are those of (left to right) a chimpanzee, a gorilla, and a modern human. The separation of the big toe and the mobility of the foot are much greater in the chimpanzee than in the human and it is easy to see why chimpanzees can pick things up with their feet and we can't. The foot of the gorilla is intermediate because the animal's size and terrestrial habits have resulted in some of the same evolutionary changes that took place in the development of the human foot. (From A. H. Schultz, "The Physical Distinctions of Man," originally published by the American Philosophical Society, in PROCEEDINGS, 94 (1950), 5. Reprinted by permission of the American Philosophical Society and the author Adolph Schultz.)

ment of the heavy muscles necessary to move the legs and keep the body balanced while we are moving. In the process, humans have acquired buttocks; apes have nothing worthy of the name. Buttocks are mostly the large hip muscles with a bit of fat to make sitting more comfortable and to provide energy storage.

The changes related to our erect posture go on up the body. Figure 5 shows the backbones of a gorilla and a human. They aren't the same. Instead of the simple forward curve of the gorilla's backbone, the human spine twists and curves several times to get to the right place—a head that is directly above the pelvis. Finally, the *foramen magnum,* the hole in the bottom of the skull through which the spinal cord enters, is not in the same place in humans as in other primates. In humans, the foramen magnum is directly underneath the center of the skull; in other primates, it is toward the back of the skull.

Even with all these structural changes, moving on two feet isn't easy. The human mind has to function automatically as a computer, continually reacting to changes in position and giving commands to the right muscles, just to keep us from falling over. Watch a baby learning to walk; walking is a great adventure and it takes a couple of years of programming to make it automatic, as well as changes in bones and muscles during growth.

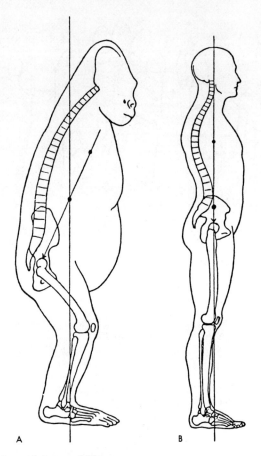

A   B

FIGURE 5   Posture of Ape and Human

The gorilla (left) is quadrupedal and rarely stands erect. Humans (right) and their ancestors have been bipedal for millions of years, with resulting changes in the skeleton and muscles. Note the differences in the shape of the pelvis, the angle of the hip joint, and the curve of the backbone. (From Dudley J. Morton, *The Human Foot.* New York: Columbia University Press, Fig. 48, p. 101.)

     As human feet lost the ability to grasp, the hands went in the opposite direction and became more flexible. Building on their prehensile character, they were perfected into instruments of superb precision. The thumb was a critical feature. It became longer and completely opposable—it could be touched to the tip of any of the other fingers, something that other primates can't really do. This made possible both a *power grip,* something all primates have, and a *precision grip,* a unique human characteristic. The difference between the two grips is easily demonstrated. Imagine using an axe or a screwdriver; that's a power grip. Write down what you did with a pencil; that's a precision grip. The two together provide an enormous range of possibilities. Why they have developed can be explained in one word—tools.

Another area of differences between us and the apes is the brain. Human brains are much larger, averaging 1,350 cc as compared to a volume that rarely exceeds 500 cc in apes. We have, then, more than twice as many brain cells as apes. That means more memory, more learning, and more thinking. We are smarter, in other words. The contrast, in fact, is even greater than the size difference suggests. The surface of the human brain is wrinkled and convoluted; that of apes is smoother. This surface area, so wrinkled in humans, is the *cerebral cortex*. It is an area devoted to memory, sense impressions, and conscious response. The wrinkling is not chance. It is an economy measure that allows the cerebral cortex to be much larger without the skull having to expand to a grotesque and impossible size.

Finally, a number of differences exist between us and the apes in the face and teeth (Figure 6). Teeth and jaws are smaller in human beings than in apes, and *prognathism,* the extent to which the jaws protrude beyond the level of the rest of the face, is much less marked in humans. Almost the entire skull of the ape is enclosed by heavy muscles necessary to operate the massive jaws and, in some of the larger apes, there is a crest of bone (*sagittal crest*) along the top of the skull to give an enlarged area of attachment for the jaw muscles.

Although humans and apes have the same number and kinds of teeth (two incisors, one canine, two premolars, and three molars on each side of the upper and lower jaws), there are differences in both the shape of the dental arch and in the shape of the teeth. In the great apes, the line of teeth has a U shape with molars and premolars forming almost parallel lines on opposite sides of the jaw and an abrupt rounding at the front. In our species, the line of teeth forms a more continuous curve. The canine teeth in many primates, including all the apes, are large, pointed teeth that protrude well beyond the level of the rest of the teeth and serve as useful tools and weapons. In human beings, the canine teeth are much smaller and less pointed, although their large roots suggest that these teeth must have been larger in our ancestors. The first lower premolar teeth in many primates are also large with a single dominant point against which the upper canine teeth sharpen; in humans, all premolars are alike and have two cusps (points) of equal size. In great apes and most other primates, the molar teeth increase in size from front to back so that the third molar is the largest. In humankind, the molars decrease in size from front to back.

The human face also has a number of unique characteristics. Because of an enlarged forehead, reduced jaws, and a chin, our face presents an almost straight line from top to bottom, whereas the faces of other primates slope backward from chinless, protruding jaws to a receding forehead. Most primates, particularly apes, have large ridges of bone above the eyes, but in modern humans these ridges are barely developed. The human nose stands out from the face with a well-developed bridge and extended cartilaginous tip. Noses of other primates are flat and broad with a small bridge.

Physical Characteristics and Behavior

The physical characteristics of an animal—human or otherwise—have to fit its behavior. It is not a simple case of physical characteristics causing behavior or vice versa; the two interact upon each other in ways that are very difficult to follow. The following brief summary will outline some of the complexity surrounding the characteristics that make humans unique.

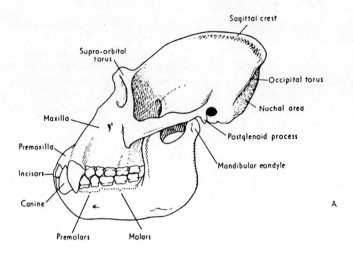

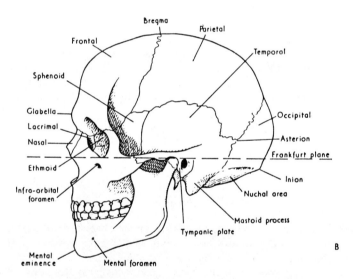

FIGURE 6   Skulls of Ape and Human

In the male gorilla (A), the massive jaws dominate the facial skeleton and the small brain case is in back of the plane of the face. In the human (B) the greatly enlarged brain case with well-developed forehead is directly above the reduced teeth and jaws. (Reprinted from The Fossil Evidence for Human Evolution by W. E. LeGros Clark by permission of the University of Chicago Press; Copyright 1955 by the University of Chicago)

We are two-legged, tool-using, thinking animals. We stand solidly on two feet because we have other things to do with our hands; we think a lot because we have large brains, and we have large brains because we think a lot. We have rather insignificant teeth and jaws, but we don't need big ones because we have developed other instruments with which to perform their tasks. All of this relates to culture.

Without culture we wouldn't look the way we do, but it doesn't matter because we wouldn't have survived. Tools are a critical part of culture, and the use of tools depends upon the fantastic manipulative ability of the human hand. A horse as smart as a human couldn't use tools or make a computer. There is simply no part of a horse's body equipped for such tasks. If we are to use and carry tools, the hands have to be free and we can't be bothered with walking or swinging with them as we move around. Consequently, the redesign of the feet and lower limbs had to be 100 percent reliable as a means of transportation and, as you can see from the list of physical characteristics discussed previously, evolution went to a lot of trouble to get the job done.

Tools do a lot of things for humans that teeth do for other animals. To defend ourselves, we substituted sticks and stones for teeth; then bows and arrows, guns, and atom bombs. It makes one wonder, sometimes. We can cut or crush food with knives and pounders or electric blenders instead of with our teeth. Teeth, then, are kind of passé except for chewing and they may become smaller.

The way in which human brains have enlarged provides a wonderful example of how complicated a seemingly simple problem can become. Our species depends on intelligence; therefore, we need bigger brains and bigger skulls to put them in. Simple? Just a few mutations to enlarge brains and skulls? Not at all. If babies' heads become large before they are born, there will not be room for them to pass through the birth canal, where they must squeeze between the bones of the mother's pelvis. We have probably reached a limit in the size of foetal heads because humans already have more birth problems, and more infants and mothers lost as a result, than most other mammalian species. To enlarge the size of the birth canal would demand a major restructuring of the female pelvis which has been carefully engineered to function efficiently for walking. An interesting question is what will happen when Caeserian sections have become so standard worldwide that they eliminate deaths from such birth problems.

An alternative to large foetal heads that makes possible much of the increased size of the human brain is having the brain grow after birth. This has a disadvantage, too, for it means that human infants are born with a much smaller fraction of their mental development than infants of other primate species. A baby ape or monkey has the ability to cling to its mother's fur very shortly after birth; a human infant lies helplessly for weeks before it can even turn over. A monkey or ape, who must walk on all fours to move rapidly, could not easily protect such a helpless infant. Consequently, the development of erect posture, leaving the hands free to carry things like babies, was a necessary part of this process.

This may seem very complicated, but that's what makes evolution such a remarkable process. Almost never is a change, even a very beneficial one, a simple matter because a modification of one part of a body almost always necessitates changes in a whole series of other parts.

The Geological Time Scale

Before we can present the fossil evidence for human evolution, we need a time scale. Geology provides that with its study of the slow changes that have modified, time and again, the face of the earth. Geologists divide the history of the earth into *eras*; only the most recent one, the *Cenozoic*, is of interest to us. Since the

Cenozoic era was sixty-five million years long, it is necessary to subdivide it into the *epochs* presented in Table 1. Table 1 presents the geological subdivision of the Cenozoic era correlated with the history of the primates as indicated by the scanty fossil material available.

The climate was very warm in the early part of the Cenozoic era, and huge areas in the Northern Hemisphere that are far too cold for primates today were populated by our tropical ancestors. A slow-cooling trend in the middle of the Cenozoic restricted primates to a smaller territory, mostly in what are still tropical regions today.

Shortly after the start of the *Pleistocene,* the most recent of the Cenozoic epochs, a strange thing happened. Climates began to fluctuate rapidly (in geological terms) from warm to cold and back. The results had a profound effect on the development of humans and their culture. During the cold *glacial* periods, great sheets of ice spread over vast areas of the Northern Hemisphere, covering all of the Scandinavian countries and most of the British Isles and extending as far south as Kansas in the United States. During the intervening *interglacial* periods, the climates became as warm or warmer than those of today.

It is hard for us to envision the amount of water that was tied up in ice and snow during glacial periods. Even today, the glaciers that cover Antarctica and most of Greenland are 10,000 feet thick in places. They contain enough water to raise sea levels 200 feet, high enough to destroy a substantial proportion of the world's largest cities. When glaciers were much more extensive, sea levels were much lower and parts of the world that are now under the ocean were dry land. England was part of the European mainland; Asia included the large islands of the Pacific, but never Australia; Alaska and Siberia were connected by a land bridge that was 600 miles wide.

Most geologists consider the Pleistocene to have ended when the last glaciers retreated about ten thousand years ago. We are now in the Holocene or Recent period. In fact, however, there is no reason to think that this is not just another interglacial period, with the glaciers simply biding their time before thundering down once again from the north. On the other hand, if the Greenhouse Effect, caused by carbon dioxide generated by our reckless burning of fossil fuels, warms the climate as is threatened, it may melt the remaining glaciers and drown our coastlines. Neither prospect is very promising.

TABLE 1   Primate Evolution in the Cenozoic Era

Epochs	Dates (in millions of years)	Primates
Holocene	0.01—Present	Modern humans
Pleistocene	1.8—0.01	Development of humans
Pliocene	5—1.8	Australopithecines and *Homo habilis*
Miocene	25—5	Variety of apes and very early humans
Oligocene	35—25	First monkeys and apes
Eocene	58—35	Prosimians similar to lemurs and tarsiers
Paleocene	65—58	Earliest primates

Ancient Primates

Primates we are, and primates we will be into the foreseeable future; consequently, a decent respect for our ancestry demands that we know something about primate evolution. The earliest primates that peek cautiously out of the fossil record go back to the beginning of the Cenozoic era about 65 million years ago. These first primates were closely related to the Insectivores and were tree-dwelling insect eaters who looked more like squirrels than like apes or humans. They were closer to prosimians than to any other living primates, but were far more primitive. They represent a stage in primate development that has been superceded, leaving no living representatives. By the Eocene epoch, 58 to 35 million years ago, recognizable prosimians had appeared, some rather like lemurs, others like tarsiers. Since there wasn't anything better for their ecological niches in the warm early Eocene, prosimians were a great success and became quite common.

About 40 million years ago, toward the end of the Eocene, a few fragmentary fossils suggest that some of the prosimians had taken steps toward monkey-like forms, and by 30 million years ago in the Oligocene there were undeniable monkeys. Monkeys were larger, had bigger brains and better coordination, and were more effective creatures than prosimians in arboreal environments. Prosimians declined rapidly in the Oligocene—a decline that has left only a few species alive today. They may have been partly outcompeted by monkeys, but even more severe competition may have come from rodents who diversified rapidly and with great success at about the same time.

Ideas about the evolutionary line that led away from monkeys to apes and humans are in a state of ferment. Some pleasingly simple interpretations that were possible when there were only a few fossils have proven untenable in the light of information from new finds. As is often the case, the more fossils there are, the more complex things become.

One of the best ways to distinguish apes from monkeys is to look at dental details, especially of the molar teeth. In addition, teeth are much more abundant in fossil collections than anything else. New fossils frequently grow like the Cheshire Cat: first the teeth appear, then a face, then the rest of the body fills in very slowly.

Looking at teeth alone, the record is quite clear. As early as 30 million years ago, in Oligocene deposits at the Fayum locality in Egypt, there were some primates that had ape-like teeth and some that had monkey-like teeth. Early in the Miocene (21 to 17 million years ago) there were apes in East Africa. At the end of this time, Africa and Eurasia drifted together and apes romped off into new territories. By about 12 million years ago, apes were all over: Africa, southern Europe, the Middle East, India, Pakistan, and China.

With this rapid spread of apes and the many new fossils that have been discovered in recent years, chaos reigns temporarily while the experts try to sort things out. The best way to summarize the situation is to make some general points. First, there were a lot of different apes between 15 and 10 million years ago, at least four genera and many possible species. Many of the species have no modern descendants and had characteristics and behaviors that are not represented among living primates. Second, some of the Miocene apes lived in heavy forests (like apes today); others were adapted to more open country. In addition to teeth, apes are separated from monkeys by characteristics of the upper limbs that relate to a greater use of the arms and hands for hanging and reaching. These features are hard to study because the appropriate parts of the body are rarely preserved as fossils. But when the limited evidence available is considered, the picture of ape evolution is far less clear than when only teeth are considered. Most of the early species that have teeth like apes do not seem very ape-like in their limbs and it is not clear when and where the adaptation of the upper limbs took place. Finally, it should be noted that apes have not been an enormous evolutionary success. After the brief flurry in the middle of the Miocene, apes have declined in both kinds and numbers. If one of the apes had not been the starting point for humanity, the whole idea of a large primate might well go down as one of those little mistakes that happens sometimes in the process of evolution.

Of all the later Miocene fossils, not one seems a likely candidate for a human ancestor. A few years ago, a fossil named *Ramapithecus* (now included in the genus *Sivapithecus*) was touted as a possible hominid—a creature in the human line— because of dental characteristics. Recently, David Pilbeam, a primate specialist from Harvard University, discovered a fossil of the genus that included most of the face. It was the face of an orangutan—as far removed from the human line as one can get among the great apes. How could such an awful mistake be made—a fossil orangutan considered a human ancestor? The answer is that the original interpretation was a bold guess based on a few fragmentary fossils. Such mistakes are common in early interpretations and every researcher knows that he or she will be wrong sometimes.

Are we, then, in such bad shape for Miocene fossils that large errors are still likely? Yes, at least in one very important sense. Although there are recent finds dating from the Late Miocene, almost none of them came from Africa. Since it is almost certain that human characteristics first appeared there, we will not know much more about our ancestry for this period until more African fossils are discovered.

Australopithecines and Homo Habilis

If the Miocene is a terrible disappointment in terms of human ancestors, the Pliocene is just the reverse thanks to a burst of startling fossil finds from Africa. What emerges, particularly for the time period between 4 and 1.5 million years ago, is an unusually detailed account of a group of creatures that beyond any doubt includes our ancestors. The creatures were hominids: that is, they were in the evolutionary family that leads to modern humans rather than in the pongid family that leads to the apes. We know now what early hominids looked like, how they walked, and the environment in which they lived. As these questions have been answered, debate has turned to the details of how all the creatures fit together into a meaningful evolutionary pattern.

The story begins in 1924 with one of these sudden discoveries that every researcher dreams about. Raymond Dart, a British-trained anatomist teaching at the University of Witwatersrand in South Africa, received two boxes of fossils from a site called Taung. The site was a deposit of ancient limestone that encased and preserved animal remains. At the time of the discovery, the limestone was being commercially mined and a mine foreman had agreed to ship chunks that contained fossils to Dart.

The first box contained nothing of interest, but at the top of the second box a suspiciously rounded lump of limestone caught Dart's eye. It was the cast of the inside of a skull. An excited search through the box led to another limestone mass within which the bones of the skull, a face and some teeth, were barely visible. The first glimpses were enough to convince Dart that he was viewing a creature the like of which had never been seen before. Ancient baboons were already known from Taung, but this was no baboon—it was an ape-like animal or something even more important.

Separating the fossils for study was not an easy task. The surrounding limestone was like concrete, far harder than the precious bones. For 73 days Dart picked patiently away until at last the fossil was exposed. Dart's enthusiasm was justified. The skull was that of a child of five or six years whose first permanent molars had just erupted. The face was flatter than that of any ape, and the canine teeth did not project beyond the other teeth.

The foramen magnum was nearly beneath the center of the skull, rather than displaced backward as it is in apes. Since this feature relates to posture, Dart reached the daring conclusion that the creature had stood erect. The brain, however, had not been of human size. Although the forehead of the Taung child was slightly more rounded than that in apes, the capacity of the skull (although Dart overestimated it) measured only 400 cc, about that of an adult chimpanzee. Dart was sure that he had discovered a missing link, a creature that stood somewhere between apes and humans.

Dart, who had named his creature *Australopithecus africanus,* published his findings in the prestigious British journal *Nature* in early 1925. Almost all of the experts concluded he was wrong. What he had found was the skull of an ape—they insisted—a new and interesting species, perhaps, but not one that stood in the line of human development. Dart had been deceived by the youth of his specimen; had it lived to grow up, it would have developed the ape-like features it lacked. Even more scorned was the date estimated for the fossil—two million years. This was admittedly no more than an educated guess, for cave deposits provide no stratigraphy upon which to base a solid conclusion about age. Not nearly that old, concluded the experts. There was a puzzle that Dart's critics could not explain, however. Other animals in the deposits showed that *Australopithecus* had lived in an open grassland, an environment totally foreign to any kind of ape known at the time.

Dart, of course, was right or there would be no reason to spend so much time on his discovery. But it is no surprise that other experts balked at his conclusions. He was suggesting a far earlier and more primitive human ancestor than anybody had ever seen, and suggesting it on the basis of a single juvenile skull. His ideas desperately needed confirmation from other fossils.

The first confirmation was to come from the work of Robert Broom, curator of paleontology at the Transvaal Museum in Pretoria. Broom was one of the few to believe Dart's ideas from the beginning and, although it was several years before he was free to begin research, he was determined to search for fossils at other limestone cave deposits in South Africa. The first break came in 1936, when Broom recovered another skull from a site called Sterkfontein. It was like the Taung skull, but was an adult. It proved that Dart's baby would not have grown up to be an ape after all. In 1947, Sterkfontein yielded an almost complete pelvis, nearly identical in shape to a human pelvis. If conclusions about posture based on the position of the foramen magnum were debatable, a pelvis left no doubt. It came from a creature that had walked on two feet.

Broom's work also provided a surprise. From the site of Kromdraai came another skull. It shared the small canines and rounded dental arch of previous finds, but was so different in other ways that it could not be the same species. It was larger, more rugged, and had immense premolar and molar teeth. There had not been just one early hominid in South Africa, but two. Both are now accepted as australopithecines—members of the genus *Australopithecus*—but, to avoid the debates on formal species names that cause specialists to growl and bare their teeth, they are often referred to informally as *gracile* for the Taung skull and similar finds and *robust* for more rugged specimens like Kromdraai.

The finds discussed are only the most spectacular; there were many others during the 1930s and 1940s. With the evidence mounting rapidly, Dart's view had triumphed. Argument over the importance of the australopithecines was capped in the early 1950s by a gracious concession by Sir Arthur Keith who had been Dart's teacher and one of his most vigorous opponents.

I am now convinced of the evidence submitted by Dr. Robert Broom that Professor Dart was right and I was wrong. The Australopithecinae are in or near the line which culminated in the human form.

The story is far from ended, but the scene now shifts to East Africa. At the Olduvai Gorge in Kenya, erosion has created 300-foot cliffs that display a layered series of ancient deposits. Here is the stratigraphy lacking in the South African caves. Better yet, there are layers of volcanic ash that can be given dates in absolute number of years by measuring the quantity of argon gas created in them by decay of a radioactive isotope of potassium.

Olduvai Gorge is inextricably linked with the names of Louis S.B. and Mary Leakey, a husband and wife team of paleoanthropologists. When the Leakeys started work in the 1930s, they discovered a profusion of early stone tools tumbling out of the steeply sloping deposits. In Bed 1, at the very bottom of the gorge, is a tool industry that they named Oldowan. The tools are very crude: choppers produced by striking a few flakes off the end of pebbles to provide jagged, not very sharp edges; flakes usable for cutting and scraping; round pebbles used as hammerstones.

For years, the Leakeys searched in vain for fossil remains of the maker of the tools. Finally, in 1959, Mary Leakey discovered a handsome skull. It was an australopithecine, although for a while Louis Leakey called it *Zinjanthropus* ("Zinj" for short). Zinj was of the robust variety; even more robust, in fact, than the South African examples.

Knowledge had come several steps further. Australopithecines had occupied a wide area, not just South Africa. There was now a solid date, for the Zinj skull could be dated by a volcanic ash layer to around 1.75 million years ago. Dart's guess date of two million that had so outraged his colleagues had been as accurate as his assessment of the meaning of the Taung skull. It also seemed that australopithecines had made tools, for Zinj was found in an ancient camp site surrounded by tools and a scatter of broken animal bones that were presumably the remains of ancient meals.

What more could be left to learn? Lots, it turned out. In 1962, the Leakeys found parts of another skull and a jaw at the same 1.75 million year level. The new skull was not robust. It was fairly delicate but—at least so it seemed to Leakey—had a far larger brain than any of the other fossils. This larger-brained hominid seemed a more likely tool-maker than Zinj, who might have been found in a camp site with tools and animal bones because he, too, was part of the menu.

Leakey, Tobias, and Napier christened the new find *Homo habilis,* making it the earliest member of our genus. This was a radical step and one that was received with caution. Louis Leakey was flamboyant, daring, and, for all his contributions, sometimes wrong. The reconstruction of the *Homo habilis* skull was an issue. The skull had been badly broken and warped so that fitting the pieces together involved a considerable exercise in imagination. If it were reconstructed to be smaller, it would not have been much different from the gracile australopithecines of South Africa. Besides, some researchers were already uncomfortable at having two different hominid species alive at the same time; to add a third seemed too much of a good thing.

The answer to the *Homo habilis* riddle came a decade later from a new location on the eastern shore of Lake Turkana, north of Olduvai. Here, the Leakeys' son, Richard, has discovered an abundance of important fossils. Robust australopithecines were there from about two million to one million years ago. They seem to have been very conservative and changed very little over this long interval. Tools and several kinds of archaeological sites date to the same interval. The key find, however, was a skull labeled ER 1470. The skull was like the *Homo habilis* skull from Olduvai, but it was well enough preserved to permit a better reconstruction. The cranial capacity was 775 cc, 300 cc larger than the average for australopithecines. The date of ER 1470, although it was originally thought to be older, now seems to be around 1.8 million years ago, coeval with the Olduvai material. Most specialists now agree that the creatures should be assigned to the genus *Homo.* It should be noted, however, that the genus designation depends almost entirely on the larger brain, for in other features these early *Homo* skulls do not differ very much from those of gracile australopithecines. Since brains were such a crucial feature in the development of our species, the conclusion to include these in our genus is not unreasonable.

Taking stock of the information presented so far shows that several important facts have been firmly established. They will not be changed no matter what future fossil hunters may discover.

Several different kinds of hominids were spread across Africa by two million years ago. The number of fossils the creatures have yielded is astounding; there are hundreds of specimens, including even such unlikely finds as an almost complete foot. All of these hominids stood erect, for the numerous parts of the body (Figure 7) that indicate posture invariably show the distinctive physical characteristics that go with walking on two feet. The teeth of all of the creatures are more human than ape-like (Figure 8): canine teeth do not protrude and the dental arch is rounded like that of humans. Nevertheless, the teeth are very large in comparison with those of modern humans, especially the molar teeth of the robust variety. Brains of early

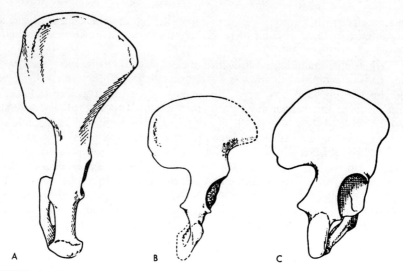

A   B   C

FIGURE 7   Evolution of the Pelvis

The close resemblance between the australopithecine (B) and modern human (C) pelves and the way in which they contrast with the pelvis of the quadrupedal chimpanzee (A) leave little doubt that the posture of the australopithecines must have been close to that of humans today. (By permission of the Trustees of the British Museum [Natural History])

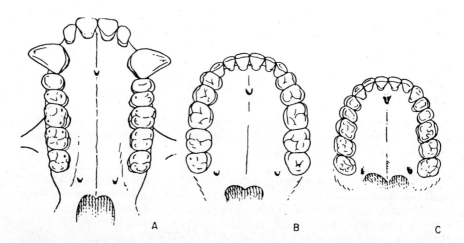

A   B   C

FIGURE 8   Evolution of Teeth

The teeth of the australopithecine (B) are very large in comparison with those of Homo sapiens *(C), but the shape of the teeth and dental arch are similar. Most notable in contrast with the teeth of the gorilla (A) are the reduction in size of the canine teeth and the more rounded shape of the dental arch.* (Reprinted from *The Fossil Evidence for Human Evolution* by W. E. LeGros Clark by permission of the University of Chicago Press; copyright 1955 by the University of Chicago)

African hominids were variable in size. Those of the australopithecines are about the size of those in the modern great apes. *Homo habilis* had more brains; the average for the few measurable specimens is 650 cc. This is still far closer to the size of apes, however, than to the modern human average of 1,350 cc.

These facts say something very important about the rate at which human physical characteristics developed. Not all human characteristics appeared at the same time. Posture changed first; the physical structure for erect posture was completely established before brain size had changed very much. It was not intelligence that made our ancestors branch off from the ape line, it was getting up on two feet. A matter that is still the subject of disagreement is exactly how many kinds of hominids the group included and what biological names to give them. These are points about which new evidence could still change opinions.

With only a few dissenters, experts seem content with the genus name *Homo* for the larger-brained East African hominids, although they are divided over whether to use the species name *habilis* or find another. There is no disagreement over calling the South African gracile Australopithecines *Australopithecus africanus*, but some would use this name in a broader sense to include East African *Homo* and some still earlier hominids to be discussed later.

Opinion is relatively uniform that the robust group belongs in the genus *Australopithecus* and that they are different enough, with their rugged features and huge molars, to deserve their own species name. But there is an almost even split over whether they are one or two species. Those who include them all in a single species call them *Australopithecus robustus*. Other use the name *A. robustus* only for the South African examples and call the even more rugged East African set *Australopithecus boisei*. A lot of the debate about numbers and names of species comes down to the basic question, "How different do two fossil groups have to be before they should be called different species?" The only way to tell for sure whether two groups of animals are separate species is to see whether they are capable of interbreeding. Since two-million year old fossils have long since lost interest in participating in such an experiment, fossil specialists are left to argue questions of species without any sure means of resolution.

A final question that remains unresolved is how many of the African hominids made tools. It is logical that the larger-brained *Homo habilis* must have done so, but this is no reason to conclude that other species might not also have been tool makers. There may never be a final answer to this question since even finding the remains of a hominid in the same site as tools is not clear proof, as the case of Zinj demonstrates.

The most recent set of fossils to be discovered carries our ancestry a step further into the past. As a site called Hadar in the Afar region of northeastern Ethiopia, American Donald C. Johanson, with French colleagues Maurice Taieb and Yves Coppens, has discovered some exciting fossils that date to around three million years ago.

The remarkable thing about the Hadar fossils is their superb preservation. In one case, 40 percent of the skeleton of a tiny hominid nicknamed Lucy was recovered, including bones from almost every part of the body. In another instance, an enormous collection of bones was scattered over a hillside in a single area. At least thirteen individuals, including four infants, were represented. This "First Family," as they have been dubbed, may have been a single social group killed by some sudden tragedy such as a flash flood. Never before has there been an opportunity to study a whole group of hominids from such an early date.

At three million years ago, a million years earlier than most of the other fossils discussed, one would expect hominids to be more primitive. That is exactly what the data show. The Hadar fossils clearly fall within the genus *Australopithecus*. All the indicators demonstrate an erect posture. (The wonderfully complete Lucy is particularly useful.) Some of the teeth from Hadar, however, are decidedly less human-like than those of later fossils. Canines are quite large and often project beyond the level of the other teeth; the dental arch is U-shaped rather than rounded. If one were to look at teeth alone, it would be hard to place the Hadar finds in the hominid line. Skulls are quite small and show several primitive features.

The large collections of fossils from Hadar show a good deal of variability. One possible explanation for the variation among the fossils is *sexual dimorphism*—a difference in size and characteristics between males and females of the same species. Females from Hadar seem to have been quite small. Lucy stood only 3 feet 6 inches and weighed about 50 pounds. Some of the larger, presumably male skeletons may have come from individuals 5 feet tall who weighed twice as much. It is also possible, however, that the size differences indicate two different species, not two different sexes.

No tools at all have come from the three-million year time levels at Hadar, although tools do appear in later levels dated to about 2.5 to 2.7 million years. This suggests that tool *making,* at least of nonperishable materials, had not yet developed, although the *use* of unmodified objects as implements seems likely.

The Hadar specimens fall closest to the general group of gracile australopithecines. Since few of the pronounced characteristics of the robust group are present, that group may have been a later specialized development. Johanson and White have given the new species name *Australopithecus afarensis* to the Hadar fossils.

What Happened and Why?

The hominid fossils can be put together into an evolutionary scheme, although there are some points at which the evidence permits several alternative reconstructions.

Before four million years ago, *Australopithecus afarensis* developed from some still unknown ancestor that dwelled in the gap in the Late Miocene fossil record. Between 3 and 2.5 million years ago, something important happened, but there are different interpretations of what it was. One interpretation is that *A. afarensis* split into two lines, one leading to the later australopithecines, the second to *Homo habilis*. The second view puts the split a little later in terms of species and sees *A. afarensis* evolving into *A. africanus* which then divides into the robust australopithecines, on the one hand, and *Homo habilis,* on the other.

As a result of whichever of these splits occurred, several different kinds of hominids were all living in the same places in Africa between 2.5 and 1 million years ago. This is something that nobody would have dared to suggest before the fossil evidence appeared. It is a biological principle that two very similar species cannot coexist in the same ecological niche because one will inevitably outcompete the other. There are several possible explanations for this puzzle. Perhaps the early hominids had ways of life that were different enough for them to coexist; perhaps we are looking at such a short segment of evolutionary time that competition had not had time to work. In the long run, the principle seems to have held because there aren't any australopithecines around competing with us today.

Later events are much clearer. *Homo habilis* evolved into a more advanced species called *Homo erectus*. This happened quite rapidly because, by 1.6 million years ago, the first examples of *H. erectus* have appeared and *H. habilis* is seen no more. The australopithecines, alas, became extinct without leaving descendant species. *A. africanus,* who was closest to us, was the first to go. The robust species, who may have had a specialized adaptation for eating large amounts of vegetation that *Homo* didn't want (a guess based upon the huge molar teeth), hung around until about one million years ago. Then, it too disappeared, perhaps because it was no match for the rapidly developing *Homo erectus*.

The most fascinating question of all is why all these things happened. What started us off in a direction that led human ancestry away from the line that led to apes? The key to the riddle must lie in erect posture, since that is the first feature that turned in the human direction. Remember that we are now dealing with a topic for which there is no fossil evidence; even by the time of *Australopithecus afarensis,* bipedalism was established, so we have no fossils of half-erect ancestors to guide us. Perhaps because of the lack of data, the number of hypotheses about postural development is large and the agreement is very small.

It is very likely that the change relates in some way to environment. All modern apes live in dense forest; none of the early hominids did so and when modern humans live in the forest they walk around the trees, carefully keeping to the ground. At some point, our ancestors came down from the trees to live on the ground where new foods were available and different physical characteristics were useful. Animals who spend a significant part of their time away from trees would be under different selective pressures from those that rarely touch the earth.

But what selective pressures? What was bipedal posture good for under such circumstances? Just standing on two feet does not seem to be the answer. Apes can move very rapidly on all fours and can get away from danger as fast as humans can. Standing erect does enable an animal to see farther, especially in country with tall grass such as our ancestors may have inhabited, but this seems a fairly small advantage.

Far more important is that an erect posture leaves the hands free, something for which there are lots of obvious advantages. British anthropologist Clifford Jolly has suggested that the earliest advantage of free hands was in gathering the small seeds that are available on the ground but not in trees. A concentration on small seeds might also explain the dental differences between hominids and apes because hominid teeth are better adapted for the grinding motions needed to eat small, hard objects.

Free hands can also be used to carry babies. Although early hominid babies were certainly not so helpless as human infants, they probably needed more care than those of monkeys and apes and would have been at risk when their mothers were threatened by predators. A baby ape is quite safe with its mother in the trees;

safety on the ground is another matter. It is certainly clear that being able to run fast and carry a baby at the same time is an advantage.

Finally, of course, hands that are free can carry and use tools that are good for a variety of things including defense and getting food. Tools used to be the most popular explanation for erect posture. With the discovery of *A. afarensis*, already erect and half a million years before the first known tools, the argument seems less cogent. It is still possible that the use of tools that cannot be recognized by archaeologists; sticks and stones to frighten predators, for example, would be advantageous enough to select for bipedalism.

"What caused erect posture?" is the kind of question where checking the box marked "all of the above" is not a bad answer. All of the suggested factors are, indeed, advantages of standing on two feet that could have contributed at some point to its development. If earlier, less erect fossils are discovered, they may help decide which factor might have been the starting point. At the moment, we can only say that erect posture was an advantage; if it hadn't been, we would all be reading this perched in trees somewhere.

We have devoted a great deal of space to the earliest known hominids. That is not only because they provide such clear evidence of an important stage in human development, but also because they are such a fine example of how the scientific record and interpretation grow. Starting from the Taung skull and Dart's remarkable intuitive interpretation—which couldn't actually be proved at the time—research moved on to add more and more evidence. This evidence demonstrated some things that are now established facts. It also opened new mysteries that specialists now argue about. In time, more fossils will solve some of these debates and open the door to new levels of problems.

Later Steps In Human Evolution

The next stage in human development was a creature called *Homo erectus*, who proves to be a logical next step considering the nature of *Homo habilis*. *H. erectus* stood fully erect as shown by all associated anatomy. The teeth and jaws were somewhat smaller than those of *Homo habilis* and the australopithecines and were more like the teeth of people today. The most important evolutionary advance was in the size of the brain case and the cultural accomplishments that went with it. The average *H. erectus* brain size was about 1,000 cc, a size roughly between those of *H. habilis* and modern brains. The largest examples of *H. erectus* heads fall within the volume range of the heads of people living today. There are many details about the skull and face of *H. erectus* that still differ a great deal from the way those features are today. *H. erectus* had a very large "brow ridge" of bone above the eyes, a low forehead, and no chin whatsoever. Pretty he wasn't (by today's standards), and it is likely that the difference in brain size would have been enough to prove a serious handicap in modern living, but nobody can doubt that *erectus* belongs firmly in the genus *Homo*.

Homo erectus lasted quite a while. The earliest finds that indisputably belong to the group date back to 1.6 million years ago, while the most recent date only about 200 to 300 thousand years ago. Finds of *H. erectus* have been made over a much broader portion of the earth than those of earlier forms. They have been found in Africa, where *H. erectus* fossils occur in later levels of some of the same deposits that contain Australopithecines and *H. habilis;* in Hungary and Germany in Europe; in China at the cave of Choukoutien (or Zhoukoudian in modern Chinese spelling) outside of modern Peking (Beijing); and on the island of Java in Indonesia. Tools that date back to this period and that must have been made by *H. erectus* (as there were no competing hominids remaining by this time) also occur in England, North Africa, India, and Southeast Asia. Some of these areas had cold temperate zone climates. It was culture that had allowed *H. erectus* to escape to these cold areas from the warm latitudes to which their delicate tropical bodies were naturally suited, for they had developed a bag of cultural tricks—including fire and living in caves—that provided the warmth needed for survival.

There are dozens of *Homo erectus* fossils, some of them very complete. In earlier days when biologists and students of early humans were "splitters" who hated to put any two fossils in the same group, each additional find tended to get a new species or even a new genus name. This accounts for such time-honored titles as *Sinanthropus, Pithecanthropus,* and the Heidelberg Jaw that appear in older anthropology books. In those days, an enterprising young researcher who found an old shoe was likely to call it a new genus. Now, most biologists who are interested in early humans are "lumpers" and all these remains get dumped into the same basket labeled *H. erectus.* There is, indeed, a good deal of variety within this group but, given the facts that they lived for more than a million years, inhabited most of the Old World, and were frequently subjected to partial isolation and extreme environmental conditions, such variation is only to be expected. If we had enough fossil remains, all carefully dated and arranged in space, we would probably be able to see varieties of *H. erectus* that might correspond to what we would today call races.

Homo erectus evolved gradually into our own species *Homo sapiens.* Therefore, it is not surprising that a number of fossils dating to the period between 300 and 100 thousand years ago are difficult to classify because they show a mixture of traits from the two species. The major difference between *H. erectus* and *H. sapiens* is in the size of brains and the size and shape of skulls that go with them. There are also differences in dentition, mostly amounting to the fact that teeth continued to decline in size as one moves toward modern humans.

Although the fossils may be hard to classify, it is easier to explain the evolution of this period than it is to explain the development of erect posture. Culture was the overwhelming reason for continuing physical change by the time of *H. erectus.* Tools, hunting, communication, and more complex social life—all parts of culture—put a premium on intelligence with resulting selection for larger brains and changing skulls. More advanced tools and methods of preparing food substituted for strength and size of teeth, and teeth became smaller. With the decrease in tooth size, the shapes of jaws and muscles changed, resulting in changes in facial architecture.

The record of human evolution is much better beginning about 100 thousand years ago because of the existence of a numerous and well-studied series of fossils called Neandertal that certainly fall within *H. sapiens.* Most specialists consider them to have been simply an earlier variety of our species and give them the name *Homo sapiens neandertalensis.* By this time, the size of the brain had expanded to match that of humans living today. Size does not correlate one-to-one with intellectual ability, however, and there are some specialists who believe that the organization of the Neandertal brain was not quite like that of people today; therefore,

Neandertal may still have lacked the full quotient of modern mental skills. Short of finding a fossilized brain, the question is going to be very difficult to resolve.

Neandertal still differed from people today in a number of anatomical details. The body build of the Neandertal tended to be heavyset and rugged; its bones were thicker; there was still a heavy, bony brow ridge above the eyes that differentiates it from today's human; and some degree of protrusion of jaws and teeth persisted. These features are often referred to as "primitive" because they are shared by all types of humans who lived earlier than the modern type, but they would not have kept Neandertal Man from functioning on Madison Avenue, if his brain were up to it.

There is also a great deal of variety among Neandertals. Some fossils look quite modern and are on the borderline between Neandertal and ourselves; others are extreme in the other direction and possess all of the nonmodern features of the group in a pronounced form. It would be very satisfying to see this variation as gradual evolution toward completely modern physical characteristics. But, as often happens in science, the facts get in the way of a wonderful idea. The fossils we can date with some security show no strong relationship between time and modernness. Some of the most modern-looking Neandertal skulls are among the earliest, and some of the most different-looking are quite late. A set of Neandertal skeletons from southern and western Europe form quite an extreme group often called *Classic Neandertal*, based on the idea that they represent the ultimate in variation of Neandertal away from the modern form. The fossils are relatively recent, pertaining to the early, very cold part of the last glacial period, 75 to 40 thousand years ago. From caves in Israel come another series of fossils that make a very mixed lot including some typical Neandertal specimens and some of mixed characteristics only a few miles from quite modern fossils. The date is probably somewhat earlier than that of the Classic Neandertals of southern and western Europe.

A lot of imagination has gone into trying to explain the variety and the lack of increased modernity as one gets closer to more recent times. One reconstruction suggests that there may have been two sharply distinguished varieties of humans; one an early example of a modern human, the other a Neandertal cousin who became extinct. In this viewpoint, the modern type lurked in eastern Europe, snuck occasionally into the Near East where they miscegenated a bit with Classic Neandertal in the obscurity of caves. They left western Europe to the Neandertals until about 35,000 b.c., when they swept in upon their befuddled cousins to exterminate them and to complete their conquest of the world. This viewpoint isn't very popular any more, although there are some respectable anthropologists who still hold modified versions of it and the evidence certainly can't be used to *disprove* it. Another interpretation is more favored today. This theory suggests that the Neandertals, like any group of animals, showed a good deal of variety; a population in one part of the world differed from that in another because of adaptation to different environmental conditions and genetic drift. Occasionally, one group would become isolated for a while and, during the separation, would diverge slightly. Then, as the circumstances that created the isolation changed, the divergent group would again interact and interchange genes with other groups, giving new mixtures. The Classic Neandertals of southwestern Europe were such a group. Because of the severe climatic conditions of the glacial period during which they lived, they were partly cut off from Neandertals elsewhere and were, at the same time, subject to strong selective pressures related to the climatic extremes. They drifted in a somewhat different direction. Some anthropologists believe that the divergence became so strong that they were genetically or culturally incapable of breeding with other Neandertals when isolation lessened and, hence, they became extinct. Others believe that the Classic Neandertals did not diverge so widely and that they simply merged with other groups when climatic conditions changed. Since the Classic group was probably few in number, their "extreme" features were simply diluted in the mass of early humans.

At any rate, Neandertals are another fine example of the way evolution works to create, augment, diminish, or blend variety, depending on conditions of the moment. We must remember that when we speak of days so long ago, we are dealing with a world in which human groups were small and sometimes widely scattered, groups whose only means of transportation were their own feet. Animals in such circumstances frequently diverge into completely different species, so it should not be surprising that human groups form strongly differentiated varieties from time to time.

Completely modern fossils—with none of the earlier primitive features—are first known from southern Europe at about 35,000 B.C., halfway through the last glacial period. Although these earliest modern fossils are sometimes called Cro-Magnon, there is no reason that they should be given a special biological name because their bones are totally indistinguishable from those of some people living in the world today.

Summary

Humans are members of the animal kingdom. Within that kingdom, we are, along with prosimians, monkeys, and apes, members of the order primates. All of the primates have grasping hands, strong and flexible arms, excellent vision, and an emphasis on social living and careful care of the young. Most primate characteristics can be explained as useful for living in trees, the place where our ancestors started. Humans differ from other primates in having a set of physical characteristics that make it possible for us to stand and move on two feet. We also have hands capable of superb precision, small teeth, and extremely large brains. Our physical characteristics make it possible for us to have culture, the uniquely human means of adaptation.

Primates are an ancient group whose evolutionary history goes back at least 65 million years to the beginning of the Cenozoic era. The earliest primates were prosimians; monkeys then developed, followed soon by the first apes. Twenty million years ago, in the middle of the Miocene epoch, our ancestor must have been one of the variety of ape-like creatures that existed. Some time thereafter, during a gap in the fossil record that does not provide a good candidate for a human ancestor, a split took place with one line leading toward hominids, the other staying ape-like and leading to the modern pongids.

At the end of this fossil gap, the record becomes crystal clear. By four million years ago, there were hominids in Africa. Their bodies had already changed to permit erect posture; their teeth were becoming human, but they still had very small brains. These earliest hominids, the australopithecines, came in several species, the number and names of which are still debated by specialists. By two million years ago, one group of African hominids had developed somewhat larger brains and the ability to make recognizable stone tools. These larger-brained specimens were the first members of the genus *Homo*.

After our genus had become established, the evolutionary line leads directly to modern humans. *Homo erectus* lived between 1.6 million and 200 to 300 thousand years ago and was the first of our ancestors to venture into colder climates. They were aided in doing so by an increased brain size and more highly developed culture. Our own species, *Homo sapiens,* appeared around 200 to 300 thousand years ago in a form that still differed in several physical details from people today. Finally, about 35 thousand years ago, humans indistinguishable from those living today appeared.

4

Physical Variety Today

It should be clear from the preceding chapter that physical variety within a species is one of the results of the processes of evolution. Populations of a species that are separated and subjected to different environmental conditions diverge slightly and foster variety. But the variety is ever-changing; it grows, lessens, merges, and may even give rise to new forms and new species. All of the early kinds of humans showed great variety; if we could see in the flesh a cross-section of the earth's early population at any single point in time, we would be astonished at the differences that could exist among people who were all part of a single species. Modern humanity is no exception to biological principles, so it is not surprising that groups living in the world today differ in their physical characteristics.

Even though variety is only the expectable, the study of modern physical variation is important for several reasons. First, physical differences tend to become the focus of cultural prejudices. The amount of race prejudice has varied from time to time and from place to place, but it has been a recurring theme in human history and is a modern social problem. Since race prejudice is usually rooted in downright falsehoods, everybody should know the biological facts about human variety. Second, individuals and groups differ in such things as inherited susceptibility and resistance to disease; their metabolism; and their reaction to heat, cold, and high altitudes. Implications for health care and nutrition are obvious. Finally, no matter what we think or do, the world's environment will change in the future, both through natural processes and through our own actions. Our response to change must certainly involve knowledge of the human body and of the variety in the ways in which it works. We are a part of nature; this is a fact that we must begin to appreciate more strongly than we have in the recent past.

Physical Variety and Race

Before considering questions of variability, it is important to emphasize the fundamental homogeneity of humankind. All living human beings belong to a single species. Considering the tremendous extent of territory and the variety of environments covered by humankind, the degree of physical differentiation is surprisingly low. Other animal species covering as wide a territory often separate into a number of quite distinct species. The prime factors in maintaining human unity are probably the use of cultural rather than physical adaptations to environment and a high degree of mobility, which fosters gene flow between populations.

Accepting this remarkable degree of similarity as a given factor, any observer can easily note that people from one part of the world differ in some characteristics from people of other regions. If, for example, one were transported directly from northern Europe to central Africa and then to eastern Asia, one would see that the inhabitants of each location are different from those in the others. If a sample of one hundred people from each of these locations were brought together, it would not be difficult to sort them out again into their original groups, although there might be a few individuals whose assignment would be in doubt.

Imagine a second journey, extending from northern Europe to central Europe, and finally to southern Europe, again for the purpose of collecting a sample of one hundred individuals from each of the three locations. An observer would note some physical differences between the inhabitants of the three areas, but the variations would be considerably less than in the former case, and the sorting of individuals from a mixed sample would include many more doubtful choices. If the distance were decreased to include three villages only 50 miles apart, it probably would be impossible to note any systematic physical differences between groups from the three locations. The message is clear: there is physical variety among humans and the variety is a function of the distance between groups.

Physical anthropologists in the first half of this century worked very hard at trying to make sense out of the obvious physical differences that can be seen around the world. They did it by classifying—taking the people in an area, calling them a race, and listing their physical characteristics. Since the people in any area weren't all alike but had a variety of physical characteristics, researchers had to choose what seemed the most typical characteristics of the group. The people of northern Europe, for example, were usually designated the Nordic race. Nordics had blond hair and blue eyes, light skin, long heads, and were tall. This was not totally divorced from reality because these characteristics are more common in northern Europe than in other places. But if you look at an actual group of people that live in northern Europe, how many of them would actually have all of the characteristics of the Nordic type? Not very many; probably far less than half. What about the others—the ones who might have brown hair or round heads mixed with Nordic characteristics? Were they another race? A mixture of races? No race at all? The answer wasn't clear.

One solution might be to make more types to take care of combinations of characteristics that fell outside of the original types. If you did this carefully enough and made enough types, it might account for most of the people in the world. Some physical anthropologists tried doing this. One researcher added so many characteristics and divided types into so many subtypes and subsubtypes that he eventually had more than 200 races. That didn't work either. The more types there were, the fewer people fitted into each type and the greater the number who fell somewhere in between, with characteristics from two or more of the types.

What was the matter? One major problem was that researchers were looking for something that had never existed. They believed that, at some time in the past, there had been "pure races"—groups of people all of whom had nearly identical characteristics, like pure-bred cattle that all look alike. Later, the pure races had broken loose and tramped around interbreeding to create the confusing mixture we see today.

These expectations made no sense in terms of evolutionary processes or human behavior patterns. Evolutionary processes have always been at work creating genetic variety; humans have always moved around; they have always interbred. What one would expect would be that at any point in time there would have been physical differences between separated human groups, but the differences would not have been fixed and unchanging. Environments were changing, people were moving, and genetic processes were working away. The result should not be pure races, but ever-changing patterns of variety, like a slow-motion kaleidoscope.

Discouraged by the effort wasted in devising racial classifications and dismayed by the fact that physical differences continue to be a source of racial prejudice, many physical anthropologists believe that the concept of race is useless and the word *race* so tainted that it should no longer be used. They are undoubtedly right that the kinds of research done in the past are not worth continuing. But, to avoid talking about physical differences that can be seen by anyone and to leave the word *race* entirely in the hands of racists seems a dubious practice.

What can be done to better understand physical variety? First, one should recognize the major groups (sometimes called *geographic races*) of humans in the world today for what they are—groups of people that have developed physical differences as a result of partial isolation from each other. There is great variety within each group; in fact, it has been estimated that 85 percent of the genetic variety in the human species today is within groups and only 15 percent is of the kind that makes the major geographic races distinct from each other. There are no sharp boundaries between groups; the characteristics that separate one major group from another shade gradually into each other. Finally, of course, there are many individuals and populations that do not fit any list of characteristics that are devised to describe racial groups.

The major geographic groups most easily recognized are Africans from south of the Sahara, Europeans, Asians from eastern Asia, native Australians, and American Indians. In some areas of the world there is even more variety than usual—variety so great that it is not possible to make the vague lists of physical characteristics that can be done in other areas. The Indian subcontinent and Oceania, the islands of the Pacific, fall into this category.

The diversity of people today is the result of evolutionary processes. Most physical characteristics that vary regionally in modern populations relate to adaptive advantages in specific environments in times past. Since, however, we relate to our environment through culture, traits that were advantageous in the past do not necessarily remain so today. In the past, natural selection might have favored the individual with superior resistance to epidemic diseases or the ability to survive on very little food; selection in modern America, on the other hand, may single out persons with superior resistance to atmospheric pollution or to psychological pressures.

Race and Ability

Race prejudice must be combated with facts. Many peoples throughout history have insisted that there are genetic differences between groups in physical or mental abilities. It was invariably *their group*, of course, that was innately superior. Colonialism and slavery were rooted in the firm belief that Europeans and their American descendants were naturally superior to all other people. Unadulterated racism peers at us out of the pages of 19th century writing. In the popular literature of the time, denigration of other groups—black slaves, American Indians, or Asian subjects of colonial nations—appears as a matter of course and without question. That this belief is far from dead is demonstrated by continuing claims of racial superiority. In the United States, this often takes the form of the claim that whites are more intelligent than blacks.

What is the truth? How, if at all, do different populations vary in capabilities or talents? A careful distinction must be made between the effects of heredity and the effects of environment in determining human capabilities. Variations in results on intelligence tests, in crime rates, or in average times in the hundred-yard dash may exist between groups, whether the groups come from different races, different religions, or different areas of the country. The important point is to determine whether the distinctions are genetic, and therefore almost unalterable, or whether they are the result of different backgrounds and opportunities. If, for example, slum-dwellers have inborn criminal tendencies, a social agency cannot use the same program to alter crime rates that it would use if slum-dwellers were merely the victims of unwholesome surroundings.

One must start with the realization that no test could ever be devised that would completely separate inherited factors from environmental factors. Any individual who can be tested has already been subjected to an environment and has been affected by it. Although tests cannot separate and measure inherited as compared to environmental factors, they can be used to demonstrate the relative roles of each. The case of intelligence tests given to blacks and whites in the United States provides a very instructive example, although who is defined as "black" and who as "white" in the statistics is based upon a definition of race that has a strong social component rather than dealing strictly with the place of origin of the majority of an individual's ancestors. A number of such tests have been given to large random samples of Americans. All of them show a range of performance within each group, a range much wider than average differences between groups. A number of such tests have also shown averages for blacks that are lower than those for whites. To consider the meaning of these differences, one must note that the tests (however well-intentioned or carefully done) were devised almost entirely by whites and given within the context of a white-majority culture. This factor alone would seem likely to affect test results.

In addition, it is immediately evident that in large random samples, black participants will display, on the average, less formal education than white participants, and far lower family incomes. If measures are taken to select samples with equivalent amounts of education, the difference between group averages in test scores lessens. The correction of differences in family economic background has the same effect—a decrease in the average difference in scores. In other words, the closer two groups are in environmental background, the closer they are in performance on intelligence tests. This proves beyond any reasonable doubt that environmental factors play an immensely important role in determining the kinds of performance that intelligence tests measure. It does not indicate what would happen if two racial groups of exactly equivalent backgrounds were to be tested, since it will always remain impossible to pick two groups whose environments have not differed in significant ways.

We can, therefore, make some definite statements about the performances of different racial groups, or any other kinds of groups on tests: (1) Within every group there are scores ranging between very low and very high, (2) the averages of groups are demonstrably very sensitive to environmental background, (3) numerous studies have shown that performance tests can be changed by training, and (4) although genetic differences among *individuals* undoubtedly exist, it cannot be proved whether there would be average differences between populations due to genetic factors if all environmental influences could be removed.

New Avenues of Research

The demise of racial typologies as an important problem in physical anthropology has opened the way for new and exciting research that stresses the way in which the human body adapts to environment. There is a lot that we do not know and the difficulties of research are immense, but some examples may help to illustrate the potential of the new avenues of investigation, There are many fascinating questions about the way in which genes affect the human body. Our ignorance of the topic is massive, largely because most physical features and physiological mechanisms are the result of the complex interactions of many genes plus the overlying effects of environment. Most of the informative results so far relate to those few human traits that result from the action of only a single gene locus.

The sickle-cell allele is a case in which we understand both the genetics of a characteristic and its adaptive results. This allele is associated with the production of hemoglobin, the protein in red blood cells that transports oxygen. There are a number of forms of hemoglobin related to different alleles (alternate forms of a gene) at two genetic loci. The sickle-cell allele is a relatively rare one that results in the production of red blood cells that collapse to a sickle-shape in the blood of the veins rather than staying round as most red blood cells do. People who are homozygous for the sickle-cell trait (i.e., have two alleles for sickle-cell hemoglobin) suffer from a serious anemia. Most of them die young, and very few reproduce. Heterozygotes with one sickle-cell and one normal allele suffer at most a mild anemia that is not a serious hazard to health or reproduction.

The loss of almost all homozygotes without reproduction is a very strong selective disadvantage, and one would anticipate that the sickle-cell allele should be very rare. Yet, there are populations scattered across the tropical parts of the Old World that have a considerably higher frequency of the allele than would be expected. The greatest number of the populations and the highest frequencies of the allele occur in a belt across central Africa, but high frequencies also occur around the eastern shore of the Mediterranean, in southern Arabia, and in central and southern India.

Why do these few populations demonstrate a relatively high frequency of a gene that has an inbuilt selective disadvantage? The answer began to surface when it was noticed that a striking correlation existed between high sickle-cell allele frequencies and endemic malaria. Medical studies that followed showed that individuals heterozygous for the sickle-cell gene had a considerably higher resistance to malaria than individuals homozygous for normal hemoglobin. Consequently, where malaria is a major health problem, homozygotes for the sickle-cell allele still die of anemia, homozygotes for the nonsickling or normal allele suffer from lowered reproduction because of malaria, and heterozygotes have enough of a reproductive advantage to keep sickle-cell gene frequencies fairly high.

An excellent example of the practical importance of understanding genetic variability had to do with the ability of the human body to use lactose, the sugar found in milk. In the United States, we have all been trained to appreciate the nutritional importance of drinking milk. This is quite appropriate, for milk is an excellent source of nutrients *for those who can digest it.* The fact is, however, that a majority of the world's older children and adults cannot digest milk. The reason is that lactose is a large and complex molecule that cannot be utilized by the body until it has been broken down into simpler forms. Almost all young children—under the age of three or four—can digest milk because their bodies produce an enzyme called lactase that splits lactose into two simple usable sugars. Whether the body continues to produce lactase at a later age is determined by an inherited allele. Those who have the allele for adult lactase production continue to produce the enzyme throughout their lives and can profitably drink milk. For those who do not inherit the allele, lactase production shuts off as they grow older. If they drink mild, their bodies will not utilize it effectively and they may suffer from gastric disturbances, including cramps and diarrhea.

The allele for adult lactase production is common in European populations and in populations from southern and north eastern Africa. It is rare in Asia, in parts of western Africa, and among American Indians. The adult lactase-production trait distribution correlates with areas where herding and milk consumption have been part of traditional subsistence patterns. The nutritional advantage of drinking milk had been strong enough to select for the presence of the allele for adult lactase production. The practical implications are obvious. Nutritional levels of populations that can digest milk can be substantially improved by the inclusion of milk in the diet. The nutritional status of older children and adults in populations deficient in lactase will not be raised by drinking milk; in fact, it may decline because of the digestive problems caused by milk. Some notably unsuccessful foreign aid programs to foster the use of milk in the wrong populations were undertaken before this genetic variability was appreciated.

The foregoing are examples of instances in which knowledge of the way genes work applies to health and nutrition. Such examples, unfortunately, are few and far between because few genes are expressed in such a straightforward manner. Information about human characteristics that are related not to one but to many gene loci will be much harder to obtain, and research progress will undoubtedly be slow. Skin color—that greatly magnified symbol of racial differences—is an example of a characteristic that is far more difficult to understand. Skin color is affected by several gene loci so its inheritance is very complicated. It has been frequently suggested that dark pigmentation, which can protect the skin from injury caused by ultraviolet rays of the sun, would be advantageous in very sunny climates, whereas light skin, which facilitates the penetration of ultraviolet rays and the formation of Vitamin D, would be favored in cloudy climates.

Another important set of research questions enters around the adaptation of the human body to climatic stresses, such as heat, cold, and high altitudes. Research has already demonstrated that the human body reacts to such stress in a remarkable variety of ways and that different groups may show quite different physiological adjustments. In one experiment, an aboriginal Australian and an American were asked to sleep outdoors, naked, in temperatures that went down to 40°F. The Australian had no difficulty getting a good night's sleep, but the American was too miserable and shivering to rest. Far more than comfort was involved, for the bodies of the two men adjusted quite differently to the conditions. The skin temperature on the Australian's feet dropped steadily from 73°F to a low of 45°F because the capillaries that brought blood to the surface of his skin contracted to prevent heat loss. In contrast, the skin temperature of the American alternately rose and fell, but never went lower than 86°F. The metabolic rate of the American rose above normal, as the heat regulating system of his body struggled to maintain a high skin temperature and suffered large heat losses in the process.

Physiological adjustments to cold relate remarkably well to environment. The Australian's reaction of lowered blood flow and skin temperature is excellent for the Australian desert where temperatures at night, although cold, never reach freezing and there is no danger of frostbite. In colder climates, different adjustments are necessary. Skin temperatures of Scandinavian fishermen and Iniut (Eskimos), both of whom need to maintain manual dexterity in daytime temperatures well below freezing, are kept high by an increased flow of blood accompanied by a higher rate of metabolism. In wonderful ways, the body does what it has to do.

Adjustments to climatic extremes, then, differ considerably between populations in ways that involve some of the major functional systems of the body. Still unresolved is whether the various adaptations are genetically based or whether they represent the range of *human plasticity*—the ability of the physical system of an individual to adjust to changed surroundings after a period of acclimatization. Considering the generations of native Australians who have lived under conditions similar to those described above, it is quite possible that there has been selection for genetic combinations that can adapt to these conditions. On the other hand, it could be that a lifetime of sleeping outdoors without clothes or covering allows them to adjust without any genetic adaptation. Research clearly indicates that the human body has remarkable flexibility. The adjustment to high altitude that most people experience after a few days in mountain country is a common example of the phenomenon. Until considerably more research has been done, we can only say that we are beginning to understand some of the processes of climatic adaptation, but we are still uncertain about the relative roles played by genetics and acclimatization.

The Past and the Future

Our past and future are inextricably linked. We are animals, but unique animals that depend on culture for survival. Neither of these things will change, and what happens to us in the future is fixed within these bounds as firmly as our development in the past has been.

A final intriguing question deals with how well we have physically adapted to the modern world. Twelve thousand years ago, the ancestors of everyone alive today were hunters and gatherers. Since that time, our species has undergone the transition to the food-producing life of farmers and herders, and, far more recently, to the further development of being city dwellers and office workers. Twelve thousand years is not much time, evolutionarily speaking, and in many ways we may still react with the physical and biochemical reflexes of the hunter. What had been useful mechanisms in an active hunting and gathering life may be just the wrong thing to promote survival at cocktail parties and in the dash for the commuter train. F. Clark Howell, a paleoanthropologist from the University of California at Berkeley, has pointed out that the body's reaction to strong emotion is to produce the hormone adrenalin, which releases extra supplies of stored carbohydrates and increases the flow of blood to the heart, lungs, and central nervous system. This causes a quick physiological high that prepares the body to react with vigor to the emotion-causing situation. For a hunter escaping a pride of lions or forced to call up reserves of energy for the kill after a long and tiring chase, the chemical stimulus is admirable; for the businessperson, whose response to emotion-packed situations may involve nothing more active than heavy thinking and eyebrow raising, the result may be disastrous. As Howell notes, "His glandular system cannot be blamed. It has responded loyally and with great efficiency to the demands made upon it; but if he is not able to behave appropriately and engage in the kind of vigorous physical activity necessary to burn up the accumulations in his bloodstream, then our businessman is in serious trouble" (*Early Man*, Time, Inc., 1965). To the extent that we still drag stone-age bodies to work in a machine-age world, those responsible for both physical and mental health had best take heed.

On the other hand, some kinds of genetic evolutionary changes have occurred quite rapidly. The sickle-cell and adult lactase-production genes must have been substantially modified in frequency in the 12 thousand years since humans became food producers. The malaria that promotes high frequencies of the sickle-cell hemoglobin allele would not have been a health problem before trees began to be cut down for gardens, since the malaria-hosting mosquito lives at the top of tall trees and rarely comes down to ground level unless the trees are cut. Similarly, the ability to digest milk is no advantage for a hunter/gatherer because the chance to milk a wild cow comes along no more often that you might guess. It is also likely that life in cities, which began no more than five or six thousand years ago, has had a great impact on disease frequencies and on natural selection to disease resistance. Epidemic diseases are rare among hunters and gatherers, for people are too scattered for causative agents to spread. The crowding and poor sanitary conditions of city life, however, were the world's great gifts to epidemic disease organisms, and the growth of such diseases must have introduced extremely strong selective pressures. Exactly how these pressures affected genes is not very clear as yet, although there are hints that some of the human blood groups may relate to differential disease resistance.

Knowledge of how the human body works, both genetically and adaptively, is obviously good. Some of the things that are learned may be practical and relevant for life today and in the future; others may be no more than curiosities. If Howell is right that our bodies react chemically in ways that increase stress, it is important for modern living. Stress is a major problem and one that medical techniques are far from controlling. Whether or not we could adapt to sleeping naked in near-freezing temperatures does not matter very much; the chances that we will ever have to do so are diminishingly remote. And, as culture makes cold tolerance irrelevant, medical technology makes some genetic "defects" irrelevant. Many of us have eyesight that would be a serious handicap if we had to be hunters and gatherers without out glasses. If our vision is corrected adequately for reading books and viewing computer screens, however, it hardly matters that we would have been at a disadvantage in a way of life that will never return.

What about the future? Potential food and energy shortages and crowding in urban areas are likely to subject our species to stress within the next few centuries. The changes that provoke this stress will probably occur too rapidly for physical adaptation through the processes of evolution to provide much help. Our salvation in the near future—if, indeed, we find salvation at all—will rest on our culture. Nevertheless, knowledge of the limits of tolerance of the human body and of the possibilities offered by our present genetic constitution will be factors that cannot be neglected in working out our destiny.

Summary

Variety within a species is one of the results of evolutionary processes, so it is no surprise that humans today vary considerably from one part of the world to another. Early attempts of physical anthropologists to understand this variation were not very successful; they were based on the mistaken notion that in the past there had been pure races sharply divided from each other by whole sets of physical characteristics. Had that been so, classifying modern humans into very precise groups would have helped to reconstruct the earlier races. In actuality, although there are differences between major world populations in the frequencies with which different physical characteristics appear, most individuals will not fit a type constructed by taking the average characteristics of their group. What we see today is a great variety of physical characteristics that make an almost infinite set of possible combinations. That is also the way it would have been in the past. There were never pure races and the search for them is useless.

Although the physical differences between people have been the source of racial prejudice, there is no evidence that different races differ in inherited capabilities or talents. Measures such as IQ tests show instead that the effects of environmental background on performance are much stronger than any heredity factors that may exist.

Research in physical anthropology today focuses on the genetics and functioning of individual physical characteristics. The understanding of a few traits such as the sickle-cell system is now well advanced, but most human characteristics are so complex genetically that it will be a long time before they are understood. The human body, however, will continue to adapt to its environment.

5

*The Rise of Culture*_____

The preceding chapters traced the development of the human body from a generalized primate base to the unique and varied configuration that we see today. We must now return to follow behavioral change along the same path. If the bodies of *Homo habilis* and *Homo erectus* intrigue us, the way in which these ancestors behaved should be even more interesting. Behavior, alas, does not fossilize. Dig as we might, mating patterns or family organization will never appear within a shovel-ful of Pleistocene sediment. How, then, can we investigate these elusive social patterns, particularly in that distant past when our ancestors were only at the verge of human status and lacked the massive amounts of cultural equipment that later humans possessed? There are two routes to understanding the behavior of long-dead creatures. One starts with the archaeological record, the imperishable objects left behind to be recovered. But these objects are only things and to get to meaning and behavior archaeologists must *infer*. The second route, observation of the behavior of living creatures, helps in the process of inference. For our very early ancestors, we can use the behavior of both living nonhuman primates and humans. Nonhuman primates provide the starting point because, at some time in the past, our ancestors were still not human. They became human, however, and the key behavioral differences between humans and other primates indicate the changes that must have taken place. This chapter will begin at the beginning, with the behavior of nonhuman primates.

The Lives of Apes and Monkeys

Humans have always been fascinated with other primates whom they have variously considered as friends, enemies, sacred beings, or just plain curiosities. An ape or monkey act is a surefire hit in a carnival, and monkey enclosures are the money-making attractions for zoos. But most of the attention has been drawn to the ways that other primates can parody human activities. Some can ride bicycles, wave at us with handkerchiefs, or drink out of beer bottles using their feet. Hilarious though these performances may be, they tell us little about the way primates normally behave.

Scientific experiments aimed at finding out what apes and monkeys do when they aren't acting like human beings have, until recently, been conducted mostly on captive animals in zoos or laboratories. Such studies are very useful for investigating some kinds of problems, but they do not tell us much about normal behavior because captive primates are far from normal. Let us hope that no extraterrestrial researcher ever comes to study humanity and returns with a report about human nature based upon detailed observations of inmates at a penitentiary. Field studies of primates in their natural habitats did not begin in earnest until the 1950s; now a substantial amount of data has been accumulated. There have been lots of surprises about the way primates actually live.

An early hope of researchers was that all primates would prove to ac t pretty much alike. If this had been so, we would have known how our own ancesto rs behaved before they started to become human. One of the first things prima te studies showed was that it wasn't so. Primate behavior is highly variable from s pecies to species or sometimes even between groups of the same species. Social gro ups among nonhuman primates range from rigorously monogamous, nuclear famili es that are very upset when they even see another of their species, to quite open and very large groups that shift easily in membership. Sexual patterns vary from uninhibited romps that a *Playboy* reporter would find exhiliarating to restraint that would please the most Victorian of Victorians. Defensive adaptations ran ge from fight to flight. Nevertheless, there are some obvious contrasts between human behavior and that of other primates. There are also ways in which other pr imates prove to be considerably closer to humans than anyone would have guessed.

One of the clearest contrasts between us and our primate cousins is in food-getting behavior. For other primates, the food quest is an individual enterprise. Each animal feeds itself, tries to steal choice morsels from others, and absolutely refuses to share. In addition, other primates eat food when and where they find it. There is no putting anything away for a rainy day or hiding nuts for winter. Primate food is, as always thought, largely vegetarian, although some species eat a lot more insects than had been realized. A great surprise is that both baboons and chimpanzees occasionally kill and eat small animals. They are not very effective hunters, but they become very excited about hunting and, for a while after a kill, may spend considerable effort trying to capture additional prey. Chimpanzees, breaking the general primate rule, will also share meat after a hunting episode by giving portions (if they feel like it) to other chimps who sit around begging. Cooperation in getting food, however, is certainly not characteristic of nonhuman primates and is not the advantage that they gain from living in groups.

It was sometimes suggested by early investigators that sex was the bond that held nonhuman primate groups together. This conclusion was based on observation of captive animals who sometimes gave the impression that sex was all there is in life except for brief lunch breaks. In the impoverished life style of a cage, where food is supplied and there is nowhere to go, there isn't, in fact, much else to do. Studies in the wild suggest a milder focus on sexual matters. In addition, the nonhuman primate female has a period of estrus, a relatively brief span during which the female is receptive to sex and at the same time is fertile and is likely to conceive. During most of the year, there are no receptive females in nonhuman primate groups and sexual activity is at a minimum. Given these factors, it seems unlikely that sex is the tie that binds groups together.

Not being eaten is important for survival and social living provides a defensive advantage for some kinds of primates. Species that are arboreal have relatively little trouble, for there are few predators that can operate successfully in trees on primate-size animals. For primates whose life style demands that they be on the ground most of the time, the situation is different for the ground is full of predators. There are several routes to defense on the ground. Patas monkeys, small monkeys who live in grassland and open woodland in Africa, show one route. The patas male (there is only one adult male in each group with a harem of females and young) serves as a lookout. If a predator appears, the male creates a terrible fuss, making himself highly visible while the rest of the troop "freezes" to avoid detection. The predator will usually chase the screaming, jumping male, who has a good chance to escape since patas are very fast. If he doesn't escape, he can be replaced. There are lots of solitary patas males waiting for a chance to take over a harem.

Baboons, who live in the same kind of open country as the patas, solve the problem of defense with organization and fierceness. Baboons are much larger monkeys than patas, and baboon males make a nasty fight for any opponent. In moving on the ground, some baboon troops have a regular marching order that places females and young at the center of the troop close to dominant males. The exposed edges of the troop consist of juvenile and young adult males with a few females without young. If trouble appears, the dominant males immediately move to the source of the disturbance ready to fight, while the females and young seek the safety of trees. Once again, those lost are likely to be adult males, a very expendable commodity since they can be easily replaced in the breeding routine. As a cautionary note about variety in the behavior of primates, it should be noted that not all baboon troops show this kind of organization for defense. Some troops simply run from predators, with the largest adult males running fastest and leading the pack while the females and young trail behind. So much for generalizations. Nevertheless, it is clear that both watchfulness and defensive tactics are helped by having a group of animals together and provide a selective advantage for group living.

Another strong advantage, in fact a necessity, of social living is that it provides an opportunity to learn from others. Experiments with monkeys raised in isolation shows that they are not even capable of learning to mate when they are reintroduced into groups later in life. Discussing learning leads into the whole question of the nature of social groups among primates.

Both the size and structure of social groups varies greatly among primate species. Interestingly, some of the greatest variation is between the different kinds of apes. Orangutans are the most aberrant, for they are the only kind of higher primate that does not live in social groups. Except for adult females, who keep their young with them for a few years, the animals are solitary. Gibbons (and some species of New World monkeys) are organized into a "nuclear family" consisting of an adult male and female and their immature offspring. Although the structure of the family and permanent male-female pairs is similar to that found among most human groups, it is almost certainly a coincidental development because the individual gibbon families are very antagonistic to each other and never come together into larger groups or cooperate in any way.

The other extreme of group size is found among Old World monkeys such as baboons and macaques, who live in huge troops that may number as many as 200. These troops are quite closed in membership and only adult males will occasionally transfer from one group to another. Chimpanzees are of great interest both because they are closest to humans in ancestry and because the flexibility of their group structure is reminiscent of that among humans. Chimpanzees form troops of 20 to 60 animals that have a defined territory, the boundaries of which are regularly patrolled by adult males. The whole troop, however, almost never comes together and the daily living units are much smaller groups that average around four animals. Membership of these small groups changes constantly as animals come and go, sometimes moving to other groups, sometimes going off by themselves for a while. The composition of groups is as varied as membership, for groups of all males, all females with their young, and mixed groups of both sexes occur.

Each group within a particular species has a *home range,* an area over which it usually travels in its rounds. The size of home ranges varies from species to species, depending upon such factors as the size of the animal, the size of the group, and the nature of the environment. Even the largest home ranges observed among nonhuman primates are much smaller than areas covered by human hunting groups. Nonhuman primate groups may be said to have a "territory" when they regularly defend part or all of their home range against outsiders of their own species. The degree of territoriality varies greatly among primates. Gibbons (the smallest of the apes) are extreme territorialists. Each gibbon family has a well-defined territory and spends a great deal of time arguing loudly with neighbors because of trespassing or over disputed ground where the territories of two groups overlap. Baboon troops, on

FIGURE 9   Grooming Chimpanzees

Chimpanzees spend a good deal of time grooming each other's fur. This pleasurable and relaxing activity contributes to hygiene and social solidarity. (Photo courtesy of Geza Teleki)

the other hand, may have home ranges that overlap as much as 80 percent onto the range of neighboring troops, and yet there is little friction. It is not true that all primates rigorously fight for their own territory, and the claim that this long-standing primate urge has given rise to warfare among humans is not supported by primate behavior data.

Within a group, the relationship between a mother and her offspring is very important. An infant remains very close to its mother for several years, and a strong and affectionate bond forms that in some species may continue for life. If we could communicate to a primate of another species what we mean by the term *mother,* they would understand instantly. What is lacking in primate groups (except for gibbons) is the role of father. Since there is no permanent male-female union, no single male is responsible for the young of a particular female.

A basic organizational principle among nonhuman primates is *dominance.* Each animal in a group has a position in the dominance order and knows exactly where it stands in relation to all other animals. Dominance involves both rights and responsibilities. The dominant male in a group has the right to choice morsels of food, receptive females, and anything else he may decide he wants. He also has the responsibility of preventing fights within the group and protecting it from outside attack. Females also have social rank and interact with both males and other females according to their positions. Dominance plays a key role in establishing order and keeping peace. Although threats and minor squabbles may be frequent, destructive violence is usually kept from breaking out by the fact that group members accept their positions within the hierarchy.

Research has shown that dominance is far more than a question of which animal is stronger or meaner than another. Coming from the right family makes a difference. If a young animal's mother is high in the dominance ranking, he or she is likely to come out well in the rough-and-tumble play among juveniles that helps establish the dominance order. In adult life, all sorts of very human-like political mechanisms—alliances, shifting loyalties, and divide-and-conquer strategies—are used to establish and maintain dominance. If some politicians in our society are not always aboveboard in their tactics, they can at least claim to be following a very long tradition.

Sweetness and loving are not complete among nonhuman primates, however, for field research has turned up occasional instances of vicious destructiveness. Jane Goodall, whose 25 years of research with chimpanzees has provided an invaluable fund of information, has reported an instance of what could well be described as chimpanzee warfare. The situation began when a small subgroup broke off from a larger group and established their own territory. Soon thereafter, the adult males of the larger group began systematic attacks into the new group's territory and continued until all the males of the smaller group had disappeared, presumably killed by the attackers. Goodall also observed a case in which an adult female and her two daughters snatched several infants from their mothers then killed and ate them. Other instances of cannibalism of infant chimpanzees by adult males have been reported, so the pattern seems to be a regular, if rare, one.

Research now shows that primate communication in the wild is quite rich and varied. Each species has a set of vocalizations (usually between 10 and 20 cries or calls) that convey information about such basic things as danger, anger, threat, and food. In addition, there is an even larger inventory of body communication ranging from facial expressions to gestures and body positions. Some of these are reminiscent of human gestures. Gentle touches on the hand, hugs, and open-mouthed kisses are all used by chimpanzees as indications of friendship and reassurance. This whole body of communication, however, lacks many of the critical features of human language. Nonhuman primate communications each have a set meaning; they cannot be combined in an infinite variety of ways as words can. Primate communication is entirely in the here and now. When a chimpanzee gives a food call, it means food now. There is no way to say anything about food tomorrow or explain that there is food over there behind that bush. Nonhuman primate communication, then, is limited: it is not language and does not have the potential for becoming a language.

Whether primates can be taught human language has always been a tempting question. The first serious attempt was when a devoted pair of psychologists spent six years trying to teach a chimpanzee, Viki, to speak. At the end of all this effort, Viki could say only four words and one had to listen with great generosity to understand them. In the 1960s, psychologists Beatrice and Allen Gardner decided that the problem might have been with the ability to make the sounds and decided to see what a chimpanzee named Washoe could do with sign language. The results were remarkable; after a few years Washoe had learned to use more than 130 signs. She could make simple sentences and even invent new words by combining signs she already knew. After this breakthrough, work has come even farther and it is now possible to have conversations with both chimpanzees and gorillas. A gorilla, Koko, knows 350 signs; she says she is happy or sad, calls her instructor, Francine Patterson, bad names, and even lies and tries to blame her mistakes on others. Some researchers, however, fear that the results have been over-interpreted and that most of the responses from apes are nothing more than clever copying or taking cues from the instructors. There can be no doubt, however, that once the barriers posed by an inadequate vocal apparatus have been breached, apes show a remarkable amount of ability with human language and probably grasp and consciously use some of the abstract concepts involved in language symbols.

Tool use and manufacturing by nonhuman primates has been another revelation from field studies. For many years, several kinds of primates have been known to demonstrate great skill and ingenuity in manipulating objects under laboratory conditions. We know that, in addition, nonhuman primates both use and make tools in their native habitats; several species make use of natural objects outside of their bodies, which is the basic definition of tool use. Most of these uses relate to threat displays during which grass, sticks, and even stones may be thrown about and sometimes even aimed quite effectively. Chimpanzees seem to be the most skilled primates at making tools in the wild; they have been noted to modify sticks to fish termites out of nests and to fashion sponges of leaves to soak up water for drinking. Nevertheless, all observed activities fall far short of the tool manufacturing of even very early human groups, and no tool system upon which the animals depend for survival has been created.

It has always been obvious that learning is very important for primates. What nobody had guessed was that learning went as far as the invention of *customs*, traits of behavior that are unique to individual groups. But the invention of such customs has now been demonstrated for Japanese macaques, a species of monkey kept in research colonies on an island near Japan and in Oregon. In the island colony, an

**FIGURE 10   Chimpanzee
                Throwing a Rock**

*As a part of their displays of anger
and threat, chimpanzees wave, and
sometimes throw, sticks and
stones. Usually, little skill or
aiming is involved, but on
occasion, as in this photo, some
chimpanzees throw things at the
object of their anger.* (Irven
DeVore, Anthro-Photo)

imaginative young female named Imo invented sweet potato washing. The macaques were supplied with food that was scattered on a sandy beach. One day Imo
was observed washing her potatoes in a nearby stream. That was much better than
eating sandy potatoes and, before long, her young friends began to copy her. Then,
one of the group discovered that if the potatoes were washed in the ocean instead of
the stream it gave them a nice salty taste. Soon, the macaques began to troop to the
sea to wash potatoes. To get them there, it worked best to walk on two feet and
carry them in the hands. From this beginning, walking erect has spread to other
kinds of activities so that this particular group shows a higher frequency of bipedal
activities than other macaques. In all these things, it is the younger members of the
troop that have proved most experimental and the customs have spread through a
network of females and juveniles. The older animals, particularly dominant males,
remain staunchly conservative and refuse to participate in the new-fangled ideas. In
Oregon, a macaque invented snowballs so that each time it snows the colony fills its
yard with huge snowballs upon which the animals perch with great happiness.

    Tool making and customs among nonhuman primates pose a problem when
one turns to the definition of *culture*. Such activities are certainly learned behavior
shared by the members of a group, which is the essence of how we define *culture*.
Does that mean that monkeys and apes have culture? That is an embarrassing question. Some anthropologists say yes, some dodge the issue with the term
protoculture, other say no, even if it means not looking very hard at the definition.
The best answer may be to say that we now realize that other primates are closer to
human behavior than we once thought. Most human behavior traits, with the notable exception of language, are present in at least rudimentary form in other prim-

ates. Human behavior differs in degree rather than in kind. Chimpanzees *make* tools, but only humans *depend* on tools for survival. Monkeys and apes have customs, but only in humans do customs become so pervasive that life would be unimaginable without them. Whether or not one wishes to say that other primates have culture, only humans have carried culture to the level at which it has become the very fabric of their existence.

The Shift to Humanity

We have seen what monkeys and apes do, and now we must ask the really important question: How and why did the behavior of the creatures that were to be our ancestors deviate so widely from that of the general primate stock from which they came? Monkeys and apes have remained monkeys and apes; we have not. The reason lies as much in behavior as in physical evolution.

The first step in behavioral change must have been the hypothesized shift from life in trees to life on the ground. This change opened new and different kinds of food resources; it altered defensive needs and made tools more useful; and it resulted in physical changes associated with posture. After the change, we weren't the same and never would be again.

New defensive needs on the ground would have changed our ancestors. Tree-dwelling primate species were able to loll in the branches at their ease with little fear of attack. The ground, on the other hand, was no place for lazy, incautious animals. Predators abound both day and night that are far faster, stronger, and better armed by nature than our ancestors were. The solution lay in both tools and cooperation. Even rudimentary tools have a threat value, as anybody who has picked up a rock in the presence of a fierce dog knows; and the largest of predators, who are in no genuine danger of injury, usually shy away from a shower of sticks and stones. Group cooperation and watchfulness are also critical. Ground-dwelling, nonhuman primates cooperate and communicate for defensive purposes, even though they do not do so for economic ends. Tool use, communication, and cooperation would all have been stimulated as early hominids adapted to ground dwelling.

The most fundamental changes, however, were those related to diet and subsistence (food-getting procedures). Primates are open-minded (sometimes to the point of being disgusting) about what they will eat. The great pleasure shown by baboons and chimpanzees after their rare successes at hunting suggests how readily they might shift their largely vegetarian diet to one containing more meat. However, procuring larger quantities of meat means substantial changes in behavior that have repercussions for the entire social system.

These changes came for our ancestors, though there are disagreements over whether they adapted gradually by starting with scavenging or moved directly to more efficient hunting. Most anthropologists tend to believe that scavenging was important because animals that were killed by carnivores or died natural deaths were fair game for anyone strong enough or clever enough to eat them. Even the simple sticks and stones that served as weapons for our earliest ancestors might have been enough to frighten carnivores away from a carcass. A few specialists have objected because they feel that scavenging is far more difficult and dangerous than most people think and that hunting is a more probable meat source for poorly equipped, early hominids. Whichever side of the scavenging-hunting argument is correct, the ability to hunt undoubtedly developed rapidly.

To obtain regular supplies of meat, especially by hunting, would demand a much larger territory than a vegetarian diet demands. Vegetarian primates in fruit-rich forests can live comfortably by endlessly circulating through the same few square miles. Human hunting-gathering groups that depend on game use hundreds of square miles. Covering so much ground draws upon one of the advantages of an erect posture that has not yet been emphasized—an enormous stamina for long-distance walking. Human beings can outwalk almost any other kind of animal. A human chasing a deer will be hopelessly outdistanced at the start; but if he can keep the animal in sight or follow its trail he can keep pushing it until it falls exhausted. The pursuit might take a couple of days, but the reward is a lot of meat.

Not all hominids in a group, however, can keep up with such a chase. Infants, young, and females in the later stages of pregnancy must be left behind and nursing mothers must stay with their infants. So, for long distance hunting a group must split. In recent hunting and gathering groups, it is invariably males who engage in long distance hunting. Among chimpanzees and baboons, as well, it is the males who hunt. This is good reason for presuming that the split of early hominid groups into hunters and those who stayed behind was a sexual split. Males hunted; females stayed with the young and gathered plant foods and small game closer to home. (Note the use of the word *home;* it is important.)

The group as a whole, however, would gain no benefit from the added meat if male hunters killed the game and ate it all at some distant location. Those who would gain most from the nutrition—the young and pregnant and nursing females—would be left out. So, for the system to work, the meat would have to be carried home and shared, the exact opposite of the nonhuman primate trait of every animal for itself in the food quest. The fact that the rare pieces of meat are almost the only food shared among chimpanzees is a preview of this change.

But the sharing would not be one way. Even the best of hunters may go for days at a time without a major kill. The plant food gathered by females would be critical for survival, as well as critical for a balanced diet. In fact, in almost all modern hunting and gathering societies, the gatherers provide more than half of the total food consumed. So hunters and gatherers need each other. There must be male-female economic partnerships that prove the basis for male-female pairs with some degree of permanence. The father who is missing in nonhuman primate society has appeared and he can play a role in the care and training of the young. The family that is characteristic of human societies has been born.

Another new feature that goes with this way of life is a home base. If hunters are to be gone for several days in a territory covering hundreds of square miles, they must know where to rejoin the remainder of the group. The place to stay must be secure and provide the group left behind with the things they need while the hunters are gone. This is why we can begin to use the word *home* for the first time. Another advantage of a secure home base is that it provides a place where the ill or injured can recover. For animals like baboons, which move continuously and do not share food, an individual that cannot keep up or feed itself is doomed. With a home base and food provided, recovery is possible. As Sherwood Washburn and Irven Devore have noted, "It is the home base that changes sprained ankles and fevers from fatal diseases to minor ailments."

American anatomist Owen Lovejoy has woven these and other themes into a scenario to account for the development of hominid physical and social characteristics. He believes that the key to this development was a new reproductive strategy. For other large primates, birth spacing is long and many infants die within their first year, perhaps in part because of the rigors of constant movement with their groups. A way to avoid this would have been to involve males in the care and provisioning of the young. Lovejoy suggests that very early, perhaps five to ten million years ago, hominid males began to range widely in search of food that they then carried back to share with females and young. Females could then stay within a restricted area, becoming pregnant more frequently and losing fewer infants to early deaths. There would be strong selection for erect posture to permit males to carry food and females to carry infants. Pair bonding between one male and one female would be advantageous because the male would then be protecting his own infants and thereby his own genes. To keep the male attracted to a single female, the continuous sexual receptivity of the female characteristic of humans developed, as well as female secondary sexual traits. Lovejoy's scheme is logical and accounts for known facts, but many parts of it are untestable and disputed by other experts. Whether the changes were as early as Lovejoy believes; whether monogamy appeared before other kinds of pairing such as one-male groups; what the exact order of changes was—these are all debatable issues. What cannot be debated is that the changes eventually took place. We must now turn to the actual archaeological evidence that shows the changes in operation.

The Australopithecus Homo Habilis Level

The evidence about the physical characteristics of the early African hominids is much better than evidence about their behavior, but the archaeological remains do supply two kinds of information. One is information about stone tools. We know what tools looked like, how they were prepared, and we can infer what sorts of tasks they might have been used for from their shapes. The second kind of information is animal bones, which can tell us something about the creatures associated with archaeological sites, and probably eaten, when *Australopithecus* and *Homo habilis* roamed the African plains.

The most ancient tools identified so far belong to a tool industry known as Oldowan, so named because they were first discovered in the Olduvai Gorge, although they are now known from even earlier deposits at Hadar. The tools are extremely crude. The most characteristic ones of the industry are large choppers made by chipping the end of a fist-sized pebble of rock to produce a jagged cutting edge. Flakes showing little standardization of shape or of cutting edge, and battered rocks that may have served as hammers, also appear in Oldowan sites. We have, of course, no information about tools that might have been made from wood or other perishable material, although the existence of such simple instruments as clubs and pointed sticks seems likely. The Oldowan tradition lasted from about 2.5 million years ago to about 1.4 million years ago.

Information about the animals eaten by early African hominids comes from a variety of sites. Some were butchering sites where very large animals were dismembered. At East Turkana, a hippopotamus was butchered, leaving the large bones and a scatter of stone tools. At Olduvai, elephants met a similar fate. It is unlikely that hominids could have hunted such large animals, so these sites probably represent instances in which they came across already dead or dying creatures. At Olduvai Gorge, some actual camping grounds occur on which Oldowan tools are found exactly as they were abandoned by their makers more than a million years ago. With the tools are the bones of animals, some showing cut marks, others smashed, perhaps to obtain the nutritious marrow within. Many species of the abundant African fauna of the time are found on the floors—antelope, elephant, pig, turtles, and rodents. The fact that the bones were found in a camp site is very important for it shows that meat was carried back to a home location, presumably to be shared. We still have no solid evidence of whether the meat was obtained by hunting, scavenging, or an opportunistic combination of both. The quantity of bones, however, suggests that meat was a more common item in the diet than it is for modern nonhuman primates.

Homo Erectus—Better Things

Our beetle-browed ancestors of the *Homo erectus* type have left considerably more archaeological evidence than the earlier hominids. Sites dating from the period when *H. erectus* was our representative on earth cover the tropical Old World and spread out into the temperate zones of Asia and Europe.

Tools show a greater sophistication in techniques of manufacturing and there are a variety of types that hint at an improved dexterity in both production and use. In Africa and Europe, industries are characterized by the *biface* or *hand ax,* a fully and sometimes beautifully chipped implement that would have served for a variety of cutting, chopping, and digging uses. Such hand-ax industries are now usually grouped under the name *Acheulean.* Asiatic tool assemblages show a different tradition that centered around chopper and chopping tools that are probably related to Oldowan choppers, but are more diverse and sophisticated. Both the Acheulean and chopping tool industries include other tools made from flakes.

Homo erectus must be credited with a major conquest in the world of nature— learning to control fire. The Greeks would have been sadly disappointed to learn that this remarkable achievement was the work of a low-browed, jutting-jawed creature who could probably not even speak, rather than their noble hero, Prometheus. Unfortunately, we can't pick our ancestors, either intellectual or physical. There is ample archaeological evidence for *H. erectus'* use of fire after 500,000 B.C. In the cave of Choukoutien, level after level of hearths attest to the careful nurturing of fire against the bitter cold of the Chinese winter of 400,000 B.C. On the plains of Spain, widespread charcoal suggests intentional burning of vegetation to drive animals to their doom. Fire was an invaluable addition to the stock of culture. It was essential to survival in the frigid winters of some of the northern climates inhabited by *Homo erectus.* It made caves a safe place to live by keeping out other cave dwellers. (A 10-foot tall cave bear makes a very uncomfortable neighbor in the dark.) Roasting meat adds to nutritional value by breaking down tough tissues and making them more digestible.

There are doubts about the hunting ability of *Homo habilis*, who may have been better at stealing carcasses than creating them for himself. For *Homo erectus*, the doubt is gone. Anything that walked—including some pretty scary creatures in those long-gone times—was fair game for *H. erectus*. At Choukoutien, the red deer, swift, elusive, and easily put to flight, made up some 70 percent of the diet. At Ambrona and Torralba, in Spain, elephants fell victim. At Terra Amata on the sunny seashore of southern France, the lowly oyster, not so much fun in the chase but equally good in the stew pot, was added to the list. *Homo erectus* himself was not immune in this sampling of nature's delicacies. At Choukoutien, burned and cracked human long bones and skulls with their bases chipped away to facilitate removal of the brains add a cannibal note to the menu. For some reason, these traces of cannibalism hold a strange fascination for our culture. Students who can remember nothing else under the pressure of a rapidly crammed for exam can always recall that *H. erectus* was a cannibal. In fact, cannibalism was rare—a slow-growing species that specializes in eating itself has a very low survival value—and some experts suggest that even in these early days it may have had more ritual or psychological significance than significance as a contribution to the food supply.

Fascinating details of the hunting accomplishments of these bygone days have come from the sites of Torralba and Ambrona in north-central Spain. Here, excavations that began as early as 1907 were renewed in recent years by F. Clark Howell to show the adaptation of hunting bands that occupied the area 300 to 400 thousand years ago. The Ambrona Valley serves as a pass for migratory animals (such as the elephants whose bones called attention to the sites) between summer homes in grassy uplands and the warmer lowlands of the south. Time and again groups of early hunters awaited them. As the beasts approached, the hunters drove them toward boggy marshlands bordering the Ambrona River. The frightened herds sank into the mud. (Once an animal as massive as an elephant is knee-deep in mud, it has little hope of being able to extricate itself again.) The mired beasts were dispatched as they became exhausted from their struggles, and the feast began. Howell's painstaking excavations show the evidence: the severed bones of the slain animals, the discarded tools that were used to dismember them, and clusters of charred and broken bone where parts of the meat were eaten on the spot. The skeletons of more than 30 elephants have been revealed at the Ambrona Valley sites, as well as remains of deer, horse, and aurochs (wild cattle). The sophistication, skill, and courage of the hunters are amply attested, but we must depend on imagination to reconstruct the scenes of happy feasting and comradeship as several bands must have come together to supply the manpower necessary for a drive of this scale.

Ambrona and Torralba are *kill sites*, not living sites. From Terra Amata, now underneath a suburb of Nice on the Mediterranean coast of France, archaeologists Henry and Marie-Antoinette de Lumley of the University of Marseilles have given us evidence of an actual camp site that may date from 300 thousand years ago. On sand dunes of the ancient beach, bands of what we presume were *Homo erectus* camped each year to hunt and forage. The de Lumleys' excavations have revealed the remains of possible brush huts, showing the patterns of the stakes that formed the walls. Inside the huts were hearths shielded by windscreens of carefully

FIGURE 11   Excavation of a Paleolithic Cave Site

The excavation of deep cave deposits is a difficult and exacting task. Here, in excavations by A. J. Jelinek at the cave of Tabun in Israel, a series of levels are painstakingly removed to follow the sequence of cultural change. (Photo courtesy of A. J. Jelinek)

arranged stones. The bones of animals and the tools of the inhabitants remained in place as they were left when the huts were abandoned. Even locations where tools had been chipped were found, indicated by scatters of waste flakes with a bare spot in the center where the chipper sat as he worked. Year after year the people returned to the same spot. In one location, the remains of 11 huts were found, one overlying the other. Food remains indicate that shellfish and some small mammals were eaten, but the majority of bones are those of larger animals, including stag, elephant, wild boar, and ibex. As is so often the case in sites of this age, tastes seem to have run strongly to large game. Again, of course, the remains are mute concerning the vegetable portion of the diet, since remains of plants have long since turned to unrecoverable dust.

The times of *Homo habilis* and *Homo erectus* and the associated Oldowan and Acheulean tool traditions are grouped together as the Lower Paleolithic stage. The entire span lasted from the time of the earliest Oldowan tools, at about 2.5 million years ago, until about 100 thousand years ago when new tool industries signal the beginning of the Middle Paleolithic. In this lengthy interval, our ancestral stock made enormous progress in cultural achievements. But, the *rate* of the progress was very slow and many tool types showed almost no change for hundreds of thousands of years; just for comparison, think of what the last hundred years have brought to our society in the way of technological change. Even by the Lower Paleolithic, culture had become a part of human inheritance, and the pace was to quicken as we move to the bigger-brained Neandertals.

Neandertal: Further Steps into Humanity

During the Middle Paleolithic stage, the time when *Homo sapiens neandertalensis* inhabited the earth, further improvements in culture occurred. Tools of older biface types continued to be used, but an increasing variety of tools were produced by the skillful detaching and reworking of flakes. Middle Paleolithic industries are best known from Europe and the Near East (where many of them are grouped together under the term *Mousterian*), but there is evidence of ample occupation of Africa and Asia as well. The Middle Paleolithic began about 100 thousand years ago and lasted until about 40 thousand years ago. During part of this period the climate of Europe was intensely cold, but cultural equipment was up to the challenge and Neandertals survived by living in caves and building shelters and learning to hunt the new kinds of game.

With Neandertal there are the first hints of more symbolic interests. They buried their dead and sometimes placed offerings in the grave as though they anticipated an afterlife when such things might be of use. There are also some interesting arrangements of animal bones—a stone cist filled with the skulls of cave bears, for example—that many anthropologists interpret as the stirrings of religious ritual or magic.

Less Tangible Thing

The story of human development so far has been reconstructed from material objects, the stones and bones that make up the archaeological record and tell us about the subsistence and technology of our ancestors. The record is solid enough to tell us that *Homo erectus* and Neandertal hunted large animals and hunted them with great skill. We can safely infer the social changes that accompany such a life style: home bases where some remain while others hunt, and male-female economic partnerships that create the role of father and the institution of the family.

But what about the intangible parts of culture? What did our ancestors think about life and death? Did they have concepts of good and evil? Of beauty? Did they sing and tell stories? Who were their gods? How important such elements are in human life will be evident in later sections of this book that deal with culture in the world today. Such abstract things are hard to see in the archaeological record, for this is a realm in which it is easy to put our own ideas into the minds of creatures whose very thought processes may have been different from ours.

Nevertheless, in all the sites through the time of *H. erectus,* there is almost nothing that does not have a utilitarian explanation. There are no burials, nothing that looks like art, no strangely shaped or arranged objects that tempt us to think of rituals. Then, for Neandertal, such things are there in profusion: dead bodies buried with offerings; bones of fearsome animals carefully buried or laid out in patterns that are certainly not accidental. At the very least, some sort of emotion or inspiration seems to have stirred Neandertal to actions that have no obvious practical purpose.

Abstract thought and language almost certainly go together. Can we somehow look for signs of language in the silent evidence that comes from the ground? Skeletal remains provide some clues, although they are highly inferential and subject to differing interpretations. Brain size and shape is one such clue. On this ground, it would seem that *Homo habilis* and, to a lesser degree, *Homo erectus* might still have been handicapped from having a language equal to the richness and variety of today's due to the sheer lack of storage capacity within the head. The second kind of evidence has to do with sound-producing organs, all of which are exceedingly perishable. Philip Lieberman and Edmund S. Crelin have suggested that the position of the tongue attachment and the size of the pharynx—the upper part of the throat that contorts during speech to modify sounds that come from the vocal cords—are critical for speech. The pharynx and associated tongue attachments are very different in the modern humans and in apes, and from an attempt to reconstruct the area from Neandertal skeletons, Lieberman and Crelin feel that Neandertals had much less pharyngeal space than we have today. From this, they suggest that vocalizations, even in the relatively recent Neandertal, would have been much more restricted than in modern humankind. Some experts doubt the validity of reconstructing the pharynx from skeletal remains. Others who accept the reconstruction insist that even a halting and imperfect speech could still convey profound messages. Most anthropologists, in other words, believe that Neandertal could speak and think abstractly.

To summarize the consensus of anthropological opinion, *Homo habilis* was a creature that we would still call an animal if we could actually observe it. A smarter, more communicative animal than any we know today, but not one of us. *Homo erectus* is more of a problem. Their sophisticated cooperation in hunting presupposes planning and communication, probably with at least rudiments of a spoken language. But if they prayed or cried for the dead or thought of beauty and goodness, they did so in a manner that leaves no concrete evidence. Although the word *human* has not been given a concrete anthropological definition, one might guess that *H. erectus* would fit just within its boundaries. The early *Homo sapiens* like Neandertal look far more familiar. They probably spoke and thought abstractly and, if we could learn their language, we could talk to them, perhaps as equals, if a time machine ever brings us into contact.

The Upper Paleolithic: The Birth of Art

About 35 thousand years ago, near the middle of the last glacial period, *Homo sapiens* of the modern form appeared in southern and western Europe, bringing a new set of cultures, called Upper Paleolithic. From the beginning, Upper Paleolithic cultures showed inventiveness and diversity in tool types. The techniques of chipping stone reached a point at which the better examples are works of art as well as useful implements. Upper Paleolithic people also learned to produce tools by grinding bone and antler, a technique that seems to have been poorly developed earlier. The effectiveness of weapons was increased by the invention of the spear thrower and bow, a mechanical means of adding to the strength of the human arm.

The grass and tundra lands south of the glaciers in Europe fed vast herds of bison, horses, and reindeer, and provided Upper Paleolithic men with full opportunity to exercise their skill in hunting. The efficiency of cooperative techniques such as driving animals into ambush or over cliffs is attested to by spectacular finds such as the remains of more than a hundred mammoths at a site in Czechoslovakia or of 10 thousand horses at the base of a cliff at a French site. Even though these bones must be the result of many seasons of hunting, it seems likely that the communal hunts provided enough food for large gatherings of people. The large number of Upper Paleolithic sites indicates that the combination of many animals and good hunting techniques permitted an increase in human populations.

Upper Paleolithic peoples are best known for their art. Drawings of animals on the walls of caves or carvings of humans and animals in bone or ivory show such feeling and excellence of workmanship that they have been called examples of the first great school of art in human history. It must be remembered, however, that these representations were more than works of art to their creators; there is strong evidence that they were intended to magically increase the supply of game animals and to aid the hunters in capturing them. Many animals are portrayed as pregnant;

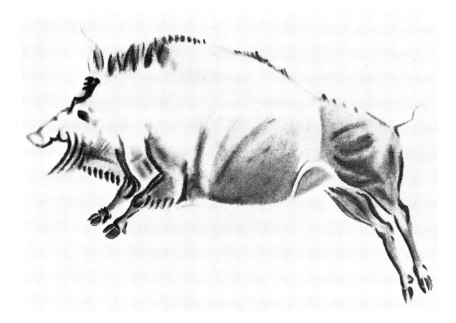

FIGURE 12   Upper Paleolithic Art

The unknown people who painted caves in Upper Paleolithic Europe were among the world's great naturalistic artists. (Courtesy of the American Museum of Natural History)

others are shown as wounded with spears and arrows protruding from their bodies. These representations are probably imitative magic—the artist hoped to bring about events by drawing pictures of them. Some Upper Paleolithic figurines carved from bone represent pregnant women with exaggerated sexual characteristics and others perhaps the male genitals; they can easily be attributed to a cult of fertility. Whatever its purpose, the art of the Upper Paleolithic demonstrates the utmost in technical skill and a genuine appreciation of natural forms.

During this stage, humans spread into previously unpopulated areas of the world as Australia and the Americas received their first inhabitants. The ancestors of the American Indians arrived from Asia by crossing the Bering Strait between Alaska and Siberia. Even today there are less than 50 miles of open water across the strait and, during the glacial periods, there was a land bridge a thousand miles wide between Asia and America. The date when the first arrivals reached the New World is still a matter of debate among archaeologists. By 10,000 to 12,000 B.C., populations had spread all over the Americas, and numerous sites show that they hunted now extinct Pleistocene mammals; but whether the first arrivals came only a few thousand years before this date or perhaps as early as 50,000 B.C. (as a few sites with still-disputed dating suggest) is still unresolved.

Adaptation to Postglacial Conditions

About 15 thousand years ago, the great glaciers that had covered Europe began to recede. As they slowly disappeared, widespread changes in climate and in plant and animal life took place. Large parts of Europe changed from open grasslands to dense forests, and the herds of animals that had fed on the grass disappeared, their place being taken by forest animals that do not congregate in herds. The Upper Paleolithic cultures that had been specialized to take advantage of the glacial environment were no longer adequate. Unlike animals specialized for one environment, however, Paleolithic people did not become extinct; they merely changed their culture to a form more suitable to the new conditions. The new types of cultures of the postglacial forest of Europe are called *Mesolithic cultures.*

At first glance, the Mesolithic cultures appear to represent a step backward when compared to the Upper Paleolithic. Most of the fine stonework, the great diversity of tools, and all the beautiful art of the Upper Paleolitic had vanished. Mesolithic tool kits were characterized by what are called *microliths*—very tiny stone blades, many of them smaller than a fingernail. Since the forest animals did not offer such concentrated hunting opportunities, human groups were generally smaller than the ones that had gathered for hunting seasons during the Upper Paleolithic, but the total population remained quite high. Fishing techniques were developed to new heights, and humanity made is first conquest in the animal kingdom by domesticating the dog to aid in hunting.

Although the problem of adjusting to the retreat of the glaciers was most striking in Europe where glacial conditions had been extreme and the cultural adaptation most spectacular, comparable changes occurred in many places throughout the world in post-glacial times. In the Americas, glacial recession was associated with a period of mass extinction. Many species of large game animals, including horses, camels, mammoths, and mastodons, disappeared—perhaps because of climatic change, perhaps because of overhunting. The Paleo-Indian adaptation, a widespread way of life that had focused on big game hunting, was extinguished and a variety of cultures, called *Archaic cultures,* emerged.

Everywhere, the post-glacial adaptations involved increasingly sophisticated and specialized use of regional resources. The process resulted in many different adaptations. In the Eastern United States, adaptation to temperate forests led to several different ways of life, some of them akin to those of Mesolithic Europe. In the American Southwest, a *Desert culture* developed in response to the possibilities of the semi-arid zone. In coastal areas scattered around the world, adaptation focused on fish and shellfish, some of them providing enough food to make possible year-round life in sedentary settlements. In the Near East, the *Natufian culture* took advantage of huge stands of wild grains to establish permanent settlements. The sophisticated use of natural resources in the post-glacial era established the setting for the major ecological shift that was to mark the beginning of food production, the topic of the next chapter.

Summary

This chapter has outlined the development of human behavior and culture. The starting point was the behavior of nonhuman primates to see what fundamental behavior patterns were shared by all living primates. It turns out that behavior is extremely varied from one primate species to another and there are few general patterns. With very few exceptions, however, all primates live in organized social groups, with dominance helping to provide the organizational structure. Organization is useful to the primates for defense and in making sure that the young survive and learn how to act as group members, but is not important in food-getting behavior.

Some monkeys and apes are closer to humans in behavior than earlier researchers had suspected. They hunt, make tools, invent customs, and can learn to talk to humans through sign languages. Humans, then, differ from other primates in degree rather than in kind, but the difference in degree is very large. No nonhuman primate uses tools constantly nor depends on them for survival, nor does any nonhuman communication system approach the complexity of human language.

In the early development of human behavior, a shift in subsistence from a largely vegetarian diet to one with regular supplies of meat was very important. When this shift occurred, it was accompanied by food-sharing, male-female economic partnerships, a home base, more effective tool use, and better communication. For the australopithecines and *Homo habilis,* the shift had begun but had not gone very far. *Homo erectus* showed great advances in culture, including better tools, the ability to hunt large animals, and the use of fire. *Homo erectus,* however, gave no evidence of symbolic behavior and probably had no more than a rudimentary spoken language.

Further cultural development was evident with the appearance of *Homo sapiens* around 300 thousand years ago. After 100 thousand years ago, intentional burials and probable rituals of Neandertal suggest symbolic thinking and are considered to be evidence of a reasonably complete language system. Finally, about 35 thousand years ago, completely modern humans appeared with their sophisticated Upper Paleolithic cultures.

6

The Change to the Modern World

Consider what humans had accomplished by 10,000 B.C. They had, by reaching Australia and the Americas, established themselves on all the livable continents and had claimed mastery of at least short stretches of the sea. They had challenged a great diversity of environments, from the parched deserts of northern Africa, to breathless heights above 10 thousand feet in the Andes and the ice-bound coasts of Siberia and Alaska. Nothing that walked, swam, or grew was safe from human predation and humans had hastened whole species to extinction. Clever chaps they, who could use mind and culture to exploit nature in a million ways, and could even survive the loss of their beloved herds of reindeer and horses in late glacial Europe and be content with nuts, berries, and the solitary elk. Feasting and glutted in good times and areas, and at least getting by when things were bad, human beings were the most effective scramblers that nature had ever seen and she had rewarded them with numbers, her own special mark of evolutionary success. Although population by 10,000 B.C. must have been at an all-time high, nature's reward was not unlimited. Vast stretches of the earth still harbored only tiny bands of wanderers who met each other at rare intervals and then moved on again. And, clever though they were, humans were still dependents. As nature prospered or suffered ill times, so did they. Drought that killed food plants or diseases that decimated animal herds affected them, and they were powerless to do other than tighten their belts and turn to prayer or magic. If population in an area grew too large, migration or starvation were the only answers.

Changing the Human Relationship with Nature

The next triumph of culture was a stage of cultural development called the *Neolithic*. From passive takers of what was there, humans became food producers—creators who themselves controlled the destinies of plants and animals and who could take an active role in what food would be available. The result was bounty beyond belief. Scattered seeds, roots, and berries could be transformed to seas of wheat extending as far as the eye could see. A few game animals disappearing over a hill on the horizon could be changed to corrals bulging with cattle. The change, as we shall see, was not a rapid one, for the new skills involved were acquired haltingly, with false starts and failed experiments liberally sprinkled in amongst the steps that proved profitable. But, compared to the scale of millions of years necessary for physical evolution or the hundreds of thousands of years for significant changes in early tool types, this change was as sudden as the magician's puff of smoke. At 10,000 B.C., there was no food production anywhere; today's green revolution is only 12 thousand years later—the wink of an eyelid in evolutionary time.

The results of this "food-producing revolution" are an awe-inspiring testimony to the magic of culture as a solution to the problem of survival. At 10,000 B.C., the population of the world was less than five million people; today it is approaching four billion. At 10,000 B.C., it took more than a thousand years for the population of the world to double. At present rates of growth, the world population will double in 33 years. Total population of our planet was not the only effect that food production had on demography. It also increased the possible size of communities. In particularly rich (and very rare) areas, nature is bountiful enough to support a few hundred people living permanently in the same place without food production. The Indians of the northwest coast of North America had such communities dependent upon the remarkable annual salmon runs that filled rivers and streams with such numbers of fish that they could be caught with rakes. But the lonely band of a few families moving continually from place to place in search of wild plants and game was the *standard* unit of hunters and gatherers, and by far the most common kind of community before the advent of food production. With food production, villages of hundreds or thousands became the standard and cities with their teeming multitudes became a possibility that had never existed before.

An associated change was the transformation from a *nomadic* to a *sedentary* life. Hunters and gatherers are forever on the move. Food in one location soon runs out and game is frightened away. Packing up and walking away to a new place is the only answer. The nomadism of hunters and gatherers is, of course, no aimless wandering, but a carefully planned routine based on detailed knowledge of where food is most likely to be abundant at a particular time of year. But, movement it is, and it affects life styles. Possessions must be kept to a minimum—a closet full of clothes would be useless and, no matter how favored a god, a two-ton statue of him would be impossible to transport. There are also health implications, for long treks are hard on the elderly, the ill, and the very young. Children tend to be widely spaced in hunting and gathering societies, for a family is heavily burdened if it has several young children to move at once. With the production and storage of food, it was possible to stay in one location year round and invest labor in possessions. Time spent in building a sturdy house and the accumulation of either large personal or community possessions were within the limits of the believable.

Food production also makes possible a regular surplus, the production of more food by a family than it can eat. A group can thereby support some individuals who do not engage in food production at all, opening the door for craft specialists, for bureaucrats, or the life of the idle rich. Spare labor becomes a commodity that can be invested in such activities as decorating houses, building temples, or regulating the lives of others. That is not to say that hunters and gatherers can never achieve a surplus. Four hunters who have just killed an elephant have a surplus beyond any doubt, but a thousand pounds of elephant meat after two weeks in the hot sun is nothing to build a village for. Some hunters do, however, have quite effective drying or smoking techniques to preserve meat and the seeds of some wild plants are

as storable as domestic grain, so it is not really fair to say that the difference between farmers and hunter-gatherers lies chiefly in the ability to store surplus. Instead, the distinction is that the sedentary lives of food producers provide more
ways to use surplus.

Full-scale food production depends on a staple crop—a crop that yields heavily and provides the bulk of the diet and the major part of the caloric intake. Staples
are always crops that can be stored in some manner and many of them are grain
crops. A number of plants became staples in different parts of the world. Wheat and
barley, domesticated in the Near East, are the staples for that region and for much of
Europe. Maize (corn) is a New World staple although, since Columbus's voyage, it
has spread throughout the world. Rice forms the basis of the diet in much of the Far
East, while millet is heavily grown in northern China. In the tropical areas of South
America and in much of the South Pacific, root crops serve as the major food
source.

Although staple crops may be necessary to provide the bulk of the diet for a
farming life, a huge variety of additional plants were also domesticated. Fruits and
vegetables, spices, and plants that provide fiber or oil were added to the list of domesticates around the world. Animals, too, were domesticated with great profit.
Where large animals such as cattle, pigs, horses, sheep, and goats were available,
their meat supplemented the diet, wool provided clothing, and their strength could
be used to pull plows and carts. In the Near East, where many of these large animals
were first domesticated, a subsistence mix of farming and herding developed that is
the ancestor of the food production system of the Western world today. In the
Americas, where there were few large animals that could be domesticated, people in
some areas developed a nutritionally complete diet that was largely vegetarian while
in others they supplemented domestic plants with carefully managed hunting or
fishing.

If food production had such an important impact on human life styles, where,
when, and how did the invention take place? Archaeologists challenged by these
questions have made remarkable progress within the last few generations. The
whole problem of domestication is made to order for archaeological research. Once
food production has started, the villages associated with food producers leave far
more tangible remains than found in the camps of hunter-gatherers. Animal bones
and many of the artifacts used in producing food are solid enough to preserve well,
and techniques for the recovery of plant remains have become increasingly sophisticated. Now, even a handful of soil from an archaeological site may be enough to
indicate vegetation in the area by means of the fossil pollen it contains.

The Near East provides the earliest evidence of domestic plants and animals.
It is an area rich in domesticable wild species. Wild wheat and barley still grow
there, thriving alongside their domesticated descendants. The wild ancestors of cattle, horse, sheep, and goats all roamed the area after the end of the last glacial period. In parts of the Near East conditions were such that huge stands of wild wheat
or barley grow naturally, without human intervention. By experimental harvesting
of such stands, University of Wisconsin botanist J. D. Harlan has determined that a
family of food collectors might gather a year's supply of grain in only three weeks
of work. In conditions like this, who needs food production? Apparently the ancient
Near Easterners felt the same way, for there is growing evidence of early villages
that seem to have been based entirely on wild foodstuffs. At the site of Mallaha,

Israel, in 9000 B.C., a group of people called Natufians built a half-acre village that included circular houses with stone foundations and flagstone pavings. At the very bottom of the great mound of Jericho, where Joshua gave his famous trumpet call, there is, dated to 8000 B.C., a remarkable village surrounded by a stone wall with a 30-foot tower. At Tell Mureybat on the headwaters of the Euphrates River, there was a village of clay-walled houses by 8000 B.C. Neither of these settlements show evidence of domestic plants and seem, instead, to have depended on unusual concentrations of wild food, although it is possible that early experiments in planting were also going on.

These were very favored locations, however, and elsewhere in the Near East domestication was necessary before people could leave their nomadic hunting and gathering routines. The site of early domestication seems to have been the foothill and mountain regions of this arid land, the only place where there is enough rainfall to grow crops without sophisticated techniques of irrigaton. By 7500 B.C., the site of Cayonu in southern Turkey had become a small village that had domesticated sheep and pigs and indications that some plants, probably even flax to make linen, were domesticated. Occupation at Hacilar in Anatolia began about 6700 B.C. with grains of wheat and barley that show the changes indicative of domestication.

Things snowballed in the next thousand years and after 6000 B.C. villages were commonplace in the rainier sections of the Near East. By about this time, Catal Huyuk in Anatolia had grown to a settlement that covered 32 acres. It was an adobe village with small rooms built together like an Indian pueblo in the Southwestern United States. Some of the rooms seem to have been shrines with paintings and sculptures of women and bulls on their walls. Catal Huyuk represents the first step toward larger, more complex communities that were to culminate in the world's first civilization a few thousand years later.

The most detailed information available about the transition from a hunting and gathering to a food-producing life style comes from the Tehuacan valley in Mexico, just south of Mexico City. There, a brilliant project under the direction of archaeologist Richard S. MacNeish has provided information so important that archaeology students everywhere have to listen to it over and over again. MacNeish chose Tehuacan for his investigation of the process of domestication because it was in the area where corn was thought to have been domesticated, and because the dry climate (20 inches of rain per year) hinted that actual plant remains might be preserved. He began by surveying the entire valley for archaeological sites and then chose a number for excavation, paying particular attention to dry caves where there was hope of good preservation. The results were even better than he had dared to expect. Layer after layer of debris in the sites revealed 10 thousand years of human occupation, including abundant samples of a great variety of food remains. The information tells the story of how human culture changed from early nomadic collectors to food-growing people with kingdoms and great ceremonial centers.

As early as 7000 B.C., the hunters and gatherers of Tehuacan had a well-established seasonal routine that involved shifting their camps from place to place as different wild foods became available. Summers, the rainy season in this semidesert environment, were the happiest times. Plant food became abundant toward the end of the dry season in May when some types of cactus fruit became available. As the rains started, more and more plants gave fruit. Tree crops, such as mesquite and guaje beans, reached the point at which their pods could be boiled and eaten. By the end of the rainy season, other species of cactus fruit became available for harvest. In good years, some kinds of produce are present in remarkable quantities, and one can imagine orgies of mesquite bean eating leaving contented bands of bloated and belching gatherers. But such success demands both good information and careful timing. Some fruits, particularly those of the cacti, change from succulent readiness to rotting soppiness in a matter of days, so it is necessary to know with great precision where the stands will be best in a given year and exactly when they will ripen. Because there are considerable year-to-year differences in such matters in semiarid climates, good advance scouting reports and detailed knowledge of how plants respond to variations in climate must be a part of the system. During the summer plethora of plant gathering, not much attention seems to have been paid to hunting. The bone remains from summer camps show that rabbits and other small animals as well as a few deer were caught in the vicinity, but even the mighty hunters seem to have had their hands full of mesquite beans and cacti.

As the rainy season drew to a close, the inhabitants of Tehuacan bid farewell to their brief life of luxury and turned to other resources. Deer hunting increased greatly in the fall, for it was mating season and a lucky hunter might even get two for the price of one. Rabbits, though not quite so abundant as during the rainy season, were still available, as were a series of year-round plant foods. These plant foods included cactus leaves (remove spines before eating!), the hearts of the maguey plant (which must be roasted in a pit for as long as five days, and even then are far short of being a gourmet delicacy), and various kinds of roots. By the end of the dry season, the food situation ranged from pretty repetitious to pretty grim, and the first spring cactus fruits must have been a welcome sight.

The details of the routine must have varied from year to year, depending on conditions. Some years may have been very good or very bad for almost everything. Other years, a single food might have been very abundant and attracted a lot of attention. In an area as large as the Tehuacan valley (70 miles by 20 miles), even different parts of the valley may have offered varying growing conditions. It is quite possible, given the pattern of summer thunderstorms, to have a serious drought in one location and a normal supply of rain 10 or 15 miles away. As long as humans depended entirely on wild plants and animals, the population could grow no larger than the number that the territory could support in its bad years.

You will notice that none of the foods discussed in the preceding paragraphs were ever domesticated. The wild ancestors of eventual domesticates were eaten, but were not important in the hunting and gathering diet. But the archaeological data from Tehuacan show that by 5000 B.C. a few plants—squash, avocados, and chili—had already been domesticated. By 3500 B.C, beans, gourds and corn, which would eventually be the staple crop, were added. The earliest corn was not very promising. Ears were tiny, often strawberry size. Each little kernel was enclosed in its own husk (glume) rather than being exposed and ready to eat. Finally, it was a popcorn with a shell so hard that it had to be popped (or exposed to some other time-consuming and traumatic experience) before the edible part could be reached. The first corn was no winner—one wonders why anybody bothered to plant it. Maybe they just liked popped corn.

In the first three thousand years of plant domestication, food production provided only a small fraction of the food eaten. By careful estimates of the quantities of different foods in the dry cave deposits, MacNeish calculates that domesticates made up no more than 7 percent of the diet by 5000 B.C, and still only 21 percent by 2500 B.C. During this period, the people continued their seasonal movement from place to place. Planting may have been no more than throwing seeds into favorable places such as moist land near streams or springs and returning at the end of the rainy season to see what had happened. It was not until 1500 B.C. that the archaeological evidence in Tehuacan shows us permanent villages whose inhabitants must have depended on food production for a substantial part of their food requirements. In Tehuacan, then, the change from wild food collecting to a reliance on food production was very slow and gradual and it took more than three thousand years from the first domesticated plants to the point at which the inhabitants could really be called farmers.

Why it took so long for food production to become the major source of subsistence in Tehuacan becomes clearer if we consider the processes involved in domestication. One can think of the processes as involving two stages. First is a stage of *experimentation* that amounts to little more than interfering a bit with nature. The activities involved are easy and simple, such things as pulling out some weeds to give a useful plant a better chance, throwing in a few handfuls of seeds, or moving a shoot from a nut tree from a bad location to a place where it may survive. These things take very little time and there is no risk because, if nothing happens, hunting and gathering routines are still in full operation. The rewards aren't very large either, only a few extra meals. There are two long-range benefits from experimentation, however. One is experience—learning more about plants and the best ways to care for them. The second is that plants may be genetically changed, even from these limited activities, making them more productive and desirable. The experiments that are successful can tempt people into more experimentation and the beginning of a commitment to growing food more seriously. It should be noted that if the presumption that women gathered plants in hunting and gathering societies is correct, it is likely that the key discoveries in plant domestication were made by women.

The second stage in domestication is developing a *dependence* on food production—reaching the point at which the loss of produced food would create a serious problem. Becoming dependent on food production is a more weighty matter and demands commitment and sacrifice. To grow a lot of food demands a considerable investment of time—time that will have to be taken away from some other activity. There may also be sacrifices in terms of land, for the best land for growing food may contain wild resources that will have to be destroyed to clear the area for fields. Risks are also increased since *dependence* is defined as going out on a limb in favor of food that is produced rather than collected. But the rewards can be very great, encompassing all of the advantages mentioned in the early parts of this section.

In Tehuacan, experimentation began early and lasted a long time. Archaeological evidence shows that it gradually improved the nature of domestic plants. Reaching the point of dependence was probably so slow because the sacrifices that had to be made to do substantial amounts of agriculture were greater in Tehuacan than in many other places. The times of planting and harvesting crops coincided with times at which some of the most important seasonal wild foods were available, so a choice between the two kinds of resources had to be made. In addition, the relatively few good areas for planting were also the best areas for mesquite trees—

one of the best wild resources—which would have to be sacrificed in clearing fields. Finally, agriculture in a place with so little rain as Tehuacan was a far more risky venture than it was in more beneficent areas.

Other areas in Mexico and Central America offered quite different conditions for the development of agriculture. Along the sea coasts, there were sedentary sites as early as 3500 B.C. Excavation of the sites produces huge quantities of shells and fish bones. Although plant remains are not preserved in the muggy climate, there is no indication that the people had domesticated plants and it is likely that resources from the sea and estuaries plus wild plants from the nearby rain forest made permanent villages possible before the introduction of domesticated plants. In this environment, the adoption of agriculture involved much less sacrifice than in Tehuacan. Most of the wild food resources are not seasonal, so foregoing them for a time to plant and harvest crops would not involve any serious loss. The zone in which crops would have been planted is an almost endless rain forest so the clearing of a few patches for fields would not seriously diminish the supply of forest plants. When more archaeological information is available from coastal zones, it may prove that the transition from experimentation with domestic plants to larger scale agriculture went more rapidly under these circumstances. As we will see, it was the coastal area that was the home of the first civilization to develop in the Americas.

Understanding the various pathways by which people reached food production still does not tell us *why* they made such a fateful choice. To us, removed by so many generations from the old ways of life, it may seem obvious—hunting and gathering seems hard and dangerous, with starvation always lurking just around the corner. This is not really so. Studies of recent hunter-gatherers show that their work is quite easy and supplies of food are secure as long as there are not too many people. Farming is far more time-consuming, with bitterly hard work at crucial parts of the farming cycle, and the risks of drought, insects, and plant diseases make famine a greater danger than it is for hunters and gatherers. Why, then, did people all over the world abandon a time-tested, easy way of life for the harder and riskier career of food production?

The first steps of experimentation with domesticates are not so difficult to understand. Human curiosity, the inbuilt primate urge to try new things, may be a part of the answer. Perhaps more important, as suggested by Richard Ford, an expert in human adaptation, was an interest in security, an attempt to insure an extra bit of food if the year should prove to be an unusually bad one for wild foods.

Harder to understand is why people ventured out on the risky limb of depending on food production. The core of the answer may lie in a suggestion made by Kent V. Flannery, a University of Michigan archaeologist. Flannery believes that experimentation with plant domestication proved to be *deviation amplifying*— one of the circles of causes where A increased B which increased A still more and so on in an intensifying spiral. In this case, investing time in domesticating plants led to more productive plants as genetic improvements were selected for. The better plants led to still greater investment in growing them, which led to further improvements, etc. At some point, population growth might become part of the cycle. If population increases—and there is evidence that population has a tendency to grow when nomadic people become sedentary—the rise of population might lead to growing more food, which might lead to more population increase in another deviation-amplifying cycle. Eventually, population would reach a level at which *producing* food would be necessary to feed the people. After this point, there would be no turning back and the culture would be committed to food production as a way of life.

Whether or not this explanation is adequate, there can be no doubt that food production was a success. Ever since it began, food producers have steadily expanded at the expense of hunting and gathering people until today only a few tiny groups of people in remote areas still subsist by the old techniques of hunting and gathering. Food production also led to further developments—the origin of civilizations or complex societies.

Social Complexity

Social complexity is like the air we breathe. We are constantly surrounded by it, reacting to it, and depending on it so automatically that we rarely stop to think what it means. Anything else is almost unthinkable to us. We may be fascinated by a planeload of boys building their own society in *The Lord of the Flies* or horrified by stories of a few survivors trying to put life back together after a nuclear holocaust, but these things are fiction; we do not really believe them. The aloneness of such worlds is too much to comprehend. But small, isolated societies are not fiction; the majority of human beings throughout history have lived and died in them. If we are to understand social complexity, we must think about what less complex societies are like.

What would life be like if we were hunters and gatherers? How many people would we meet in a lifetime? Our band might contain 50 people. There might be a half dozen neighboring bands. We would know the people in them well and many of them would be relatives. We would sometimes meet members of the bands from the other side of our neighbors. We would at least have heard of their groups and have a place for them in our scheme of life. A few times in a lifetime, we might meet a real stranger—someone from a band so far away that we did not know it existed. It would be an event to talk and speculate about. How many people would this make for a lifetime? Probably less than a thousand.

The contrast is clear. In our society, we can look out over 50 thousand people at a football game; in a day of Christmas shopping we will pass thousands. Most of them will be people we have never seen before. Every day, we must interact with strangers. If we refused to speak to anyone who is a stranger we could not function as members of our society. This is what complexity means.

Think now about the number of people we depend upon for our survival. If we were hunters and gatherers and our band were suddenly cut off from everybody else, life would go on. We could get our own food and make all of the things we absolutely needed. Suppose, on the other hand, that an American city were suddenly cut off from the outside world by an alien force field erected at the city limits. What would happen? Very soon, people would begin to die. Armed bands would roam the streets, trying to capture the remaining supplies of food. The worst dreams of the survivalists would come true. A very few might survive and begin to plant crops in vacant yards or perhaps everyone would die.

How many other people do the inhabitants of a modern city need to keep life going as usual? There is no realistic way to make the calculation, but the number is certainly in the millions. We need farmers in Kansas wheat fields, Texas cattle ranchers, the crews in factories that make trucks, and the oil producers in Alaska and the Near East. If the people who print money or the bankers in New York were removed, the economy would stop. One could go on endlessly thinking of people across the nation and around the world who have to participate if the things we use and need are to keep coming. This is what complexity means.

Another way to think about complexity is to consider the number of roles in a society. If we were hunters and gatherers, what we did would be different depending on whether we were men or women, children, adults or elderly. We might also be an individual who had special knowledge about curing or the only one in the band who knew how to make a particular kind of basket. The total number of roles would make a very short list—a page, maybe a couple. In our society, governments and large organizations have reasons to classify different jobs. The classifications can fill great books and almost nobody can understand the classifications, much less the jobs.

Think what this means about knowledge. In a hunting and gathering band, almost everybody knows everything. Although they may rarely do it, women know how to hunt large animals and men know how to gather nuts and berries. A large percentage of the information about the society is shared by everyone. In America, most people know a great deal about some tiny specialty that the majority of people know nothing about. The famous assembly line that has been at the heart of our manufacturing system symbolizes this specialization. An automobile worker may tighten the same few bolts on an endless procession of engines without knowing what happens to the engines next. Nobody in the factory can actually make a whole automobile, and even those who might know where to look it up in manuals do not have the training to do so. This is what complexity means.

We have fashioned a remarkable system. Thousands of different jobs, millions of people, books full of regulations, and uncountable bits of information must all work together, reliably and consistently, day after day. If they ever stop working, life will change and most of us will not survive. Who makes the system work? Nobody. The system runs by itself. Humans can provide the things it needs, try to change it, or attempt to make corrections when things go wrong. But any part of the system they touch interlinks with things far beyond their control or even knowledge. In essence, humans have created a system that has a life of its own. We do not really know how it works (to test this, ask a dozen economists how to control inflation or a dozen sociologists how to decrease crime) and can only hope that it will go on working.

How did human beings fashion such a strange creation as modern social complexity? First, a base had to be established upon which a civilization could be built. There had to be enough people depending on food production, so civilization was impossible until food production had been established and population increased. But not more than a thousand or two thousand years after that had happened in various parts of the world, the first signs of complexity began to appear. We will trace the increase of complexity by examining three case studies of cultural development in Mexico and Central America.

The Olmec

Our journey to the start of civilization begins at 600 B.C. near the Atlantic coast of southern Mexico. It is the tropics—rain drips from giant trees and the hot greenhouse smell of rain forest fills the air. Sluggish tropical rivers bend and twist their ways to the ocean a few miles away. On an island in one of the rivers is a site called *La Venta,* a center of the culture called the *Olmec.* The island is small and could have held no more than a few hundred habitants, the same size as an early farming village. But there are things at La Venta that were not present at any early farming village, things that show that the Olmec were on the path to complexity.

We can see at once that La Venta is dotted with stone statues, an impressive display of outdoor sculpture. There are giant stone heads, nine feet tall. They show individuals with thick lips and puffy cheeks wearing what look like old-fashioned football helmets. Other carvings portray humans holding infants in their arms, but a closer look shows that the infants are not human; their faces are contorted into snarls and the fangs of jaguars project from their mouths. Tiny carvings of jade show the same strange infantile beings with human bodies and jaguar faces. In one or two Olmec sculptures there are scenes that seem to depict copulation between a human female and a jaguar. They perhaps tell of a legend that accounts for the were-jaguar infants.

The workmanship displayed in the carvings is superb; it is undoubtedly the work of specialists carefully picked for their talent and then trained in their craft. The large statues are carved from basalt, a volcanic stone that is not found near La Venta, but must be brought from outcrops in the mountains more than 80 miles away. The largest statues weigh more than 20 tons. For a culture with no carts or

FIGURE 13   Olmec Figurine

The great skill of Olmec artists leaves no doubt that they were trained specialists. Here, a figurine of a god or mythical being indicates the kind of portable art objects that were traded widely throughout Mesoamerica. (Courtesy of the Andre Emmerich Gallery, New York)

draft animals, 20 tons is a very big stone and one can imagine the number of puffing, panting people necessary to transport it.

The buildings of La Venta, carefully arranged around a long plaza, have no parallel in early farming villages. At one end of the plaza stands a cone-shaped mound more than 100 feet tall. Along the sides of the plaza are low mounds and at the other end a compound of buildings surrounded by a wall of adobe bricks from which project seven-foot columns of basalt. The strangest find of all lay buried beneath two platforms within the compound. Before the platforms were built, pits 20 feet deep had been dug. Within the pits, blocks of the greenish stone serpentine had been laid, mounting up layer after layer until the pits were filled. One thousand tons of serpentine were place in the pits, all of it hauled with enormous labor from volcanic areas miles away. On top of the serpentine offerings, masks of a god were created by arranging stones and colored clays. The pits were then covered, never to be looked at again.

The Olmec were the first people in North America to show such telltale signs of social complexity as large public buildings and specialized artists. They had actually begun their civilization well before the time of La Venta, for a site called San Lorenzo had large stone carvings and somewhat less impressive public buildings as early as 1200 B.C. What the Olmec had not yet achieved were large settlements, and the labor for building and hauling stone must have come from gathering together farmers who lived scattered through the nearby forest. As we will see from the next example, the Olmec represent only the first step to complexity and their accomplishments were soon surpassed by other people in Mexico and Central America.

The Maya

The scene shifts to northern Guatemala, the home of a people called the Maya who built a literate and sophisticated civilization that continues to tantalize archaeologists with its mysteries.

It is A.D. 457, nearly a thousand years after La Venta. We are at a site called Tikal (Figure 14) in the center of a plaza larger than a football field, dazzled by the sun reflected from the white stuccoed surfaces that surround us. To the north is a giant platform more than 40 feet high; on the top of the platform, 11 great pyramids sweep upward to a sky of tropical blue. Stairways so steep that only half the foot will fit on the steps climb the fronts of the pyramids, leading to stone buildings with single doorways. The buildings are temples and the mysteries that take place in their small, dark rooms are not for the sight of common people. To the south, more buildings greet the eye—lower buildings with many doorways. They are palaces where the Maya elite lived and carried out their business. La Venta suddenly seems dwarfed, for here there are dozens of buildings larger than the single pyramid there. Complexity has reached a new level in the years since the death of La Venta.

Carved stone slabs taller than a human being catch the attention of the visitor to Tikal. As we become accustomed to the elaborate style, we see that the carvings depict human figures. The figures must have been important people—they stand stiffly, as if for formal portraits, wearing costumes fit for kings. Great feather head-

FIGURE 14   The Maya Site of Tikal

The photograph shows the Great Plaza as seen from the steps of Temple 1. Temple 2 is at the opposite end of the plaza with Temples 3 and 4 rising above the trees in the background. The buildings of the North Acropolis are at the right. (Photo courtesy of Philip L. Shultz)

dresses sweep upward; necklaces of precious stones fall upon chests; belts with strange objects dangling from them hold up richly decorated loincloths.

More fascinating yet, columns of glyphs surround the figures. Most of the glyphs are only shapes to us but some—a clenched fist, the head of a jaguar—are recognizable objects. There is no escaping the conclusion that the Maya had a system of writing. They did, indeed—the only full writing system ever invented in the Americas. Recently, after decades of painful but fruitless research, stunning breakthroughs have led to deciphering the glyphs and we now know what the Maya wrote about more than a thousand years ago. The inscriptions are royal records that give the names and dates of kings and tell of their ancestors, births and deaths, marriages, and battles.

The Maya inscriptions guided our choice of the year A.D. 457 for this example. In that year, a very important ruler of Tikal, a man named Stormy Sky, was buried. He was only 42 when he died, but he had already ruled Tikal for 30 years. During his reign, Tikal had become enormously powerful, by far the most important of Maya sites. Stormy Sky had built great temples and told of his accomplishments in stone carvings. He may, however, have met a violent end, for when his body was buried both his head and hands were missing.

Had we been at our vantage point in the main plaza of Tikal in mid-March of 457, we would have seen a magnificent funeral ceremony. A gaping hole had been dug through the stairway of the central temple on the north side of the plaza and a tomb prepared for the bodies of Stormy Sky and two young men, probably slaves or war captives sacrificed to accompany their master into the afterlife. A treasure trove of objects filled the tomb: knives of the volcanic glass, obsidian; shells imported from the distant ocean; a carved and stuccoed alabaster bowl. Richly decorated pottery vessels were among the marvels. Some had figures of gods brightly painted on stucco; one was carved to show two birds flanking the head of a monster; one had a lid with a handle modeled in the form of a Maya head. And one can only guess at the remarkable objects of wood, textiles, and other perishable materials that had disintegrated into the brown dust that covered the floor of the tomb when it was opened by archaeologists.

Maya kings could surround themselves with a splendor that takes away the breaths of those who discover their tombs. But, like kings everywhere, their splendor depends on the labor of their subjects. The Maya upper classes were only a tiny group and the vast majority of the people were simple farming folk. Archaeology also tells of these humble people. They lived in houses of poles covered by thatch. Small clusters of such houses arranged around paved courtyards occur every 50 to 100 yards throughout Maya sites and for miles around; the open spaces between house clusters were probably filled with gardens and shade trees. As many as 50 thousand people lived within two hours walk of the center of Tikal, plenty of hands to provide the labor for building the stone structures for the gods and the rulers.

Tikal, like La Venta, is in a rain forest. Before population became high, food probably came from corn fields on the hills and ridges which provide fertile, well-drained land for farming. Even by the time of Stormy Sky, however, the Maya were becoming so numerous that they were forced to find alternate means of farming. One of their alternatives was to develop low-lying land between the ridges—land that collects water and becomes swampy during the rainy season. This land could be farmed only by the laborious process of digging networks of drainage canals and piling dirt between the canals to create what are called *raised fields*.

Eventually, high population and overexploitation of the delicate environment were to prove their undoing. By the eighth century, Maya population had reached enormous levels and every available inch of land must have been under cultivation. The environment proved incapable of withstanding such stress and Maya civilization collapsed, the great sites were abandoned, and 90 percent of the enormous population had disappeared. The Maya case is a frightening example of overpopulation and overexploitation that provides a gloomy reminder of the dangers of worldwide overpopulation that threatens us today.

Teotihuacan

Our final scene from ancient America is in the Basin of Mexico, only 20 miles from where Mexico City now teems and pollutes. This is high country, 7,000 feet above sea level, dotted by volcanos that still send plumes skyward and wrench the countryside with earthquakes. It is a dry, dusty land lying brown most of the year waiting for the summer rains to provide a spell of growth and greenness.

It is A.D. 400. In the Basin of Mexico, Teotihuacan has already begun an urban tradition that will culminate a few years from now when Mexico City becomes the largest city in the world. Unknown to the civilizations of Europe and Asia, Teotihuacan is one of the great cities in the world of A.D. 400. There were eight square miles of construction and 150 thousand inhabitants. In Teotihuacan, one could have walked for hours without setting foot off of pavement or seeing anything except buildings and people. One could have walked down great avenues, straight as strings and laid out with an engineer's precision, or wandered through narrow lanes between the walls of apartment buildings. The trees, gardens, and open spaces of Maya sites are not there; Teotihuacan is a true city.

The center of Teotihuacan is the Street of the Dead (our name; nobody knows what the ancient inhabitants called it). It starts from the towering Pyramid of the Moon and within a few hundred yards passes the Pyramid of the Sun, even larger—more than two hundred feet tall. But the great pyramids are not the only construction, for the entire street is lined with platforms (Figure 15). The buildings that sat atop the platforms, almost certainly temples festooned with decorations, were of perishable materials that leave no trace after a millennium and a half.

The Street of the Dead is a very public place. Spacious enough to accommodate thousands of visitors and more than three miles in length, it has nothing to block the view or hinder the free passage of the multitudes. René Millon, the archaeologist who mapped the ancient city, believes that Teotihuacan was a pilgrimage center that attracted pious visitors to seek the favors of the gods. But in meeting the gods, the visitors, like modern tourists, must have left their money behind. At the side of the Street of the Dead in the exact center of the city is a huge marketplace. Although it is risky to project modern values into the past, we cannot resist imagining Teotihuacan merchants promoting temple construction and ceremonies as investments with tangible, as well as spiritual, returns.

The image of the hard-headed Teotihuacan businessman grows even stronger when the rest of the city is considered. Anyone who walks through the site today will notice areas that are covered with chips of black or greenish glass. They are pieces of obsidian, a glass that forms during volcanic eruptions and is available as pebbles or outcrops in only a few locations in Mexico and Central America. Teotihuacan is near two of the most important obsidian sources and used the stone, the broken edges of which are remarkably sharp, for making tools. The huge areas of the site covered by obsidian are remains of workshops that turned out obsidian tools. There were more than 400 obsidian workshops in ancient Teotihuacan that produced enough blades each year to serve the needs of 10 million families. In other ancient sites, some of them hundreds of miles away, the obsidian blades from the city appear, mute testimony to the size of Teotihuacan's trade network.

FIGURE 15   Teotihuacan

*Teotihuacan, a few miles north of Mexico City, was one of the great cities in the world
in the first centuries* A.D. *The Street of the Dead is in the center with the Pyramid of the
Moon in the foreground and the Pyramid of the Sun to the left.* (From *Urbanization at
Teotihuacán, Mexico,* v. 1, pt. 1, by René Millon. Copyright © 1973 by René Millon.
Used by permission of the author.)

Even today, feeding 150 thousand people is a major enterprise. It was possible at Teotihuacan because springs just outside the city provided water to irrigate 10
thousand acres of fields. Irrigation is hard work; canals must be dug, then regularly
cleaned of accumulated silt. But, in a climate as dry as that of the Basin of Mexico,
it provides the vital difference between an agricultural system that will suffer serious losses from drought in one year out of two and one that will produce abundant
crops each year from the fertile volcanic soil.

A city as large as Teotihuacan needed leadership. Administering to the needs
of so many inhabitants provided careers for organizers; fortunes were to be made
from directing the huge workshops and the far-flung trading expeditions; somebody
had to supervise the irrigation system. It is likely that Teotihuacan had conquered at
least the neighboring valleys of central Mexico, so there were military forces to be
led. Those who wielded power at Teotihuacan were addicted to living well, for the
city is full of sumptuous residences decorated with splendid hand-painted murals.
But, unlike the Maya, the leaders of Teotihuacan were not given to personal
glorification of any kind that can be recovered by archaeologists. There was no writing system to tell of their glorious deeds; they did not carve or paint their pictures
for posterity; they did not expend their goods on lavish burials. They were a different people with a different style of life.

What do these examples tell us about the development of complexity? First, it is clear that complexity develops gradually. The Olmecs were only at the edge of civilization. We can infer that they had leaders, because somebody must have had the authority to organize laborers to haul stone, carve statues, build public buildings, and deposit the offerings of serpentine slabs. There were also some craft specialists to do skilled jobs such as carving. But the Olmec still had no cities and supported themselves by the simplest kinds of farming routines.

In the thousand years that followed the Olmecs, Mesoamerican cultures became far more complex. The size of population and grandeur of public buildings in Tikal and Teotihuacan is vastly greater than at any Olmec site. Economic specialization had become far more complex, especially at Teotihuacan with its vast obsidian industry and trade networks that stretched for hundreds of miles. For the Maya, there is clear evidence of leaders who can be called kings, with all the implications of power and splendor that the term implies.

The differences between the Maya and Teotihuacan are also instructive for they demonstrate that complexity can take different forms. The Maya developed writing; Teotihuacan did not. Teotihuacan was a huge manufacturing center; the Maya, desite many specialists, did not have an economy of such scope. Maya kings proclaimed their glory for future generations to see; the rulers of Teotihuacan seemed more concerned with gracious living at the moment.

Studying civilizations that were not a part of the Western tradition also shows that things that we might consider essential for complexity are actually incidental. Mesoamerican civilizations had no beasts of burden and did not use the wheel. They had no metal and did even the most complicated stone carving and construction using stone tools. In tracing the history of Western civilization, it is easy to focus on the importance of such technological features. For Western civilization, which always had a strong technological bent, wheels, animal power, and metallurgy may have been critical, but the data from Mesoamerica prove that complexity is possible with other, and simpler technologies.

Ancient Mesopotamia and the Rise of Western Civilization

Like agriculture, social complexity appeared independently a number of times in human history. The roots of our own Western civilization go very far back. They lie originally in the civilization of Mesopotamia in the ancient Near East—the earliest civilization to arise anywhere in the world.

Mesopotamia is a parched land—a land of deserts, camels, and palm trees. The sun beats down and rain never falls. Human habitation would be impossible there were it not for the life-giving water of two great rivers, the Tigris and Euphrates. River water makes the desert a rich land and, as early as 5000 B.C., settlers moved into the plain between the rivers and began to build what was to become Mesopotamian civilization.

Glimmers of complexity came not long thereafter—small public structures that seem to have been temples. About 4000 B.C., people suddenly drew together into much larger communities, the earliest cities in the world. Although still small, with only around 10 thousand inhabitants, the cities were complete with the signs of civilization—large public buildings, specialized craft production, and the concentrations of wealth that indicate social classes.

With developing complexity went a series of technological innovations that were to set the pattern for Western technology. Animals were put to work: oxen pulled plows, an advance that allowed more effective cultivation of the flat lands of the river valleys; horses were used for riding and to pull wheeled vehicles since the wheel had also been added to the list of inventions. Copper had been used since 6000 B.C., but copper alone is too soft to be good for tools; by 3000 B.C., however, the process of alloying copper and tin to make bronze provided a harder metal for tool manufacture. Irrigation works become larger and larger as engineering skills developed. Trade burgeoned because the river valleys lacked important resources; they had no metal ores, no large trees for construction, and almost no stone. So all these things were obtained from surrounding regions in exchange for the food and textiles that the cities produced in abundance. To keep track of the increasingly complex economy, writing appeared by 3400 B.C. and the abundant clay tablets on which records were kept tell of the doings of the Sumerians, the first civilized inhabitants of Mesopotamia.

Before 3000 B.C., the temple was the center of Mesopotamian society. Far more than a place of worship, it owned lands and herds, employed specialized craftspeople, engaged in trade, and, in effect, functioned as a giant corporation. Eventually, however, perhaps under the pressure of increasing warfare that demanded professional military leaders, an office of king arose and grew in power.

At the start of Mesopotamian civilization, each city was a separate state, often fighting bitterly with neighbors over land and power. For a long time, the continual wars led only to short-lived conquests of one city-state by another that lasted only until the conquered city gathered enough strength to rebel. In 2370 B.C., a man named Sargon founded a dynasty at the city of Agade (Akkad) that was to change the rules of the political game. Sargon built a great army and conquered rival after rival until he had created an empire that covered all of Mesopotamia. The empire lasted for Sargon's lifetime, but his less-skilled successors soon saw it crumble into nothingness. Nevertheless, an ideal had been established and every ruler thereafter dreamed of conquering the whole of Mesopotamia once again. As the centuries passed, Mesopotamia was now and then united as more and more powerful and long-lasting empires rose and fell. The cost of ruling such large empires was enormous and great bureaucratic organizations flourished, as well as great irrigation works to support them. With empires and their enormous ruling organizations, cultural complexity had come a step further.

Although the early civilizations we have discussed are a long way from the remarkable complexity that envelops the world today, they show the trends that led to it. Greater and greater numbers of people under a single rule, ever more sophisticated technology, and larger and larger bureaucratic organizations were linked in a spiral of increasing complexity. Finally, in the 18th century, the Industrial Revolution brought machinery to the front in the economic process and changed the structure of the Western world, leading inevitably to the worldwide network of civilization that we see today.

Summary

Ten thousand years ago, all the people in the world lived by hunting and gathering, a way of life that limited them to whatever population the supply of wild food permitted. Then, a fundamental transformation in the relationship between humans and nature took place—the invention of food production. This invention opened the door to the possibility of greatly increased population, sedentary life, and the production of a surplus that could be used to support people who did not grow their own food.

Domestication occurred earliest in the Near East where by 7500 B.C. there were already sedentary villages growing wheat and barley and raising animals such as sheep, goats, and cattle. The transition took place later in the Americas where archaeological research in the Tehuacan Valley of central Mexico provides the details. In Tehuacan, hunters and gatherers depended on the desert resources available in the area—domesticated corn, squash, and beans, the key food crops of native Americans. Although the first domesticated plants appeared as early as 7000 B.C., this was followed by a long period of experimentation during which the people continued to rely on hunting and gathering for the major part of the food supply. Not until 1500 B.C., more than five thousand years after the first domestic plants, did the inhabitants of Tehuacan settle down in villages to become full-time farmers. The reason it took so long for the people of Tehuacan to become dependent upon farming was probably that the environment there poses severe risks for farmers and serious conflicts between farming and hunting and gathering.

The next major step in human development was a social transformation—the appearance of civilization or complex society. Complexity involved the creation of networks of interdependence of vastly greater scale than had existed before, the proliferation of the number of jobs and roles, and the uneven distribution of wealth and power between social classes.

Three examples from ancient Mesoamerica illustrate the slow growth of complexity. The Olmec, between 1200 and 400 B.C., created a society with public buildings, massive offerings, and stone carvings done by specialists, but without the congregation of large numbers of people. By the fourth century A.D., the scope of complexity had increased. The Maya had developed a civilization with enormous stone temples and palaces and had invented a writing system that enabled their king to boast of their glory and to leave records that can be read today. In the Basin of Mexico, the people of Teotihuacan had built a capital city and pilgrimage center that contained 150 thousand inhabitants and served as a manufacturing and trade center.

The tradition of Western civilization is even more ancient. It goes back to ancient Mesopotamia, where the world's earliest cities and system of writing began between 4000 and 3000 B.C. The Mesopotamians introduced such important technological inventions as metallurgy and the wheel and harnessed the energy of animals for human use. Through the centuries, these civilizations and others became even more complex until today complex society covers our entire planet.

7

Culture as a Tool

We speak of culture as a tool in two different senses. The preceding chapters have shown that culture is a unique tool among humans. Indeed, in large part culture is what makes hominids such distinct animals. A primate heritage gave a remarkable hand-eye dexterity which was the potential for tool using. As tools became an important part of being human, their use doubtless affected the course of evolution. Thus, tool use and certain biological traits fed back upon each other in evolutionary development.

From the beginning, however, culture was more than the wood, bone, or stone tool. People regularly made or fashioned a particular type of tool so that we can speak of a tradition. There was a way of making tools, a mind's eye tool or ideal, a concept of what a tool should look like. Culture was a definition of things, a concept that existed in the minds of people. What they fashioned or made was direct evidence of the thoughts they had about what should be.

Some social scientists easily ignore the distinction between the evidence and the idea by defining *culture* as everything that people have, do, or think. One early anthropologist saw culture as a "complex whole which includes knowledge, belief, morals, art, law, custom, and any capabilities and habits acquired by man as a member of society." A later anthropologist stressed simply the evidence for culture by defining it as "the man-made part of the environment." However, most anthropologists today would lean toward definitions that stress culture as thought or as a mental process. One such definition says culture is all the "historically created designs for living, explicit and implicit, rational, irrational, and nonrational, which exist at any given time as potential guides for the behavior of man."

This latter definition stresses regularity, pattern, or design in culture. The design will be for a culture; that is, when we think of the differences between Mesopotamia and Mesoamerica, we are thinking of the mental constructs these two different peoples had about what life should be like. In practice, of course, there was a Mesopotamian pattern of culture. Prehistorians have reconstructed this pattern of culture from physical evidence; we can go a step farther and infer patterns for culture also. We can reconstruct the mental guidelines that Mesopotamians and Mesoamericans must have had in order to do the things they did.

In this sense, we are speaking of cultures as two different tools, one a Mesopotamian and the other a Mesoamerican. Commonly, anthropologists will refer to

FIGURE 16

This Chinese coke maker agrees with others of his commune about what his product should look like, but the commune members are still working out norms as to how the product should be distributed. (Photo by Ernest Schusky)

the two, when comparing them, as two different cultures. However, the definitions supplied above suggest that culture is only one thing, "a complex whole" or "an explicit and implicit design." At this level, culture becomes a tool of anthropologists, the most important one in their work kit. That is, culture is a concept about human behavior. It must be an abstract from all human behavior, one that can be applied to understand all humans, living or dead. Thus, anthropology becomes so inclusive as to claim to study human behavior of all people, at all times, in any place.

Culture and Evolution

To learn about culture as a human process, anthropologists feel it is necessary to look for cultural origins in our biological background. The potential for an origin seems to lie with the mammals. One important trait of these warm-blooded animals is that they are dependent upon their mothers during the nursing period. This time gives them the opportunity to observe and learn from a parent animal. In line with this potential is the development of a more convoluted brain, one more capable of learning.

Among the primates, an arboreal life intensified the parent-child relation. The mother concentrated her attention upon the single offspring; the infant had an unusually long period of dependency, and an increasingly convoluted brain gave special emphasis to the process of learning. Additionally, arboreal life selected continuously for visual acuity, good hand-eye coordination, and an ability to make fine discriminations.

When some primates left the trees to live in the savanna or grasslands, other adaptation must have been required because ground-dwelling primates face a new danger, one of predators. Predation is rare in the rain forest, but predators abound in the grassland with its herds of grazing animals. Some primates adapted along the lines of other savanna dwellers. For example, sexual dimorphism became pronounced among baboons. That is, males became much larger than females, male incisors became like fangs, and many males became brightly colored. Some species of ground-dwellers learned to flee when other species, such as zebra or deer, became alarmed. These animals depended on their sense of smell. With keen eyesight, the ground-dwelling monkeys sometimes spotted predators and gave their own alarm cries.

Most importantly, these primates developed a strategy for coping with predators. This strategy suggests an origin of social life. Although present species of ground-dwellers, which are mostly baboons, have each worked out their own strategies, a common theme is for some males to be on the periphery of the group. They first sense danger and give an alarm cry. Large, nearby males rush to the danger while other males scurry off with the females and young. A half dozen screaming males, with large incisors and bright colors, are enough to discourage leopards, cheetahs, and hunting dogs. This baboon offense defends a group against anything except lions and humans.

For such a complex group reaction, natural selection must have favored certain kinds of animals. The physical traits of sexual dimorphism are obvious; but there must have been just as much selection for the more subtle traits contributing to social life. An ability to communicate would be of obvious importance; today, many of the ground-dwellers have a dozen or more different cries that communicate a specific meaning such as danger. Some baboons even have a cry that communicates a danger cry was a false alarm. Some animals also distinguish as to whether a threat is from a predator or from other baboons. These sounds must have some genetic base but, since the cries do vary among different groups of the same species, it is clear that learning has become important in the communication.

Likewise, a combination of learning and genetic change must have occurred in all the factors that contribute to an enduring social life. Glandular changes must have been a part of selection as the ability to get along with others became a necessary part of life on the savanna. We will never know all the changes that were necessary, but whatever contributed to the ability to share learning was important.

Such a selection for shared learning would have been vital for the primates ancestral to the hominids. Some adaptation surely put much more value on learning ability and ability to live in complex groups. This adaptation was hunting. As noted earlier, the shift from being the hunted to being the hunter is a likely part of bipedalism. It would also intensify selection for a certain kind of intelligence. In short, a long distance runner-walker that can carry some of its food supply has a special hunting ability. This ability also requires an unusual degree of intelligence; one must keep on the track of animals for hours or even days. Thus, it is necessary to make the fine discriminations that allow one deer track to be distinguished from another.

Anthropologists could learn more of the adaptation by studying it in similar animals, but there are no other hunting primates nor any similar bipeds. We must be content with hunting dogs that are probably the closest analogy. The study of their behavior shows they are remarkably cooperative. The pack chases a herd, singling out one of the slower animals. This scared creature, once separated from its herd, begins to run in a wide circle. The fastest dogs stay at its heels; slower dogs will begin to short-cut across the arc of the circle. As the fast dogs tire and fall back, they, too, begin short-cutting once revived. Eventually, the tired animal, such as the zebra, comes to bay. While some dogs hold its attention in front, other dogs bring it down from behind. An even more remarkable cooperation occurs when females bear litters. The dogs dig holes where the females give birth. Males hunt around this area, gorging themselves on a kill, then return to the females. When the females nuzzle the males, they regurgitate part of the kill, thus feeding the females and the young.

Most of this behavior is obviously genetic; indeed, so much is genetic that we hesitate to call it cooperation; yet it is close to it. Something like it must have occurred among the early hunting primates. Surely even the first hunting primates had something that was closer to a true form of cooperation; that is, they had a learned process. Based on what is known of modern hunters or food collectors, the early hominid group or band probably consisted of 10 to 20 adult men, about the same number of women, and 10 to 30 children plus a few elderly. Variation on this size and composition occurs according to environments; for the savanna, it was likely close to the average. Since women do not have a sexual receptivity cycle like hunting dogs, human females of the band would be pregnant and giving birth at different times. Also, the much longer period of infant dependency would seem to require that males be wide-ranging hunters while pregnant women and lactating mothers remain close to a base camp gathering vegetation. Thus, among humans, hunting results in a regular division of labor based on sex and a focal point, the base camp.

On the hunt, men must frequently make decisions about what and how to hunt. Once an animal has been targeted, for instance, men will make a series of predictions about what it will do. In turn, they must decide what they will do based on their predictions. In contrast to hunting dogs, which simply react to the immediate behavior of the quarry, human hunters operate under a number of predictions or conditions. They must communicate such thinking as, "If the animal circles, then we split into two groups; if the animal plunges into the forest, we fan out to cover a large area." Such planning for the future must be based on past experience. Modern hunters often talk in terms of, "When we entered the forest single file, the animal escaped to our flanks; when we fanned out, one of our group scared the animal to run into the spear of another of our group." This kind of conditional thinking, a consideration of past and future, seems particularly appropriate for what is known about past and present hunting patterns among humans. Likewise, women must know much about the plants and small animals they collect. They, too, will continually make predictions based on experience. They will profit from extensive discussions or communication about their labor just as men do. Of course, both men and women must participate in decisions about locating a base camp or meeting at some future site. Quite often they will meet according to certain conditions; individuals must be able to learn the variety of expressions necessary for such a way of life. In sum, food collecting became an important selective factor for the hominids just as certain hominid adaptations, such as bipedalism, made hunting and gathering possible as an adaptation.

Language in Human Communication

Since 1970, we have learned that other animals have far more complex systems of communication than we ever imagined. Some insects, such as bees, communicate to the extent of giving directions to a food source, indicating both direction and distance. Chimpanzee communication has surprised us even more. A few animals have mastered a large vocabulary and complex concepts of grammar. These laboratory animals reveal great potential but, in their native habitats, communication has been as much through body and facial gestures as through sound. Thus, human and nonhuman communication still remains on quite different levels.

First, in using sounds nonhumans strictly limit particular meanings to specific sounds. Nothing like "waste" and "waist" occur. Nor are sounds combined to generate new meanings. That is, almost all sounds are monosyllabic. Second, communication is almost always about feelings or emotions. Third, these emotional states are always contemporary ones. An animal can show by sound, facial gesture, or body posture what it is presently feeling. Hunger, danger, or sexual urgency are readily communicated, but it is difficult to find any evidence that an animal ever thought about such things or discussed having such feelings in the past or future. Finally, most of the communication is expressed in gesture or by other means depending on sight, which is a hallmark of the primates. Humans, in contrast, rely largely on sound in their communication. Indeed, language is thought of almost entirely in terms of sound.

No one knows when sounds became the primary means of communication among human ancestors. The vocal organs of *Homo erectus* and even the Neandertals are similar in some details to those of gorillas and to preverbal infants, suggesting that they, too, might be incapable of speech or language as we know it because of the vocal tracts and not necessarily because of the lack of mental ability. On the other hand, the cultural developments of *H. erectus,* if not the Australopithecines, suggest that they must have had language. That is, the cultural achievements are hard to imagine as being produced by anything but a symbol using, speaking, thinking human. Until more is learned about the physiology and mental processes of speaking, we must depend on the fundamentals of known languages to understand the relation between thought and culture.

When considering all that must occur in speech, it is logical to conclude that such an activity is clearly impossible. Only the evidence of billions of speakers negates the logic. Speech must begin as a thought in the brain of one person. This thought consists of some chemical or electrcal impulse, or a combination of them. The pattern is then converted to air pressure through the vocal tract where it is modified by the vocal cords, the glottis, the tongue in relation to the palate or the teeth, and the lips. Then, only half the process is complete. The speech now consists of sound waves. These waves must strike a listener's ear drums where vibrations are converted to a nerve impulse that feeds into another brain. The impulse must stimulate another chemical or electrical impulse similar to what occurred in the first brain. The process is so complex that it seems likely no identical impulse is ever received as it was begun. Even a simple "yes" or "no" probably does not mean exactly the same thing to two different people.

Such complexity of language allows far more than simple communication, such as the posturing of baboons. It allows prevarication, or lying, for example. Aside from its moral aspects, consider what is involved in lying. It requires considerable imagination to communicate quite different events from those that actually occurred. In short, lying is a form of imagination. Just as it is difficult to imagine baboons imagining, one cannot think of them as lying. If a baboon gives an alarm call when no predator is present, we do not think of it as lying. It has simply made a mistake in its communication pattern.

In thinking about thought and such features as lying and imagination, it is obvious that a great range of diversity must exist in order to deal with such abstractions. Thus, the complexity of language begins to make sense. Linguists, or the people who study this phenomenon, have long been aware of the complexity and of language's potential for diversity. With the development of linguistics as a science, linguists began to discover many basic similarities among all languages.

Structural Linguistics

The universal features of language are illustrated by an examination of basic elements that occur in all languages. Linguists call the most basic element a *phone*. It is the minimal unit of sound. Any human voice is capable of producing hundreds of different phones; likewise, the ear is capable of distinguishing among the differences. Note that hearing or reception of speech is just as important as speaking or producing sound.

In any particular production-reception system, that is a particular language, speakers-listeners select fewer than a hundred of the sounds to make a language; English has about 50. A language is then built on this selection. A community of speakers must agree that these, and only these, sounds will constitute their speech. Still, on one level, minor differences are recognized so that hundreds of individual differences in sound production register in our brains and allow us to identify individual voices. For example, recall how many people you recognize on the telephone from just a few words. How people learn to recognize the many voices that they do is beyond present explanation. Logically, the task is impossible, but all humans do it with ease. In sum, an immense diversity of sound is produced and heard, one that allows recognition of individuals; at another level, these differences are ignored where the sounds are heard simply as those of a particular language.

For some unknown reasons, all languages have a kind of economy built into their sound systems. Just as we combine all the individual differences into one system, we also combine many different phones into a set, called a *phoneme*. That is, the production of phones is stylized or modified according to the other sounds that come before or after it. Speakers are never aware of what they are doing, but speakers of all languages do it. An example of a phoneme (a combinaton of two or more phones) is perhaps the best way to describe it.

In English, the K in "kid" and the K in "skid" are assumed to be the same sound. Even if you pronounce them aloud and think consciously about it, you are unlikely to discover a difference. But, if you hold your finger close to your lips and say the two words aloud, you will feel a hard breath on your finger when saying "kid" but only a modified one when saying "skid." Now feel the pronunciation of "kick back." Again, the initial K sound is felt on the finger, but the second K never produces a breath, that is, the sound is never exploded. The final K may or may not be exploded. Selection of an appropriate phone depends on what follows. If one were to say "kick back boss," the final K would be as breathless as the internal K. If the word comes at the end of a sentence, it probably will be an exploded phone. These two different phones, which are quite different sounds in some languages, are really just one sound in English, but a sound that has variations under various sound environments. The variations are phones; each can be easily recognized by a linguist, but they combine into a phoneme. The phoneme has a meaning in a sense that each of the letters of the alphabet has a meaning. We can use these sounds or sets of sounds in our communicaton. Thus, a definition of a phoneme is that it is the minimal unit of sound with meaning. Realize that this kind of meaning or mental set is a category of thought; it does not carry a dictionary kind of meaning. No one yet understands why phonemes are necessary, but all languages make use of them and all have complex rules as to how phones are regularly combined into phonemes.

Phonemes are combined to make *morphemes*. These units do have a dictionary or semantic meaning. *Free* morphemes are words; *bound* morphemes are units such as the "un" or "non" positioned at the beginning of English words to signify a negative or opposite meaning. The "s" sound added to the end of English words signifying the plural is another bound morpheme. Bound morphemes can occur in the middle as well as the end or beginning.

Morphemes are formed on the basis of rules just as complex as those formulating phonemes. No language allows the combination of just any phonemes; only certain combinations are permitted. These complex rules are learned at an early age even though few people are ever aware of the rules. For example, no morpheme in English ever begins with the sound represented by the letters "ng." If an English speaker is asked to pronounce "ngsi," the tongue is tied and the speaker complains that it is impossible. If the sounds are rearranged to "sing," the same person manages the morpheme with no trouble. Although numerous combinations of phonemes, consonants, and vowels are permitted, numerous other combinations are prohibited.

Structural linguists have established systematic methods for the study of phonemes and morphemes. Common processes occur in all languages, and *phonemics* and *morphemics* have illustrated the universal nature of language. However, language does most of its work at the level of combining or, as linguists say, stringing morphemes together. This process of stringing morphemes is called *syntax*. Grammarians long studied the process, but many of the rules they devised were as misleading as they were insightful. For instance, grammar tells us that "John is eager to please'' is the same kind of declarative sentence as ''John is easy to please.'' Both sentences have ''John'' as the subject or actor with ''is'' as the predicate or verb. The grammarians should really never be forgiven for claiming that John is the ''actor'' of ''John is easy to please.'' Clearly, the intended meaning of this sentence is, ''It is easy to please John.'' John is a kind of receiver of the action.

What is truly interesting about this sentence is the process by which an obvious original string of morphemes was transformed. The original sentence must have been the thought process equivalent to, ''It is easy to please John.'' A speaker then not only converted the brain waves to a flow of air in the vocal tract but also transformed a direct expression of the thought to a more complex one, but a kind of reversal, making an object appear somewhat as an actor. Think of how interesting the problem of analysis becomes. What are the rules for taking a string like ''It is easy to please John'' and transforming it to ''John is easy to please.'' What is the relation of this transformation to the one that asks, ''Is it easy to please John?'' Surely such questions are more interesting than ones the grammarians posed about subjects and predicates. Consider, as a further example, the differences between ''red on green'' and ''green on red.'' A child learns to make these differences in meaning by changes in stringing while so young that grammarians have never considered them. Yet, a complex difference in meaning arises from a simple reversal of strings. Could a chimpanzee or other animals make such distinctions? Is language necessary for such a distinction?

If earlier scholars had recognized such issues they might have moved on to the even more intriguing problems of how semantics enters into the ordering of morphemes. As it is, this current issue is barely recognized let alone understood. However, its fascination is easily appreciated by this example. Consider these two sentences:

1. They are playing shoes.
2. They are playing horse shoes.

Clearly, in sentence 1 the ''they'' is the same as the shoes, while in sentence 2 the ''they'' are some people while the ''horse shoes'' is something else. How do all English speakers know this to be true? The ordering of the morphemes is identical but, because of semantic differences in the words, the sentences are fundamentally different. Interestingly, the semantics and the order of the morphemes need not give clarity; they can also yield ambiguity. In the sentence, ''Flying airplanes can be dangerous,'' we do not know if it is low-flying planes that endanger us or if the occupation of pilot is dangerous. Think of the questions that such problems pose. What are the rules for constructing such expressions? How are they learned? Are there similar rules in all languages? Are there any universal rules? And again, the overriding problem: How is it possible that a thought in one brain gets into another brain almost instantaneously when so many complex processes occur in the transmission?

While we are far from having answers to this problem, we have some insights into a solution by thinking of the initial step occurring as a *deep structure*. That is, the brain waves or reactions must have some patterning, a system that gets transformed into sound waves that yield a *surface structure*. This surface structure is the subject matter of linguists. Through the study of language and discovery of all the rules for language production, we may come to know something about the deep structure. Presently, what does seem likely is that the brain is not just a vast storage unit which is filled by simple conditioning in order to learn a language. Rather, the human brain contains some genetic program so that bits of learning are readily transformed into an infinite array of information. Thus, four- and five-year old children, regardless of language spoken, are capable of producing understandable utterances they never heard before.

Although linguists are recognizing that all languages have more in common than previously realized, they are also learning how a common genetic program might produce different kinds of thinking because of greatly different types of information fed the program. In this work, the importance of cultural differences is striking. In a field called *metalinguistics* or *psycholinguistics,* investigators are asking how a particular language might shape the thought process rather than the reverse. For example, an English speaker must be quite time conscious since the verbs in any sentence must be expressed in the past, present, or future. In contrast, Navajo verbs are formed on the basis of the nature of the object rather than tense. The verb for moving will change depending on whether the object moved is thin or thick, soft or hard, large or small. In other languages, the verb form will depend upon whether the speaker saw the action, whether someone else witnessed it, or whether it was something that is traditionally taken for granted. Imagine how differently one would see the world if one's language forced thought along these lines deemed essential by the syntax of language.

Such study has demanded a close working relationship between linguists and cultural anthropologists. While the study has produced some very thought-provoking exercises, it has not taken a firm direction. The relation between thought and language remains unclear, but it is certain that cultural anthropology cannot ignore the study of language in all its aspects.

Cultural Regularities as Seen in Prehistory

Perhaps the earlier hominids had simpler rules for transforming deep structures. The communication work with chimpanzees and gorillas should eventually clarify this possibility. Even with simpler rules, considerable variation could have occurred, but a limited range may explain the remarkable persistence of a simple way of life throughout the long Lower Paleolithic. Possibly, Neanderthal communication was also limited since the Middle Paleolithic, likewise, exhibits relatively slow change.

With the appearance of fully modern humans in the Upper Paleolithic, the rate of change becomes impressive. It is tempting to explain this change as a result of biological evolution. Perhaps, modern humans finally achieved a brain structure allowing the symbolic thought and full transformations from a deep to surface structure that are typical today. Yet, the Upper Paleolithic and Mesolithic cover thousands of years; by today's standards the continuance of a food collection subsistence seems oddly persistent. The stability of these first cultural forms, scattered over most of the Old World and long-enduring, suggest that technological change may depend on accumulation of culture, not on a particular brain size or shape.

The issue deserves special attention and some review is in order. One might recall the notable change in art form of the Upper Paleolithic. Art is absent in the Middle Paleolithic; once it starts, it develops quickly in cave paintings and in carving and sculpture. Yet, while art was flourishing, stone-working technology continued simply as core and flake productions. Flaking is perfected in the Upper Paleolithic, although these skills diminish when antler, wood, and ivory are added to the materials for tool making. Once again the question arises: Why was change so slow?

Conversely, why was change so rapid once the Neolithic Revolution began? It is soon followed by the Urban Revolution and, although change slows for some centuries until the Industrial Revolution, change has been the capstone of the past three centuries. In addition, the past 30 years have witnessed as much technological change as the preceding 300 years. Analyzing such change reveals much about the nature of culture.

For instance, it is now clear that the technology part of culture grows at an accelerating pace. When the technological base is simple, little change can occur. Given a greater technological base, greater numbers of combinations are bound to arise. More variation in technology is inevitable in the next generations. Since change is built into the technological foundation, persons born today will know more technology in their first 20 or 30 years than their grandparents learned in a lifetime. In contrast, other areas of culture such as religion or politics do not build or change simply because of their base. These areas do change as a way of adapting to new technology. Thus, they remain a step or two behind. The resulting difference in rate of change is called *cultural lag*. Exceptions occur, of course. A revolution can radically change politics, religion, or family life while technology remains the same; the Chinese revolution well illustrates the fact. Environmental and population changes also alter politics, the family, and religion. However, the theory of culture lag gives us a cultural perspective on much of human history.

This history, especially the prehistoric or unwritten portion, must be based on considerable inference. Archaeological finds can establish a sound record of economic life, particularly for types of production. Exchange patterns and consumption can be inferred without treading far from established fact. In short, we can form a fair perspective of the human place in prehistoric ecology.

A greater degree of inference occurs as we attempt to describe the social life of food collectors. From what is known of contemporary hunters, the past ones must have been organized into equalitarian bands, with only age and sex specialization. Marriage seems likely to have an early beginning in establishing fundamental ties among a number of bands. Where a husband and wife lived was flexible and there were no large, permanent kin groups. Possibly, one or two individuals knew more about curing and supernatural events than others, so they led in curing or looking for game. Another individual may have led the hunt, however, because leadership depended on context. It also fluctuated over time and was never backed by force.

Some variation of this pattern would occur depending largely upon size of the band which in turn correlated with ecology. For example, where people hunted large herd animals such as mammoth on the tundra, band size might be several hundred. Leadership was probably more regular and some specialization might have occurred among hunters and craftworkers, although it is unlikely that any full-time specialists ever occurred. Where people hunted smaller, solitary animals such as

FIGURE 17

These Eskimo drying fish live in small groups since they depend on sea mammals and fish much of the year. (Photo courtesy of the A. R. Schultz Collection, University of Alaska)

deer or boar, the band might have only a dozen members. It would be difficult to pick any adult out of the six or seven who could be called a leader. We make these assumptions on the basis of contemporary food collectors and we should be cautious. For example, the sex division of labor usually excludes women from hunting today but, in prehistoric times, such a division might well have been lacking.

Inferences become even less certain if we try to describe a typical life cycle or generalize a personality. Some inferences may be drawn about child care on the basis of house structures and dwelling patterns. Children confined to a relatively isolated household will differ from those reared in larger settlements. A readily available, abundant food supply must indicate a different life style than when resources are scant and scattered. At this level, inferences will abound but it is necessary to recognize strict limits to their validity.

Still, on the basis of contemporary evidence, one might even hazard some guesses about the value systems of food collectors. For instance, they almost surely valued their mobility more than material goods. By not needing material goods, they approached affluence, that is, they had all they needed because they needed very little. Value systems such as this might be refined into what social scientists define as *institutions*. Institutions are general ways of doing things. Politics, education, religion, family, and economics are major institutions. The more specific rules for behavior within an institution are called *norms*. Norms are any kind of guidelines for behavior. Norms include etiquette, customs, taboo, and law; in short, norms are any proscriptions or prescriptions. The rewards and punishments that govern the norms are called *sanctions*. Positive sanctions range from a pat on the back to awards of merit; negative sanctions include everything from a frown to imprisonment and execution.

The patterning of norms and institutions provides an individual within a culture with a view of the world or a perception of surroundings. A world view may define the outside as friendly or hostile, as a good or an evil place. In reconstructing the culture of early humans, we can accurately determine what the norms called for in making a projectile point. We can even infer to a degree when aesthetics were a part of the normative order. However, no direct evidence is available for how Paleolithic peoples viewed the world. No one can say if a people deemed the world threatening or safe; yet, it seems quite likely that they disdained accumulation of material goods. Thus, values may have been a contributing factor to scarcity of artifacts in the prehistoric record. Nevertheless, prehistorians continue to fill in more and more details about the growth of culture and its analysis.

Ways to Describe Culture

Even when working with contemporary peoples, anthropologists must continue to infer many interpretations. The inferential process is well illustrated by considering some of the ways by which anthropologists describe the parts of a culture. For example, culture has been divided into *material* and *nonmaterial* aspects. Material forms are described without inference, but as soon as one ascribes aethetics to tool-making, one must make inferences. To describe the nonmaterial aspects of economics –the choice-making among scarce resources—inferences are unavoidable.

Another early way of describing culture was to divide it into trait, trait complex, and pattern. An automobile is a trait in American culture. It is one part of a trait complex that includes highways, traffic legislation, automobile dealerships, certain taxes, and even drive-in movies. This complex may be joined with similar ones of rail and air to form a cultural pattern of transportation. Description of this pattern reveals much about the American economy and values such as time and mobility. This has been valuable for describing the simpler cultures, and it has been the basis for a number of museum displays. It has not been as helpful in understanding larger, more complex cultures; it was useful generally because it emphasized how various parts of any culture are closely intertwined.

A more widely used way of describing culture is one that calls for an analysis of *form, meaning,* and *function.* The forms of an American automobile could be described by blueprints, a series of pictures, or lengthy description. It is a fairly easy task even when the object is completely foreign. An analysis of meaning becomes much more complex but essential. Imagine describing a car to a Martian ethnographer without telling what it means to have an automobile. Any ethnographer should find that cars are part of the American prestige system; the form and age of an automobile help define the relative standing of its owner. An ethnographer with a psychological background might even delve into the erotic meanings that cars hold for some persons. Even the less psychologically oriented observer surely would conclude that autos have a special meaning in American sex and courtship patterns. While meanings must be determined largely by talking with informants, that is, people of a culture, some inferences will also be necessary. In determining the full meaning of automobiles for Amercians, an ethnographer would make conclusions about American life ranging from its social class system to courtship and family life.

At the final level of description, an anthropologist must analyze the functions of cars. One conclusion might be that use of cars, together with other practices, allows for an increasing independence among young people. One danger in such analysis is that functional explanations may be interpreted as causal ones. The car, for example, has been blamed for immoral sexual behavior among the young. Functional analysis, by contrast, not only avoids value judgments but also refrains from cause-and-effect description. Instead, a functional analysis ties practices and beliefs with the rest of culture wherever links are found. This type of description was borrowed from biology. Early biologists realized they could not describe the circulation system as caused by the digestive system. Biologists must describe how intestines supply the blood with food—how the two systems are related and work together. Any overall picture must be given to show mutual interrelationships and interdependencies. Such a focus is a *functional analysis.*

Cross-Cultural Description and Comparison

After description and analysis of a particular culture, the next step is to compare cultures or parts of a culture. For example, one early anthropologist, Edward Tylor, became interested in a practice known as mother-in-law avoidance. A husband has stylized ways of avoiding contact or conversation with his wife's mother. It is a custom that occurs in cultures scattered around the world. Tylor found that most of these cultures had a custom or norm which prescribed that a newly married couple live with the bride's family. Today, social scientists call this a *correlation.* Early anthropologists did not know the term, but they realized that mother-in-law avoidance and residence with the wife's family were mutually related; one did not cause the other. They had learned to appreciate the nature of many cultural phenomena even if they lacked the word *functionalism.*

Partly, they failed to develop the concept because their comparisons aimed to discover stages of cultural evolution. In such comparison, the culture of Australian aborigines was assumed to be at a low level; European culture was thought to be the peak. Comparisons of these two cultures should reveal something about the intermediate stages. The difficulty with this approach was that parts of some particular culture often resembled the aborigines while some other part was close to European culture. That is, cultures as a whole did not readily fit a social evolutionary continuum from primitive to civilized.

Opposition to social evolution comparisons began in America early in the 20th century, with some anthropologists denying that there could be a comparative method. Yet, these anthropologists, in developing an historical approach, began making their own comparisons in order to reconstruct history where no written records existed. Such comparisons were on a much smaller scale, directed largely at traits or trait complexes instead of total cultures. For instance, a history of the Sundance of Plains Indians was reconstructed by comparing it to all tribes. At the center of the area, the Sioux had the greatest number of traits in the complex. Tribes close to the Sioux had almost as many, but tribes farther north and south had fewer traits. Comparison led to the conclusion that the Sioux must have originated the

Sundance; tribes on the periphery with the fewest traits had been the last to acquire the trait complex. While this method, called the *age-area* approach, is a way of reconstructing particular details, it is of little help in making generalizations basic to the development of science.

In contrast, more recent functional descriptions of particular cultures force cross-cultural comparisons and carry a necessity to generalize about culture as a human phenomenon. For example, functionalism asks if control of technology, such as driving a car, is a regular way of demonstrating manhood. Are there cultures that do not relate technology to social definitions? Similar comparisons of economic systems showed which systems existed in conjunction with other conditions; comparisons of many religions allowed generalization about religion itself. Above all, the comparative method and functionalism produced questions about the relations among social practices. Anthropologists asked, ''What kind of kinship practices occur with what types of economic organizations?'' The comparisons led to generalizations such as, pastoralism correlates with kin groups formed around males while small horticultural groups are organized around females. Analysis of the mutual relations between such factors constitutes a major part of cultural anthropology.

Contemporary comparisons pinpoint the essential similarity of human behavior in all cultures. Despite anthropology's recording of continual diversity among cultures, the generalizations from comparing differences lead to conclusions about how much alike all humans are. The fact that all cultures are functional wholes is basic to the similarity. Understanding this point is essential to recognizing what culture is. With some idea, now, of the nature of culture, it is worthwhile looking at how anthropologists go about collecting the data they analyze.

The Technique of Participation-Observation

The first anthropologists depended on the observations of early explorers, missionaries, and government agents for the data from which to form cross-cultural comparisons. They realized the many defects of such work and devised some means of correcting for bias in the reports of nonanthropologists. However, these ''armchair'' anthropologists recognized that first-hand observation by a trained anthropologist would be most valuable. At the end of the 19th century, various expeditions were organized to remote parts of the world such as the Bering Strait between Alaska and Russia and the Torres Strait between New Guinea and Australia. In the United States, a few men, such as Henry Schoolcraft and Lewis Henry Morgan, made contact with Indians on an immediate and personal basis. Their fieldwork was brief and the large expeditions were usually dominated by medical experts interested in physical rather than cultural comparisons. Nevertheless, much more reliable data began to become available to anthropology at the turn of the century, and the need for first-hand observation began to be keenly felt. In the United States, Franz Boas set an example for his students by working among the Eskimo or Inuit, as they call themselves, and Northwest Coast Indians. In England, A. R. Radcliffe-Brown and Bronislaw Malinowski set a similar precedent. Malinowski spent a year in the Trobriand Islands near New Guinea when World War I broke out. After a year in Australia, he returned to the Trobriands for a second year of fieldwork. Through such intensive experience and by becoming fluent in the language,

Malinowski delved into areas of culture, such as sex and religion, that had been explored only superficially before. Such experience made it apparent that anthropolgists in the small community could not be simply objective observers. It was necessary that they participate as well as observe.

Anthropologists are justly proud of their technique of being a participation-observer. It requires patience, tact, and endurance. On the other hand, it is simple and varies only slightly from what a reporter does, except in aims and usually in time expended. The length of time allotted by the anthropologist allows the initial months to be spent in building rapport. *Rapport* is a closeness, or a kind of easy-going relationship, that allows one to participate and observe as fully as possible. These initial months can also be used in the tasks of learning the language, drawing maps, compiling a census, and recording how everyone is related to each other. Relationships are recorded by gathering genealogies, and much of social life is revealed as informants discuss their ancestors and relatives. During this period, the anthropologist is obligated to explain, as well as possible, what his or her goals are in studying the community. For example, in studying a Sioux community, one of the authors was introduced as "doing a survey." It took weeks to assure some people that this surveyor was not there to help build a dam.

Fieldworkers must also ensure that the results of their work cannot harm members of the community. Gossip that accumulates in the fieldworker's notes could embarrass an informant with their minister or even be used by police. The anthropologist must respect rights to privacy. This responsibility becomes increasingly burdensome in the modern world when even a simple map may be used by either rebels or government forces in their efforts to involve villagers in obtaining nationalistic goals. Consider how damaging a description of local political leadership might be. Indeed, anthropologists became aware of this problem because the CIA used anthropological description to recruit villagers in the highlands of Vietnam. Still, extensive records must be kept and recording is as essential as observation. Written records are basic, and typed notes allow multiple copies for cross-filing. Most of us compile a daily record, abstracting from it data on individual informants and on specific subject matter. Regularly, one carbon is sent out for safekeeping. Notes are supplemented with tapes and photos whenever possible, and fieldworkers can never learn enough about photography and videotaping.

Besides a number of technical skills, some ability in learning another language is useful. Just as in fieldwork, acquiring a second language depends primarily on motivation and willingness. In learning another language, the fieldworker is motivated by making mistakes because they are useful for building rapport. The anthropologist may be the first member of a dominant society to show an interest in an exotic language; even more, the mistakes indicate that the anthropologist is indeed human and can be laughed at. Some members of the Sioux community mentioned previously finally decided that the anthropologist was not an FBI agent because no FBI agent had ever tried to learn their language. Otherwise, the anthropologist, by simply asking a lot of questions and not doing anything useful, does resemble an FBI agent.

After rapport is built, the fieldworker begins more systematic data collection. Anthropologists may use a questionnaire and gather information from a sample of households. If a community is small the questionnaire-survey may include all households, so statistical analysis of a sample is unnecessary. However, most anthropologists rely on a directed interview. We know there are some questions we want answered but, while pursuing these answers, informants take us in new directions that raise new questions. During this phase of fieldwork, it is probably necessary to make great effort to interview the individuals who have not been as friendly as others. It is a good time for fieldworkers to reflect on how their own personalities may be influencing their data gathering. A short time away from the field can be helpful. Upon returning, people will be welcoming, and more isolated informants can be interviewed. It may be useful to decide who is representative of the community and to collect their life histories. Women are likely to be poorly represented in the field notes, especially if the fieldworker is male, and special attention should be given to ensure coverage of both sexes and all ages.

Obviously, none of the techniques of participation-observation are mysterious or difficult; the only prerequisite for using them is some degree of maturity and commitment to ethical concerns. Since anthropology practices no standardized technique, fieldwork varies widely between the extremes of participation and observation. A quiet introvert may record in detail the way pottery is made or cloth is woven, while the gregarious extrovert becomes embroiled in political feuds leading to insights into political organization. So much of participation-observation is a part of one's personality that the technique is as much an art as it is a science. Not surprisingly, much variation in technique has accompanied a wide variation in method and theory. Indeed, anthropologists do not even agree as to what should be called *method*; some would describe participation-observation as a method. Here, by *method* we mean a general approach to understanding a culture.

Anthropological Method

The differences among participant-observers are partly a result of different personalities but in large part they are the result of a variety of anthropological methods. While anthropologists speak of writing ethnographies as if they consisted of a catalog description of each area of a culture or community, few, if any, such works have ever been produced. Instead, the descriptions of each anthropologist have been based on a particular theoretical viewpoint that limits as it focuses. Thus, many different perspectives are reflected in the best-known ethnographies.

An *historical perspective* is perhaps closest to the idealized all-inclusive ethnography. Yet, even a history must be composed of actual events, particular individuals, and selected locales. A strict chronology is unnecessary, but a descriptive chronicle cannot help but provide some insight into processes such as culture change while introducing most parts of a culture. Some anthropologists call themselves ethnohistorians, intending to picture culture as it persists over time and recreating what existed before written records. Many descriptions of American Indians are ethnohistories, and the distinction between the work of an historian and the work of an anthropologist is based largely on the ability of anthropologists to reconstruct the culture of the past on the basis of the present. Generally, the anthropologist does try to relate a history portraying a culture as a whole, but we do not have a monopoly on such an approach.

Another method for analyzing a culture is to focus on the relationship between human behavior and the environment. Emphasis is on mutual relations rather than cause-and-effect ones. The concept of ecology is useful for emphasizing relations with other species as well as with the physical environment, leading to an *ecological method* in anthropology. It is illustrated by the work of E. E. Evans-Pritchard among the Nuer of East Africa. The Nuer herd cattle, an activity that shapes their lives in many ways. A man's prestige is measured by the cattle he owns, and individuals establish kin ties with their cattle. A good overall view of the Nuer pictures the continual adaptation they must make to accommodate their herds. In the rainy season, Nuer congregate in large villages on hilltops to protect their cattle from marsh insects; in this time of dense population, social conflict is frequent and the means of social control are complex. These social complexities diminish in the dry season when the Nuer scatter their cattle over large areas to follow drying up streams. Life in the dry season differs radically as Nuer divide into individual households. A vivid picture of Nuer life emerges as it is described in terms of wet and dry seasons.

A second ecological view has recently developed, one centering on the production and uses of food. It interprets culture as adaptation. Ritual, taboos, and the rest of life are analyzed for their adaptive value. Primarily, these adaptations are interpreted as ways to ensure an adequate food base. For instance, in parts of highland New Guinea, pig feasts are essential parts of ritual life, and warfare cannot be undertaken without such ritual. Six or seven years are needed to raise sufficient pigs for a proper feast, so long periods of truce limit the destructiveness of warfare. This new ecological perspective offers a theoretical orientation known as *cultural ecology*. The field claims to have moved anthropology much closer to biology and its evolutionary theory.

A concentration on the *social structure* of a community is another common focus for anthropologists. In all human communities, society is divided on the basis of age and sex. The nature and details of this division are a convenient starting point for describing a culture. Much more of social life is organized around kin groups. In some communities, individuals depend on a few kin for all their needs, relating to others through marriage. Elsewhere, large kin groups organize most of one's economic, political, and religious life; marriages serve as links among such kin groups. Still other social groups are organized in terms of power or prestige so that social strata provide further organization. In short, analysis is of interrelations among individuals and among groups, with life emerging as human interaction. Since so much of human life is composed of interactions, a social-structural approach provides a comprehensive perspective of culture.

The generalizations from a structural approach tend to ignore the individual. To compensate, other anthropologists have collected biographies or *life histories* to illustrate the detail of individual life. Sometimes an anthropologist has trained informants to record so much of their own life that the reports are more autobiographical than biographical. Their accounts provide rich introspection and speculation, aspects rarely encountered in an ecological or structural analysis. Thus, life histories are valuable supplements to other methods. Many are now available for North American Indians; others cover African and Latin American peoples. A common criticism of the life history is that no one can tell how representative a particular person is of a culture. Some autobiographies do seem to have stemmed from extraordinary individuals; on the other hand, Oscar Lewis appears to have portrayed much of Mexican life in his popular description of *Five Families.*

To allow for greater representation while still covering points made in life histories, anthropologists may portray cultures in terms of typical *life cycles.* They generalize from a number of particular births. Infancy is usually described at some length. Child care practices are particularly important because of their influence on adult life and the formation of personality. The period of adolescence introduces subjects such as ritual when rites of passage occur. Marriage carries with it some description of family life and kinship while adulthood gives a picture of economic and political life. Death is almost always a reflection of religious life, and attitudes toward death reflect a people's view of the world. In sum, much of culture can be dramatically revealed from the perspective of a life cycle.

Akin to the study of life cycles is analysis of *culture and personality.* Studies of culture and personality illustrate how normative patterns for adults are expressed in child-rearing practices. The child-rearing methods are analyzed to discover the ways that teach adults to carry on the kind of culture defined by the norms. The circularity of the method is its notable weakness. Yet, in *Patterns of Culture* Ruth Benedict revealed much about the Kwakiutl, Zuni, and Dobuans when she used the method. By showing how Zuni children were reared to be restrained, cooperative, and ever mindful of others, she showed why a common pattern emerged among Zuni politics, economics, and religion. The approach became an integral part of American anthroplogy, resulting in close ties to psychology. As the method widened, it has developed into what is now known as *psychological anthropology.*

The focus on personality still retained the perspective of an outsider. That is, culture and personality were constructed as observed entities. The next move was an attempt to enter the minds of individuals from another culture and to see the world from their perspective. For example, Mayan ecology and social structure had been described by early anthropologists; then observations were made on Mayan personality. However, when Robert Redfield lived among the Maya, he wanted to go a step further. He began asking the question, ''How do the Maya view the world they live in?'' Do they see the world as essentially friendly or hostile? What is their world view? Others of us raised similar questions in analyzing value systems. What were the most important norms a people chose to guide their everyday actions? What central premises formed a people's perception of their world? At this level of interpretation, the anthropologist relies on inferences, but results provide valuable additions to the other more common methods. The world view method and value analysis led toward defining culture as located in the heads of people.

All these methods are practiced in part by anthropology. None is exclusive of another. Each anthropologist has generally approached fieldwork emphasizing one of the methods. Each method has also been influenced by the general setting of anthropology within what may be termed *theory.* Three notable stages of theory will be described here, but no sharp distinction can be made between theory and method. What we are calling *theory* might be better understood as *perspective, outlook,* or even *assumption.* In short, we do not see much theoretical development for the field; nevertheless, anthropology has come a long way in its understanding of culture.

Anthropological Theory

Anthropologists do not always distinguish clearly between anthropological theory and method. Social structure analysis or culture and personality may be called theoretical approaches. But these methods or theories can be set within some more general developments in anthropology that this book will describe as theory. For the beginning student, this theory will give an idea of how anthropology developed and where it is going.

What we call *theory* in anthropology resembles much of the theory of natural science. It explains much while it is cast in fairly simple terms. It does not make value judgments; it appears objective and rational. Yet, it was difficult to build upon and expand anthropological theory, in contrast to physics or chemistry. There may simply be a different path for the development of anthropology and the other social sciences.

However, anthropology has passed through several stages regarded as theoretical, even if these developments might be called assumptions or even hunches. What something is called is not important; the fact is that anthropological thinking has yielded important insights into the cultures of Africa, Asia, Europe, and the Americas. It is work that has been important for understanding the past of these peoples, and it is vital in understanding them in today's changing world. At an introductory level, it is necessary only to look at the major developments in anthropological thought and to examine only the esssential features. Here we will look extensively at current thinking, but appreciation of it requires some historical perspective.

Origins of Anthropology: Social Evolution

Edward B. Tylor and Lewis Henry Morgan are regarded as the founders of anthropology. Tylor established the study in English universities, but his emphasis on culture had a lasting influence on American anthropology. Morgan remained a lawyer and had no students, but his interest in social systems inspired much work in English anthropology.

Both anthropologists were strongly influenced by the evolutionary thought of the late 19th century. Darwin's theory permeated all of intellectual life which documented the evolution of law, religion, family, weapons, marriage, and politics. All of these human products came to be subsumed under the term *culture* as Tylor defined it: "A complex whole which includes knowledge, belief . . . and any other capabilities . . . acquired by man as a member of society." Morgan studied the social part of the definition, bringing the world's attention to relations between forms of property and forms of social organization. In *Ancient Society*, he described three stages of social evolution: savagery, barbarism, and civilization. These stages correspond to the current divisions of food collecting or the Paleolithic, food producing or the Neolithic, and the Urban Revolution. Morgan realized that a number of changes occurred in social life when economic systems changed. In this study, he became particularly interested in kinship changes. Through questionnaires to missionaries and government agents around the world, plus some fieldwork of his own, Morgan compiled a global survey of kinship systems that inspired generations of anthropologists.

In contrast, Tylor focussed on a wide variety of topics ranging from technology to religion. By comparing techniques of fire-making, for example, he established an evolutionary continuum of the technology. In sum, he believed the human past might be reconstructed by comparing present-day peoples. His enthusiasm led him to collect proverbs, study children's games, learn the sign language of mutes, and record myths. This work is reported in *Primitive Culture,* a book that covers all of human history in a unique way. It made mundane, everyday activities the subject matter of anthropology.

While social evolution lasted only from about 1870 to 1900, the work did make culture the prime concept of the discipline. The concept included all of human activity, and Tylor had suggested that all the parts of any culture have close, mutual relations. Tylor and Morgan, along with other early anthropologists, appreciated that what other peoples did made sense in terms of their own cultures. Anthropologists could not be *ethnocentric* in their work. That is, peoples everywhere judge their own ways as superior; this ethnocentrism prevents an objective view of other cultures. As a result, these first anthropologists laid the foundation for *cultural relativity.* This position asserts that any particular behavior or value can only be judged relative to its own culture. In objective study, the standards of one culture cannot be imposed on another culture. Although there are difficulties in following cultural relativity to its logical conclusion, the viewpoint is essential for anthropology. Thus, the social evolutionists contributed a solid foundation for the growth of anthropology even if their major idea that all cultures follow a single or unilineal continuum of development was dismissed at the turn of the century.

History and Diffusion

While theory in biological evolution continued to advance in the 20th century, the idea of social evolution was generally dismissed. In the United States, the reaction was a revolt. Far too many discrepancies had been found in the stages; that is, some societies were ranked high on the evolution continuum because of their religion, but these same people had a family life regarded as primitive. No general social evolutionary scheme had been found that was intellectually satisfactory.

A rejection in the United States was fairly easy because Morgan had never taught; he left behind no department or students. Instead, anthropology got its start as an academic discipline under the direction of Franz Boas, who saw a need to record American Indian culture without the bias of social evolution. Thus, he trained his students in an historical technique, believing more data were necessary before establishing theory. Rather than speculate on a history inferred by worldwide comparisons, Boas used archaeology, physical anthropology, and comparative linguistics to build cultural anthropology along with participant-observation that concentrated on gathering recollections of older informants.

Students of Boas combined these fields to focus on a particular community, describing their group as whole, while often concentrating on a particular trait complex. The Sundance is an example of one such study. This historicism was much more objective and empirical than the speculation of the social evolutionists. The work built a highly reliable record that is useful even today, but concentration on detail diverted attention from the nature of culture as a complex whole. The historical approach made a culture appear to be composed of many historical accidents. It required nearly three decades to rediscover culture as a pattern of mutually related parts.

In Europe, the revolt against social evolution followed a similar trend, although the theories to emerge were equally speculative. One theory in England had everything of importance originating in Egypt and diffusing to the rest of the world. A more serious theory saw most basic inventions occurring in a remote part of Asia because *Homo erectus* fossils were then the earliest known humans. Supposedly, peoples on the margin of the area who had acquired the earliest traits were pushed still further out as more developments brought an expanding population. Further developments involved still more spread. The cultural developments were reflected as a series of concentric *cultural circles,* or *kulturkreise,* with the earliest or outer circle at the margins of the world. Geographic barriers could distort the circles so peoples of the outer circle were represented by Tasmanians, Pygmies, and Negritos of the Philippines. Proof that such peoples were related was derived from physical, linguistic, and cultural comparisons.

In this way, German interest paralleled the American development. Surprisingly, similar details do occur in mythology and technology among some peoples such as those reported on the outer circle. The kulturkreise theorists accepted these few similarities as proof. The rest of anthropology regarded them as coincidence because some cultural practices are limited in terms of a range of possibilities. In retrospect, the diffusionists contributed less than the evolutionists, but they did compile an impressive catalog of cultural traits and customs and, in America, the historicalists had established a traditional tie among physical anthropology, linguistics, archaeology, and cultural anthropology. The next generation of thought used this tradition to revive the social evolutionists' concept of culture as a functional whole.

Functionalism

In England, Bronislaw Malinowski and A. R. Radcliffe-Brown rejected history and diffusion as theories of anthropology. They turned to the work of French comparative sociologists, such as Emile Durkeim, who were still engaged in evolutionary thought, but picturing society in a new way. Emphasis was on a complete picture, necessitated by close ties among the parts. Society was seen as an organic whole with Durkheim tracing the evolution of this organism. Malinowski and Radcliffe-Brown rejected a search for the evolutionary past, but they looked for a theory to describe how the parts of a whole were interrelated.

Both men called their work a functional approach. Malinowski concentrated on how culture functioned to meet the needs of society and individuals, while Radcliffe-Brown demonstrated the necessity of showing how cultural parts must be analyzed in terms of a whole. Although the two sometimes criticized each other, their work turned British anthropology toward strict synchronic analysis; that is, it examined contemporary culture without historical explanation. Malinowski well demonstrated how such work should be done in his description of the Trobriand Islands. His comprehensive account of their culture, by fitting parts into a whole, laid the basis for functional theory.

In the United States, some students of Boas likewise turned against historical theory. Boas encouraged them and some of his writing reflects his change of thought. The new theory is best seen in Ruth Benedict's *Patterns of Culture*. This book was read widely outside of anthropology because it vividly describes and compares three different cultures, the Zuni of the American Southwest, the Kwakiutl of the Northwest Coast, and the Dobu in the Pacific. Benedict vividly portrayed how a kind of person or personality was necessary for a culture. If the common personality type was one valuing cooperation and constraint of emotion, such as Zuni, then processes of cooperation would be reflected in government, economics, religion, and other institutions. Culture had to be patterned.

Margaret Mead, younger than Benedict but a contemporary of hers, did much the same thing in Samoa, where she was able to give greater attention to detail by concentrating upon a single culture. In *Coming of Age in Samoa*, Mead pictures the growth of a personality well adapted to the kind of culture in which it must function. She, too, offers a pattern or configuration of Samoan society and culture. This approach has been called *configurational* and equated with functional theory but, in this book, we see the focus on a relationship between personality and culture as a method within functional theory.

British anthropologists criticized this method claiming anthropology must concentrate solely on culture. Yet, they realized that Americans were coming to recognize the importance of seeing cultures as wholes. Agreement on this point laid the basis for the new approach in anthropology that assumed culture was a complex whole as defined by Tylor. By the 1930s, anthropologists realized the great complexity of culture meant mutual interrelations of parts. Borrowing the concept of functionalism from biology, they saw social institutions as thoroughly related to each other as the digestive system is related to the circulatory system.

The wholeness or interrelatedness of cultural parts is convincingly demonstrated by Trobriand culture in Malinowski's account or by Zuni culture as described by Benedict. Yet, the overall picture remains a subjective one, supported in part by the style and presentation of the authors. Since no one has ever devised an objective method to determine that cultures must be composed of mutually related parts, one hesitates to call functionalism a theory. Nevertheless, functionalism remains anthropology's basic way of viewing culture. Despite recurrent arguments claiming the demise of functional theory, most social scientists remain functionalists. They continue to assume culture is a complex whole whose intertwined systems are functionally related. Anthropologists may break these systems apart in their analyses, but a final picture must be composed of a reconstituted whole. Thus, the basic theory of anthropology, functionalism, is relatively simple and limited in explanatory power. Its value can be appreciated, however, by comparing it with the assumptions of the diffusionists or historians who made culture a jumble of historical accidents.

Current Theories of Structuralism and Ecology

The anthropologists who disclaim functionalism proclaim either structuralism or cultural ecology. The *ecological view,* in many cases, is clearly an expansion of the older functionalism to include mutual relations with other species and the environment. This ecological analysis can be considered a method. However, some ecologists break with functionalism to cast culture as a wholly adaptive response to the environment. Adaptations are seen as caused by environmental conditions. According to this theory, human behavior is a reaction to a particular environment, and norms that allow an effective exploitation of resources survive, while ineffective norms become extinct. This theory of culture as adaptation resembles an earlier environmental determinism; however, today's theory is exceedingly more sophisticated. Whether it is simply an outgrowth of functionalism or a radical departure from it must be left for future evaluation. Presently, it offers an additionally interesting perspective, one to be explored in greater depth in the next chapter and in the chapter on religion.

Likewise, *structuralism* is interesting as an alternative to functionalism. The term itself is confusing because Radcliffe-Brown frequently used the term along with functionalism. He saw anthropology's major concern to be structure of status relations; functional analysis was an examination of the functional relationships within social structure. Like Durkheim, Radcliffe-Brown concentrated on social structure and explaining these social relations only in terms of other social facts. Currently, Claude Lévi-Strauss claims a renewal of Durkheim's structuralism but takes it in a new direction.

Previously, social life seemed to be structured by the nature of human social life. People have to be able to expect what others will do if they are to live in complex groups. Consider how many people you interacted with today, knowing well

FIGURE 18

Extensive exchange of pigs and pearl shells in the Highlands of New Guinea seems to many observers to be unproductive. Anthropologists have shown the adaptive value of such practices. (Photo by Larry L. Naylor)

FIGURE 19

This Canadian totem pole indicates its owner's place in society. Lévi-Strauss suggests that its form is a product of the mind. (Photo by Ernest Schusky)

how they would respond to you. A wide range of such expectations—of a normative code—is possible because of a complex symbolic system. The symbolism of language facilitates the symbolic systems of religion, economic exchange, or even forms of greeting. The symbolism common to a group, giving it its unity, was termed a *collective conscience* by Durkheim. Social scientists assume the collective conscience arose from the consequences of group life.

Lévi-Strauss reversed this reasoning by arguing that the structure of human behavior is a product of the way the brain works. The structure of human behavor, especially the rules or norms for it, is shaped because the mind works through structuring, both in conceiving the norms and again in perceiving them. Lévi-Strauss bases his argument on analysis of a variety of customs ranging from face painting through totems and kinship to mythology. Mythology is particularly appropriate for revealing how structured thought operates, and his analysis of myths ranges through four volumes. The theory has attracted much attention in the arts and humanities as well as in the social sciences. It has probably stirred more controversy in intellectual thought than anything since Freudian theory. Obviously, it is not yet possible to judge how far reaching the effects of structural theory will be.

Summary

This introductory survey of the basics in anthropology is meant to facilitate analysis of economics, social organization, and symbolic organization as presented in the following chapters, but its essential use is for a more complete understanding of the *concept of culture*. One should now fully appreciate that a major reason for the diversity of definitions of culture is that many different people have had quite different perspectives and theoretical approaches to what anthropology is all about.

Any starting point must emanate from the origins of culture which lie in the adaptation to grasslands and the transition from being the hunted to being the hunter. A complex social life probably arose as a protection against being hunted; bipedalism combined with cultural growth for hunting. The nature of human hunting put a premium on communication for past and future behavior leading to language, a unique step beyond communication of presently felt emotions.

The complexity of language grew at the levels of sounds, their combinations, and the attachment of meanings to sound. The minimal unit of sound, the *phone,* is combined by patterning into a set, or *phoneme.* Phonemes are two or more phones, but they are produced and heard as a single sound, one with a conventional meaning. Phonemes are combined into *morphemes,* sounds that have semantic or lexical meanings. In all languages, rules specify how phonemes can be combined. For expressions of thought, morphemes are strung together. Complex rules govern this stringing; the pattern of stringing is called *syntax.* A syntactic expression begins in the brain which must give shape to a *deep structure.* It is then expressed in sound waves known as *surface structure.* Language is a combination of deep and surface structure.

The regularities in language, discovered by structural linguistics, suggest that culture, too, must be regularly patterned. Systematic growth is sugested by the study of prehistory recording a regular change in technology that precedes change in the rest of culture, a difference expressed as *cultural lag.* The persistence of nonmaterial culture is studied at the level of *norms,* or all the rules for behavior. The importance of norms is measured by their *positive* and *negative sanctions,* the rewards and punishments for following or breaking the norms. Norms regularly group together as major ways of doing things, or *institutions.* All societies have institutions of economics, politics, family, religion, and education.

In describing these institutions and the rest of culture, anthropologists analyze their *material* and *nonmaterial* aspects. Material culture is whatever can be seen and felt; it is what is customarily displayed in museums. Nonmaterial culture is the norms and institution or thinking behind material culture. Most definitions of culture now emphasize the thought processes that generate culture. Culture may also be divided into form, meaning, and function. *Form* is an expression of culture, be it in type of family life, e.g., a husband and several wives and their children, or a pattern for a projectile point. *Meaning* is an examination of what is in peoples' heads, or an inquiry into what a spouse means to one. Is he or she primarily an economic asset or a companion? *Function* is an analysis of what some part of culture does for society. Is the family a producing or consuming unit? What does it do for the education of children?

The study of form, meaning, and function in any one culture is facilitated by *cross-cultural comparisons.* We may see nearly identical forms of culture among different peoples, but the meaning and functions of these forms can differ widely. The contrast gives us perspectives on how culture operates. Cross-cultural comparisons are also important for understanding relationships among institutions.

Such a comparative approach allows a diversity of methods. An *historical* method comes closest to straight description, but even here selection occurs in order to present a viewpoint. Another method illustrates culture as adaptive to environment. This *ecological* view began in the 1930s and is prominent today because of important discoveries in related fields. *Social structural analysis* likewise continues to be basic. It emphasizes social relations and the reasons for their regularity. These methods contrast with those of the life history, the life cycle, and culture and personality. *Life histories,* either biographical or autobiographical, bring out the rich complexity of an individual life but do not sort out idiosyncratic from patterned responses. *Life cycles* thoroughly detail childhood experiences along with major points, such as rites of passage, but they may miss significant points about society. The method of *culture and personality* brings out how the early life cycle fashions an adult personality and how personality fashions behavior in all situations, thus creating a pattern among them. All these methods present an outsider's view. In inferring an insider's perspective, the *world view* method attempts to picture culture as seen by a participant. This method requires considerable familiarity with another people and lacks objective measurement.

Despite an abundance of viewpoints deriving from such diverse methodology, two major trends may be noted in developing a concept of culture. One begins with the *social evolutionists* and continues through today with *cultural ecologists.* This trend emphasizes culture as an adaptive device and assumes that humankind is unique because the species largely replaced biological adaptation with cultural adaptation. Each part of culture and even the norms are regarded as responses to the environment.

The *diffusionists* rejected this view, particularly Boas. The early *functionalists,* largely overlooking the environment, also did not see culture as adaptive. Malinowski was an exception because he recognized that some cultural traits functioned to meet individual needs such as hunger, but like other functionalists he believed most of culture was an elaboration upon societal needs. In sum, the functionalists' focus on culture and society largely excluded the natural environment.

This view was part of a general intellectual climate before World War II that stressed the importance of learning and the ability of humans to devise all sorts of solutions to almost any problem. Humankind went so far beyond the problems of survival that culture had to be something more than just adaptation. It was too complex to be only a response to the environment. For a while, the environment hardly qualified as a factor in human behavior.

Since 1960, most anthropologists have settled somewhere between these two viewpoints. The *cultural ecologists* have been convincing that much of culture can be understood as adaptive. Ensuring an adequate food supply for a population is no simple matter; the complexities of culture are necessary to perform such a task among humans. Additionally, of course, it must also ensure some protection against the elements, hostile populations, and the diseases that take children's lives. Nevertheless, anthropologists continue to record parts of culture that appear to have absolutely no link to any possible adaptive response. Particularly in the area of symbolic organization, it seems far-fetched to conceive of some verbal play or highly elaborated art style solely as adaptation.

What is much more likely is that, in the selection for an intelligent, symbol-using primate, a species evolved that solved most of its problems through culture rather than biology. Culture is adaptive beyond doubt, but the human animal went further and elaborated culture. Much of culture is more than adaptation; it is an elaboration based on mental capacity that has far more potential than what is needed simply for survival.

8

*Ecology and Economics*___

The two poles in anthropology about the concept of culture—first that culture is solely adaptation and second that it is elaboration through time—are nowhere better illustrated than in the study of the human relationship with the environment. As we will note in a moment, the cultural ecologists have demonstrated their case by studying food taboos and ritual associated with food production. This area is also one extensively studied by earlier anthropologists who found they could trace long routes of diffusion or migration in their histories of food taboos.

While the initial diffusionist studies did not clarify fully the nature of culture, the work moved anthropology and the other social sciences in new directions. In the early 19th century, differences among humans had been explained on the basis of biology. Racial differences were the most notable assumed causes, and assertions of one race's superiority to another justified policies from colonialism to slavery. Biological differences between the sexes were also used to rationalize further inequities within the same race. Even individual peculiarities were explained away as biological. The child who did not turn out as expected was a "black sheep," a reversion to some primitive, undesirable form caused by some unknown biological quirk. In sum, behavior was supposedly a fixed entity where learning and, therefore, culture were inconsequential. Ironically, it was a viewpoint of an intellectual world that had not yet even discovered the field of genetics.

By the late 19th century, when Darwin made his case for biological adaptation, the first anthropologists were beginning to wreck the argument for biological determinism of human behavior. While these first theorists are now called social evolutionists, they were making the case that it is society and culture that evolved and that these two factors are the overwhelming determinants of human behavior. In their search for documentation of evolutionary stages, the social evolutionists discovered that the innumerable differences among humans could not be explained on the basis of race or any other biological fact. In this thrust, they were joined later by the diffusionists and the cultural historians of the early 20th century who recorded cultural events in even greater detail.

What the growing record showed was an incredible amount of variation even in regard to problems that would seem to require a simple, uniform solution. For example, clothing in a hot climate ranges from a penis gourd and necklace for a man in New Guinea to layers of cloth covering the body from head to toe in the Arab

FIGURE   20

Clothing in the New Guinea Highlands is usually scant, even in an initiation rite such as this. In Guatemala, each Mayan village has its own distinct style of dress. (New Guinea photo by Larry L. Naylor; Guatemala photo by Ernest Schusky)

world. Almost any variation in style and amount appears in between. Yet, as studies accumulated, anthropologists found they had to answer questions about similarities. Everywhere people use clothing in symbolic ways. Everyone, for example, has some ideas of modesty, although just what parts of the body should be covered or exposed is not agreed upon. Likewise, everywhere people have norms that specify clothing for males that differs from females, norms that often require males to wear more colorful and flamboyant costuming than females. It is also common that clothing will be used to designate other statuses, often ones having to do with religion or ethnicity, and clothing generally says something about the prestige of the wearer.

The consumption of food shows even more variation than the wearing of clothing. Probably every digestible food is eaten somewhere by some group of people, but when it comes to animals, someone somewhere says the flesh is taboo—that is, it should not be eaten. Hindus will not eat beef while Moslems scorn pork, creating a problem for the British in feeding their Indian troops. Most Westerners reject the idea of eating horses, dogs, or insects. Fish with scales are rejected by Tasmanians while Jews are forbidden fish without scales. While plants are not disapproved on such a scale, some of them may also be taboo. The reasons people give for their taboos vary as much as the forbidden foods. Proscribed foods may be "unnatural," "dirty," or cause illness or skin blemish; their consumption may offend the supernatural in a variety of ways.

While some foods are *proscribed*, consumption of other foods is *prescribed* with norms designating their use in quite specific ways. Hosts are limited in what they can serve guests, and other elaborate etiquette guides the serving of food. Guests may be served from china or well-woven banana palms but, whatever the setting, it marks off the occasion as extraordinary. As with us, guests are often served first, but in some places hosts may not even share in the meal. Besides using food as a special symbol for social relations, almost all peoples also use it during ritual. Frequently, the ritual occasion involves eating a food that is taboo any other time. Australian aborigines, for example, consume the animal that is the symbol of their kin group only when they gather for a major ritual. Otherwise, the meat of this animal is repulsive to them. The practice resembles the Christian one where human flesh is repulsive, but in partaking of Communion, bread is the flesh of Christ and wine, the blood.

Anthropologists still cannot explain satisfactorily why such great diversity exists in detail, yet such similarity is found at a general level. Obviously, people everywhere go far beyond what is necessary to meet their biological needs for food and shelter. What is most curious are the close parallels among very different cultures in the elaborations that are made. The extras in food and clothing almost everywhere denote social status in age, sex, and prestige or leadership while also having religious significance in a great many cultures. Thus, it is a pressing question why so much symbolic significance is attached to what would seem to be simple activity required to meet basic biological needs.

Cultural Ecology

The fact that humans show considerable similarities at a general level suggests principles of adaptation similar to ones that occur in the biological realm; yet, no satisfactory explanation of the principles occurred until cultural ecologists began to stress the need to see culture as adaptive. The first major effort in this direction was made by the late American anthropologist, Julian Steward, who pointed out the close relationship between the Shoshoni Indians and their Rocky Mountain environment.

The Shoshoni, Ute, and other Indians in this area depended on small game and a few limited vegetation products such as pinon nuts. Population density was quite low as a result, and people lived in bands or groups of as few as five to ten. A husband and wife with their children and an odd relative or two comprised the typical local group. Such bands came together into a larger group only once or twice a year. These occasions were prompted by an antelope, rabbit, or a locust drive; they were also times to perform major rituals. Steward uses their basic ecological adaptations to describe a core of social structure for bands. This structure is typical wherever people practice food collecting and depend on small game and scattered vegetation.

Steward also makes a good case for a core organization known as a *tribe* where people are organized around big game hunting, pastoralism, or even some forms of horticulture. The generalizations about social structure for tribes are not as precise as for bands, but anthropology does recognize that bands and tribes have much in common in their social organization. These types of organizations are well tied to the ecological adaptations of food collecting and simple forms of agriculture.

In the 1960s, some anthropologists began to argue that adaptation was reflected in all parts of culture, since all of culture must be adaptive. This point of view was initially expressed by Marvin Harris and others at Columbia University. Harris illustrates his argument with an examination of the sacred cow in India. First, he notes the wide range of factors that must be considered in evaluating the Hindu proscription of beef which stems from high regard of the cow as a sacred animal. This point is in line with what ecologists are continually discovering, that the relationships among species and their environment are incredibly complex.

Would India's hungry really have more food if the people were to eat their sacred cows? Harris searched for a practical answer to the question. He ignored the symbolic value of the cow for providing social cohesion or yielding some kind of psychological satisfaction. These were the factors often described by social scientists but impossible to measure. Instead, Harris argued that the value of the cow could be measured in terms of its manure and milk production, along with the ox's value as a plow animal. In India, manure is a valuable fertilizer but it is equally important as a fuel and often is useful as a building material. As a means of traction, oxen are absolutely essential since mechanization is just beginning and fuel costs have risen rapidly. By Harris' estimate, India is actually short of cattle for farm traction, largely because the monsoons require all villagers to be plowing at the same time. This estimate contradicts the views of many nutritionists who see an overabundance of cattle competing with humans for edible grains. Yet, we do not fully know the diet of Indian cattle. They can consume grass and forage that are inedible by humans, and many Indian cows never eat grain. Finally, it is interesting to note that the untouchables and other low caste groups are accused of eating the meat of dead cattle when they process the hides. If they do consume much meat, it is about their only source of protein.

Thus, the taboo on beef looks as if it is not simply a useless elaboration of culture surrounding food consumption, but rather it may be a highly valuable form of adaptation. Further, Harris' questions suggest that such issues may be empirically tested. No one can measure an increase or decrease in group solidarity, but one could measure manure and milk production or amount of meat consumption from carcasses carried off by untouchables. Practically, of course, it has not been possible to make any of these measures because of the size of the Indian population, both human and bovine. Thus, some students have looked to smaller societies where measurement might be practical.

In the Highlands of central New Guinea, Roy Rappaport lived with the Maring, a small isolated group who had an interesting taboo on the flesh of most wild animals. This taboo was intriguing because the Maring are short of protein, and the meat of the small game and reptiles would seem to be vital in their diet. Pigs, likewise, were seldom eaten although the Maring devoted considerable time and effort to pork production. For a people short of protein, the taboos seem worse than simple, useless elaborations. When the short supply of pork is consumed, it is at rituals that require gorging. Any nutritionist would advise that a short supply of protein be spread out over a period of time. In short, the norms regulating meat consumption appear to be maladaptive, not simply useless.

Rappaport's ecological analysis suggests otherwise. The taboos on wild animals restrict their use by men and older women. Such food is unfit in the proper diet of the influential person. It is scorned food, fit only for those people with little or no prestige. Thus, this small quantity of protein goes to young women, many of whom are pregnant or lactating, and to infants and young children. In sum, the taboo ensures that the scarce protein goes to that part of the population most in need of it.

The norms constraining the use of pork are quite different. Pigs are almost never slaughtered except for a major ritual that marks preparations for war. This ritual cannot be held until there are scores of pigs that will enhance the prestige of leaders who direct their donations at feasts. Guests will be expected to be allies of their hosts so the celebration must be impressive and must obligate all those who participate. For a typical group, the accumulation of pigs takes seven years so the use of pork seems to reduce dramatically the incidence of warfare among the Maring. Interestingly, the massive consumption of pork just before a battle is accompanied by a taboo that forbids warriors to drink water. This act gives an initial burst of energy, but it would quickly lead to exhaustion. Thus, Maring wars are not only infrequent but of short duration when they do happen. The elaboration of norms about pork consumption may be interpreted as an adaptation, not as just an accumulation of historical borrowings from neighbors.

Another cultural ecological interpretation brings new understanding of a well-known custom that previously was seen as a result of diffusion and elaboration. On the Northwest Coast of North America, tribes practiced the *potlatch,* an elaborate ceremony featuring feasts and gifts of blankets, carved wood, and raw copper pounded into sheets. The energy invested in the production of goods used almost entirely for display, give-away, and accumulation of prestige was one of those curious facts known by every anthropologist, but regarded only as elaboration. However, Stuart Piddocke, another cultural ecologist, argued that the potlatch was adaptive because of microecological conditions on the Northwest Coast. The rivers and coastlines there fluctuate over time in their production of fish and shellfish. For five to ten years, Valley A may be highly productive while Valley B is unproductive. Then the valleys may change in their production. The problem for human adaptation is how to even out access to food resources when regions fluctuate in productive value. Piddocke's answer was that when a human group was well off, it hosted groups from other areas, bestowing food on them and acquiring great prestige for being generous. The greatest prestige was reflected in titles that went with the copper sheets. When the physical resources of a rich region dwindled, groups there were able to give up the wealth they had accumulated in titles, copper, and other nonfood resources when they became guests of villages that now enjoyed greater than usual food production. Piddocke is the first to admit that conditions have so changed today that we cannot prove his hypothesis, but it is certainly worthy of examination. It offers a valuable alternative to the earlier explanations of history and diffusion.

Are all the seeming elaborations truly some sort of subtle adaptation? It seems unlikely. Surely, some practices that were once adaptive are no longer so because of changed conditions. Further, humans probably have to elaborate in numerous ways in order to discover a few ways that are adaptive. That is, many customs may be like mutations where numerous maladaptations are necessary to find one that is useful. The value of the ecological approach is that it has given a new appreciation for interpretation of behavior within particular environments, both physical and social. This appreciation has been helpful for understanding culture in general, and economic organization in particular.

FIGURE   21

This reconstructed model of a Northwest Coast Village indicates that culture can be highly elaborated; some anthropologists are showing that the "elaboration" is often more adaptive than first thought. (Photo by Ernest Schusky)

Economic Organization

One of the striking differences between humans and all other animals is the division of labor. Among baboons, for instance, all of them feed independently. Except for a brief time when mothers help their young, each animal pulls up a shoot or gathers seeds and eats them without sharing. It is impossible to see a baboon troop as engaged in production and then in distribution or in consumption. Their feeding is a single act. All human communities engage in these three acts because each of them divides work between the sexes and among age groups. Such a division requires one act of production, such as males hunting and females gathering roots, and a second act of distribution when the sexes come together and share their production.

The separation of tasks results in a complex of norms about who is to do what, when, so that humans must begin making many decisions about how they are going to maximize their satisfactions, or what the economists call *utility*. Men must decide every day if it is better to hunt and produce calories or to stay in camp and conserve calories. Likewise, women will waste energy if they go gathering when adequate food may be left from the day before or if time would be better spent in improving shelter. In sum, individuals must continually make decisions about how to use their time and effort.

This economic organization of human beings has come to be understood via two different viewpoints. They are well reflected in the differing definitions of the science of economics. One field tends to focus on the decisions that humans must make in using their resources; thus, *economics* may be defined as *the science of how humans allocate scarce resources to maximize their utility*. This viewpoint emphasizes the sameness of all human beings, and stresses that all economic organization is alike. Harold Schneider of Indiana University has illustrated this view by showing how a people in Africa, in using cattle as an exchange for brides, are making decisions akin to those of a stock broker on Wall Street. A second viewpoint of economics stresses overall organization. An economist using this view defines *economics* as *the study of the system of production, distribution or exchange, and consumption* of goods and services within a society. Since the focus is on social system, this latter definition has usually appealed to sociologists and anthropologists while the first viewpoint has attracted psychologists who may join with an economist in the study of decision making.

The study of economic organization as system has tended to emphasize the differences among humans. Differences in production are most notable, such as the contrast between food collecting and modern industry. However, it is in the study of exchange that anthropologists have been struck with apparent differences in what motivates people to undertake tasks that would seem to yield little or even endanger their lives. This activity deserves thorough study and will be detailed after an examination of human production.

Systems of Production

In the highly technological world of today, almost everyone assumes that the production of goods can be infinite and that people's desire for goods is infinite. During the energy crisis of the 1970s, the view of unlimited production was severely criticized, and discussion began about the possibility of changing the seemingly infinite wants of humans. Some social scientists noted that a huge investment in advertising is necessary in the West in order to create many of the "needs" that are considered innate and, in anthropology, much light was shed on the human condition through the study of the different forms of production, especially food collecting.

A classification of the forms of production closely parallels the stages of prehistory. The simplest form, like the earliest form, is food collecting or hunting and gathering. A second form, resembling the Neolithic, is agricultural; this form is divided between pastoralism and horticulture with horticulture subdivided in several ways. An industrial form of production, coinciding with the Industrial Revolution, has vastly complicated economic organization in the past two to three hundred years and can be but briefly treated in a later chapter on political organization. It is an area of analysis that requires pulling insights from all the social sciences and has been neglected by anthropologists until recently.

Food collectors, a preferred term for hunters and gatherers, are the most misunderstood group. They have been stereotyped as people almost always on the verge of starvation and constantly engaged in the pursuit of food. Today, they have been pushed into some of the least desirable land in the world, such as the Arctic or the arid lands of Australia and Africa, or dense tropical forest. Yet, even in these locations they have been found to be living comfortable lives, scarcely ever in danger of famine, and needing only about 20 hours a week to produce everything they need.

They manage to be affluent, or have everything they need, first of all by not needing much beyond food and shelter. James Woodburn, who studied the food-collecting Hadza, writes that they valued mobility more than pottery or other material goods that would have to be carried. They simply scorned most goods except for a few simple tools. He further noted that the Hadza rarely accumulated any foods. This living from day-to-day was condemned by missionaries, but Woodburn saw that the Hadza always shared food wisely. In effect, they stored their food in other people's bellies.

The little time spent in production was a surprise to Woodburn; it was brought home to him dramatically during a gambling season when one or two Hadza had won all the arrows of their fellow hunters. The men simply could not hunt; then he noticed that men over 40, complaining of poor eyesight, seldom hunted, while some inept individuals rarely hunted. Similar variations also occurred among the women. And, while they usually did collect vegetation, they often caught small game so the sex division of labor was not rigid. It was neatly complementary, however, with the women supplying most of the calories from roots with carbohydrates while the men provided most of the protein.

Both sexes were able to accomplish their tasks in a 20-hour week because many more foods were available to them than they used. That is, women identified many plants as edible but chose only a few to harvest because of taste preferences. Likewise, men acknowledged that they sometimes ate animals that they normally passed up because of their taste or because of minor taboos. Such practices made sense to Woodburn when he viewed them from an ecological perspective. Ecologists have found a principle that a species must adapt to the minimum conditions of an environment. That is, a population should be able to exist when food sources are at their minimum. This means that most species have found ways of regulating their population so it does not grow when food is in abundance because starvation would occur in times of scarcity.

As a result, during average or good times, food is found readily and can be procured with minimum effort. As confirmation that the Hadza follow the principle, Woodburn returned to them when Africa was experiencing a drought. He found some farming people had joined his food collectors who were now eating all the edible foods known to them and spending much more time in food procurement. However, they were not starving like some of the farming peoples, nor were they yet spending all of their time in production. The danger in their future was that a national government intended to settle them and teach them farming in order to overcome their "primitive" behavior.

Once people start farming, they probably begin to violate the principle of adaptation to minimum conditions. At least, more than 99 percent of today's population is agricultural, and a great deal of it is in continual threat of famine or malnutrition. Further, many of these people live in exploding populations. Thus, it is important to examine carefully the various systems of agricultural production. Like food collecting, the simpler systems have been grossly stereotyped, and we probably have more misinformation than facts about what goes on in pastoralism and horticulture.

Pastoralism is probably the least understood system, although since the 1970s, famine in the Sahel regions of Africa has affected hundreds of thousands of camel and cattle pastoralists. While drought is often blamed for their deaths, it is obvious that social and political factors are far more important. "Drought" has been a constant feature of semi-arid areas, and is not the drought usually pictured by Westerners. In fact, semi-arid areas usually experience much variation both by region and over time. That is, microecological conditions affect behavior, and pastoralists have devised many ways to meet environmental changes, just as Indians did with the potlatch on the Northwest Coast of America. Among the pastoralists in Africa, the good times saw an active production of highly ornamented jewelry and brass work along with elaborately designed rugs, known in the West as Persian rugs. Such wealth was then traded for food during dry spells. The exchange was familiar to us; food was purchased with the luxury goods whereas the potlatch was a give-away; but, the results were the same. Food was spread equitably over large areas where no overall government existed that could redistribute resources. After the imposition of centralized governments under colonialism, the traditional adaptations were disrupted. There is no way, of course, to return to former practices in order to resolve the starvation and malnourishment of contemporary pastoralists, but the research on pastoralism reveals it as far more effective than once judged.

A similar view of "simple" horticulture has been discovered by agricultural economist Ester Boserup. The stereotype of primitive farmers is that their lack of technology makes them poor producers who frequently face hunger, work long hours to have barely enough to eat, and are often malnourished. People of the Neolithic are often portrayed like this, along with many contemporary peoples farming in isolated parts of the tropics. They practice what was once called *slash-and-burn* horticulture; now it is more often called *swidden farming*. Swidden farmers cut a part of the forest and let it dry thoroughly before burning it. If the farmers clear only five percent of the land available to them, they can use it once and let it grow up again in brush and saplings. While the land is idle, it is said to be in *fallow*. If people are clearing land that has long been fallow, such as 15 to 25 years, they have dense vegetation spread over their fields. By letting it dry thoroughly, they can create an intense fire that will kill all weeds and insect eggs. The ash from the vegetation is the only fertilizer necessary for the fallow land. In short, the vegetation or biomass that grew for 20 years was an accumulation of solar energy. By cutting it and burning it, swidden farmers used solar energy in their gardens and reduced labor energy considerably. During the one or two months of cutting, they worked long and hard, but planting vines of yams or sweet potatoes requires little more than dropping them on the ground. Seeds of plants, such as dry rice, are dropped in soil broken up only an inch or two by a digging stick, because the soil's nutrition is in the ash on the top of the ground. Fighting pests is a minimal task because of rapid growth, and harvesting is an effort spread out over a long period that can be done by all age groups. Typically, the gardens contain a wide variety of plants; the variation ensures a nutritious diet as well as a reliable one, since a plant disease can infect only a small portion of the crops. Finally, we can see that the only necessary tools are an ax or machete plus a digging stick where long-fallow agriculture is practiced. The technology is simple but all that is needed.

Today, such swidden farmers are found only in remote areas visited by missionaries or anthropologists. Other types of swidden farmers exist and are important

FIGURE 22

The Guatemalan hillside is rapidly eroding as short-fallow swiddeners continually intensify their farming. (Photo by Ernest Schusky)

in the economics of most developing countries in the tropics. These farmers practice short-fallow farming. They can leave their fields idle only three to five years; they will clear mostly grass and only some brush. In effect, the fields have not been able to accumulate much solar energy in the biomass. Before they burn the fallow vegetation, they spread it carefully and may go into distant forests to cut limbs and add them to the dried vegetation. Or they add mud from streams or lakes or use other sources of natural fertilizer. Obviously, their task requires considerably more labor. Further, the fire will not be as effective in destroying weeds and people will have to work hard at weeding. This step involves use of a hoe, usually made in several varieties; other tools may be added in order to cultivate the variety of plants.

Both long- and short-fallow farmers are not only regarded as backward but as inefficient because they use only a fraction of their land. Thus, governments today discourage swidden practices but it appears that, even before this pressure, many farmers began to plow their fields annually. This change is drastic because it gives up entirely the energy of a biomass and substitutes the energy of a draft animal, such as oxen, buffalo, or horse. The obvious need is for deep plowing to use nutrients from deep in the soil but, as these are depleted, animal manure becomes a necessity. The use of animals means they must be cared for year-round. They must be fenced in pastures or fields must be fenced to keep the animals from eating crops. If they are stabled, labor is involved in building and maintaining the stables, but manure is concentrated. If animals are pastured, collecting manure involves labor. Of course, farm technology becomes far more complex. Plows must have at least an iron, preferably steel, point; the rest of the plow is fairly complex even if wooden. Harnesses and hitches are necessary and usually require specialization in blacksmithing and leather-working. As tools specialize and become more complex, it is tempting to reduce the number of crops grown and depend more and more on a few, usually the grains. Thus, corn and beans became major crops in Latin America, while dry rice and chickpeas were important in parts of Asia.

We see immediately that the shift to annual plowing will likely contribute to a less nutritious diet. Moreover, the change violates an ecological principle. In the tropics, many different species live in small populations. Think of a rain forest where all sorts of grasses, bushes, and trees are surrounded by many types of insects, reptiles, and mammals. There is abundant life but no herds of animals. Near the poles, the principle is reversed and a few species exist in large numbers. In between, in temperate zones, a moderate number of species live in moderate-size populations. Interestingly, the "primitive" gardens of fallow farmers were a domesticated duplication of the ecology of the wild forest. A more "modern" farmer plowing fields annually with only a few crops violates ecological principle in the tropics.

Analysis further reveals that annual cropping requires far more labor than swidden farming. Because of animal care, farming must be a year-round task. Plowing is as strenuous as cutting and fertilizing is far more time consuming. Cultivating and harvesting also become more labor intensive because the grains must be stored and they require greater food processing. Thus, a major question arises as to why people ever change from swidden farming to annual cropping or why they change from long-fallow to short-fallow methods.

FIGURE 23

Annual plowing of semi-arid lands becomes hazardous when emphasis is placed on cash crops for export and traditional variation is replaced by a single crop. (Photo courtesy of the U. S. Agency for International Development)

Boserup has noted that population density greatly increases between long-fallow populations and those who crop annually. Past explanations have said that the technological advances that accompany the changes allow greater production and, therefore, larger populations. However, one should ask immediately why anyone would want larger populations when it means working two to three times harder. In short, the changes that have been regarded as "progress" make no sense. Boserup's answer is that populations must have grown first and farmers were forced to increase use of their land. Likewise, they were forced to add hoes to their technology when they had to weed short-fallow fields. And, when they had to plow all their land, they had to come up with technology for plowing. The evolutionary changes in agriculture show that people have produced more food per unit of land, but they have had to work much harder because they have been producing less food per unit of labor.

With the advent of modern agriculture in the 19th century, a change occurred that was even more radical than converting to animal power. Most often, the change has been attributed to breakthroughs in technology. The tractor, with all its associated machinery, is certainly impressive. But, all this machinery is powered by fossil fuel, and the major advances in agriculture since World War II are due to chemical fertilizer and pesticides, also requiring abundant use of fossil energy. In short, modern agriculture is unique because it is so energy intensive. Always before, any people who put more calories into farming, in the form of labor, than they produced in food would starve. Today, it is estimated that North American farmers use about seven calories of fossil fuel for every one calorie of food produced. This ratio does not include all the other energy needed to transport, store, and process food, let alone the gas or electricity that goes into preparing a home meal. The system makes sense only where fossil calories are very cheap and food calories are expensive. In an age when fossil calories are becoming scarce, "modern" agriculture clearly is inappropriate for the traditional world and may well be modified in "modern" cultures.

Yet, something called a *Green Revolution* is being used to help the poor nations produce their own food. This revolution is described as one that depends on botany to develop highly productive plants for the tropics or semitropics. New varieties of wheat and rice have doubled production in favorable areas, but the new plants are all highly dependent on fertilizer. A high use of chemical fertilizer also requires intensive irrigation. Most irrigation systems are powered by pumps, operated by fossil fuel; the manufacture of chemical fertilizer, likewise, requires much energy. Thus, the Green Revolution is a parallel to North American and European farming. It cannot possibly be expected to solve the world food shortage in the long run.

Fortunately, new techniques are being worked out that depend more on human labor and less on fossil fuel. Even in North America, innovations in management are reducing energy inputs and making greater use of natural products. For example, the natural enemies of insect pests are being raised, and rapidly growing crops that crowd out weeds are developments that reduce the need for pesticides. No-till cultivation reduces the use of tractors. Such developments have not brought about any rapid increases in food production, but they clearly indicate that future trends can be away from a dependence on intensive energy use.

Systems of Exchange

In the modern world of high technology, consumers' health is threatened by the variety of chemicals used on the farm while farm profits are threatened by the rising cost of their use. Even so, modern agriculture has become incredibly productive, although its gains are dwarfed by the production of industry. Today, Europe and America must fear a dwindling resource base, but an even greater problem looms from the byproducts of this production. The pollution of land, air, and water has never occurred on such a scale, while radiation and exotic chemical poisoning are entirely new phenomena. Despite such novelty, the truly revolutionary development of modern times may be the creation of consumers with infinite needs and desires.

So many people have developed an insatiable appetite that it is assumed to be a part of human nature, although one should immediately question why so much advertising is needed to spark such demand if it is innate. In fact, however, the demand stems primarily from a comparatively recent system of exchange known as the *market*. In the market, which is a concept rather than a physical place, individuals or groups such as business firms meet solely to exchange goods or services. You have something that I may want, and you are willing to give it up for something I may have. Money, of course, will facilitate the process, but we could barter. The important aspect of the process is wholly impersonal. You and I need not know each other; only our needs and products are of importance to the transactions. With the convenience of money, or what is an agreed-upon unit of value, people in the market do not even need face-to-face contact. Indeed, mail order catalogs and electronic processing suggest a future market totally without human contact. Even grocery stores are being designed to be operated by robots.

The future may eventually eliminate *money* but, since it has come to have such symbolic value, it is likely to persist for a long time even after it is no longer necessary. Its symbolism has created problems in defining it, and anthropologists do not always agree on what peoples have money. If it must be portable and easily exchanged, then some giant stone rings called money are probably something else even though they are units of value on some Pacific islands. If money is a means of storing wealth, then woodpecker scalps that deteriorate do not qualify, although they too have been thought to be money among some California Indians. The issue cannot be settled here, but it is useful to see money as characteristic of the highly impersonalized transactions of the market. True money is not found where personal relations are part of the exchange.

The market is so prevalent and internalized in the Western world that social scientists once assumed it was the only way of exchanging goods that could be considered as economic. Time and again anthropologists recorded complex systems of exchange but, since the flow of goods did not follow standard market practices, the distribution was called *ritual exchange* or the motives for it were described in psychological terms. However, these examples of "ritual" trade or "acts of tribute" were quite obviously systems of exchange that stood between systems of production and acts of consumption. They simply could not be ignored as economic, although it took an economic historian, Karl Polanyi, to describe their part in economic organization.

FIGURE   24

*Four markets around the world: New Guinea Highlands, China, Guatemala, and India.
Barter still occurs in the Highlands; money is the medium of exchange in the other three
cultures.* (New Guinea photo by Larry L. Naylor; others by Ernest Schusky)

One of the classic examples of an economic practice that stood in limbo until
Polanyi was the Kula ring of the Trobriand Islands, northeast of New Guinea. In the
kula, men made long, dangerous trips to neighboring islands to bestow a necklace
on a partner. Long speeches were given by the Trobriander about the value of the
gift. This value derived from traditions—what great people had held the necklace
before giving it away. Such value occurs in our culture; a cherry bedstead that was

owned or even just slept in by President Washington is far more valuable than the same piece without the history. Sometime later, the man receiving the necklace makes a trip to the Trobriands and presents his partner with a shell armband. The Trobriander displays the armband and gains prestige by telling about it, but his way to fame is to take the armband to another island and bestow it on another trade partner who will later present the Trobriander with a valuable necklace.

Over the years, armbands traveled among many islands in roughly counter-clockwise fashion. Necklaces followed the same circuit but in a clockwise direction. Trobrianders did not know all the islands involved in the exchange nor were they even curious. They did realize that they got necklaces from one direction and gave them in the other and, with some talent and luck, they could build up their prestige by acquiring notable necklaces or armbands. Partners, whose fathers usually had been partners, never haggled over the value of their items, although they did bargain over smaller items such as pottery and tobacco. This type of trade clearly followed the market principle, but the kula exchange was different.

How is it to be analyzed? The oratory and other practice suggests it is ritual, although there is no obvious connection to religion. Many observers recorded the Trobriands as giving necklaces to their partners. One long description of such exchange, by Marcel Mauss, is titled *The Gift*. But, to the Western mind, "giving" implies altruism, suggesting that the practice is not economic. However, to describe the practice as barter or trade is even more misleading. The Trobrianders are nothing like entrepreneurs when engaged in kula. Clearly, the goods are of little consequence or use; what is important is social ties among individuals.

The study, *The Gift,* provided the data for Polanyi to make it clear that this type of exchange was interwoven with the fabric of social life. To avoid the connotations of *gift* the items exchanged are now called *prestations*. A prestation is without question part of an exchange, but it is important to understand the motivations for the exchange. Social relations totally regulate the flow of goods; the goods or services themselves are only symbolic of the personal ties. Mauss termed such exchange reciprocity and Polanyi showed how widespread it was. The value of the goods is quite secondary to the exchange itself. Social relations exist; they are perpetuated, intensified, or moderated through reciprocity. When Western peoples practice reciprocity, they usually describe it as gift-giving and attribute the exchange to generosity or altruism. The anonymous gift is so motivated, but much of our gift-giving is actually a prestation. Most wedding, anniversary, and birthday gifts are "given" knowing full-well that they obligate the recipient to return "a gift" to the donor. Note further that Western presents, such as wedding gifts, are much like Trobriand shells. Silver and crystal are of little practical use; their exchange is delayed, often for several years, and one would never think of returning a crystal goblet to its original owner/giver.

Typically, in reciprocal exchange some period of time must elapse before a donor receives a return prestation. The time in between the exchange maintains an obligation that cements a social relationship; an immediate mutual exchange would tend to cancel a social bond. A second characteristic of reciprocity is that the goods exchanged are of a nonessential nature and, while they are much the same in nature, they are never identical. Crystal glassware returned for silverware meets these requirements just as shell necklaces and armbands. Consider how you would feel if you had given someone an expensive present and a year later it was returned to you.

You would sense that the social relationship is broken. For confirmation consider the man who gives a woman a diamond engagement ring and she later returns it.

Reciprocity is likely the earliest form of exchange to occur among humans because they lived in nearly identical communities. That is, one Paleolithic band or a Neolithic village produced the same goods and had equal resources. Despite the lack of any reason for trade, it is known that goods and services continually circulated in such situations in order to maintain social relations. Another important characteristic of reciprocity is that the exchange must match the social relations. When two individuals are peers or of approximately equal status, the value of the goods they exchange must be roughly equal. For example, in our society, gift exchange between males and females is about equal whereas a few generations ago men were expected to give far more expensive gifts than they received from women. Consider how you would feel if a friend suddenly began giving you much more expensive gifts than you could reciprocate. You might well accuse your friend of one-upmanship rather than generosity. In contrast, if the father of a young son was to expect a birthday present from the son equal in value to his gift, the man would be considered miserly. A differential of this type is called *skewed reciprocity*. In societies with little formal political organization, leadership is generally determined by skewed reciprocity. Leaders must consistently give more than they receive; consequently, they sometimes are the poorest in a village, poor in goods at least, but wealthy in prestige.

Reciprocity is not limited to exchange between individuals. The potlatch of Northwest Coast Indians is a classic example of reciprocity, and major potlatches that occurred between villages were often cases of skewed reciprocity. As we saw earlier, a region with material wealth gave it to poorer people, thus accumulating prestige and a kind of superiority over others. Then, in hard times, this prestige was traded off for food. Likewise, the pig feasts of the Maring are seen as reciprocity. The bestowal of pork creates an obligation to support a host even in warfare, although it should be remembered that the guest was a potential ally before being invited as a guest. Indeed, the guests had likely once given their own pig feasts, making allies of the present hosts.

It is interesting to ask just how much prestige can be built up through reciprocity. Why should there be any limits to it? Yet, if prestige were infinite, there would be no value to it. It would be worthless if everyone could be assigned immense amounts of prestige. Some hard-nosed economists who believe that prestige cannot be measured refuse to acknowledge that allocations between goods and prestige can be included in the science of economics. That attitude may make life easier for them, but the omission of such exchange means they fail to understand some fundamentals of human behavior.

Reciprocity is a part of all human behavior to be viewed from many perspectives, including religion, kinship, politics, education, and especially economics. This point is dramatized in an ethnography by Edward Schieffelin on the Kaluli of New Guinea. These people practice an exotic custom known as the *Gisaro*. In the Gisaro, a village invites neighbors who compose nostalgic songs to be sung while dancing, the lyrics causing much sorrow for the hosts. The sorrow is so great that the hosts become exceedingly upset, seize torches, and burn the dancers' backs. The dancers suffer the pain stoically, knowing that the more they are burned the more their hosts have appreciated the power of their performance. The burning, however, is not sufficient reciprocity; later, the dancers will use pearl shells or other prestations to compensate their hosts. To achieve full comprehension of the Gisaro, Schieffelin had to analyze all the reciprocity involved in the ritual not only from the perspective of the exchange of goods and services but also from the perspective of religion, kinship, and politics.

Reciprocity is the essence of life among many peoples in the nontechnological world while also remaining a vital part of social life in the modern world. However, other systems of exchange began to emerge with the growing complexity of society. Skewed reciprocity suggests the beginnings of differentiation. One who gives more than others stands above them. At some point, prestige becomes equated with power. Just how individuals acquire power or convert prestige to power is unclear but, in many horticultural societies, goods begin to circulate in ways other than by reciprocity.

The African kingdom of Bunyoro offers a prime example of a process of exchange known as *redistribution*. In everyday life, Bunyoro commoners provide feasts for each other, exchanging grain and beer by reciprocity; but, in addition, they set aside some grain, beer, and cattle for the village head. These leaders use some of the produce, but pass on most of the goods to the district leaders, who pass it on to regional leaders, who pass most of the goods to the Bunyoro chief, known as a king to many Africans. The king or chief is a wealthy man compared to others. But how much grain, cattle, or even beer can one person consume? Such concentrated wealth does an individual very little good, except to enhance power. Food is sent back down to the villages in time of need or to men serving in an army in time of war. The chief uses cows to give for brides, and he has a large harem. The many marriages make him a brother-in-law or son-in-law to many of the commoners who thus are obligated to support his rule because he is relative as well as chief.

Clearly, this system involves much production, exchange, and consumption but obviously operates outside the principles of the market. Nor does it resemble skewed reciprocity since it is not social ties that direct the flow of goods. Goods and services flow up and down the hierarchy because of the power of the Bunyoro chief. This power derives in part from mythology and tradition, but the essential motivation is the power of the chief. The chief has power because he directs so much of the flow of goods up and down the hierarchy. It is not easy to break into this circular explanation, but it does give some idea of how the system works and it is useful to illustrate the close relation between economics and politics.

In the Western world, taxation is sometimes described as a system of redistribution. Governments often do redistribute wealth, supposedly from the wealthy to the poor, but not always. Since taxation is backed by force or power, goods do circulate as in a chiefdom and, obviously, taxation is not a market process. Yet, taxation is not redistribution either. The differences lie largely in the nature of the goods. Tribute must be in the form of consumer goods so that they cannot be accumulated. Moreover, the goods are usually limited in type, reflecting the personal relations involved in their transfer. Only certain forms of wealth satisfy the needs or demands of the hierarchy, just as only cows could form the bride wealth in Bunyoro. Typically, when colonial governments encountered redistribution, they tried to simplify the system by substituting money. But, when chiefs discovered that money could be stored in unlimited amounts in Swiss banks, they no longer directed wealth to the commoners. They quickly lost power because they no longer acted like great chiefs; moreover, commoners discovered all sorts of uses for money that grain and beer did not serve.

To summarize, all societies have developed economic systems because of a division of labor. However, all societies have gone well beyond an economic system within their immediate group. They have established social ties with neighboring groups through reciprocity. Such ties make good sense for food collectors who must have access to wide and changing territories. Reciprocity is also an excellent way of tying together various groups of pastoralists who must be able to move to different territories when their own experiences a severe dry spell. Horticulturalists, too, need social ties beyond their own communities so that population can be adjusted to microecological change. With some specialization, centers of power grew up, as often occurred with the intensive cultivation of annual cropping. Redistributive systems often accompany such a form of production. Still further specialization, especially as reflected in urban life, leads to impersonal relations and sets the stage for the market. Possibly, no markets existed until the first cities of 5,000 years ago; even then, the vast majority of goods seemed to have circulated in the early empires on principles of redistribution and reciprocity.

Clearly, adaptation to an environment through the elaboration of particular economic systems results in an economic-political complex that provides a core of social relations. Kinship and religious groups must be compatible with this core so that cultures within an environmental area generally show considerable similarity. It is tempting to suppose that the similarities are due to environmental influence, but it is important to realize that peoples within an area always have considerable contact, even when they are hostile to each other. It is the opinion of most anthropologists that it is this contact or what is called *diffusion* that brings about most of the important similarities. Obviously, diffusion must be the major influence in the ways of life that have to do with religion, value systems, or aspects of personality. It should be emphasized that culture traits do not diffuse automatically. People consciously borrow from others, making deliberate choices about selection and rejection. They are, of course, unlikely to borrow traits that would be incompatible with their environment or with their own values.

Culture Areas

In the initial stages of anthropology, cross-cultural comparisons were often made on a group-by-group basis; but, as data accumulated on thousands of groups, it became necessary to classify them into larger units. Such a step occurred first in anthropological museums where anthropologists realized that their displays were more meaningful when they employed a *culture area* concept. For example, rather than have a separate exhibit case for each of the Cheyenne, Dakota, Crow, and other Plains tribes, one general display could represent all the tribes between the Rocky Mountains and the Mississippi River because of the many similarities among them. Another display could well represent the dozens of tribes living along the Northwest coast from Oregon to Alaska.

Cultures within an area must show some common adaptations, particularly in their economies and associated political organization. Thus, in grouping peoples within a culture area, the political economy is a major consideration; however, no one would exclude religion, education, family type, or even art styles. Thus, a major criticism of culture area classification is that anthropologists have never agreed on objective characteristics to determine precisely what constitutes significant similarities. As a result, border regions between culture areas are sometimes hazy. In short, culture areas are imprecise, and criteria for forming them are subjective. Culture areas also are imprecise because of *acculturation* or the major changes that occur when a dominating society comes in contact with subordinate societies. The dominating societies are the ones that have described subordinated peoples so such contact was essential for anthropology. But the discipline tries to reconstruct cultures as they were before contact. That is, there is sufficient contact to establish a significant record, but not too much change to distort the precontact period. This point of time is called the *ethnographic present*. Obviously, the ethnographic present must also be imprecise. As illustration, the Indians in northeastern North America were fairly well described through a long period of contact with French fur traders and missionaries. Such contact does not lead to great change, and the ethnographic present well represents aboriginal life. In contrast, southeastern Indians in North America faced the colonizing English and, to survive, they had to develop well-organized political confederacies in a short period of time. For Cherokee or Creek, then, the ethnographic present pictures a complex political system that never existed in aboriginal times.

The culture area concept remains useful as a way of organizing materials on the various continents. However, ethnographic data has increased to such magnitude that it is now stored in computers. Data known as the *Human Relations Area Files* may be handled on a worldwide basis. For example, one might look for correlations between all long-term fallow farmers and certain child rearing practices. How much time do fathers spend with their children when they do not have to work very long? How do they differ from men practicing annual cropping? Other cross-cultural comparisons may be made within a culture area. An anthropologist might concentrate just on the Pueblo Indians of the Southwest in order to examine in detail a multitude of historical, cultural, and environmental factors. In short, a wide range of cross-cultural comparisons are practiced.

Summary

In looking at all the human adaptations to the environment, anthropologists concluded that culture represented far more than obtaining sufficient food and shelter. Culture was play-like in that it consisted of much more than was necessary. It was elaboration. This perspective was probably carried too far; it has been countered by *cultural ecologists* who maintain that we must see culture as adaptive. Humans now use cultural change rather than biological change in adapting to their environment. The cultural ecologists have shown how food taboos, once thought to be pure elaboration, may be adaptive.

In studying the choices that humans must make in their adaptations, anthropologists join with economists in an analysis of behavior. From economics, one perspective has developed that focuses on the individual or a group, studying how this unit makes decisions about *the allocation of scarce resources*. Another perspective on an economy is that it is *a system of production, distribution, and consump-*

tion. The latter view has been popular in anthropology with early analysis of various kinds of production, usually put into stages that parallel prehistory.

Food collectors, for example, live much like peoples throughout the Paleolithic lived. We now know that this life is far easier and more healthful than once thought. Since food collectors need very few material goods, they are able to produce them quickly along with the food and shelter they require. Gathering a variety of vegetation plus hunting yields a well-balanced diet so that, generally, food collectors enjoyed a leisurely, well-nourished life, seldom experiencing hunger, despite existing in some harsh environments.

A change to *horticulture* usually means an increase in the hours spent in productive activity and may mean some decrease in nutrition. Some horticulturists have little access to animals but, if they are able to engage in *long-fallow cultivation,* they likely will have a considerable variety of plants, especially in the tropics. Since the technology of long-fallow horticulture requires only an ax and a digging stick, tools are easily made. Clearing a forest is the only difficult work; burning the dried brush serves to weed and reduce insects while the ash fertilizes the soil. Where horticulturalists are forced to use land more often and have only a *short fallow,* they must engage in weeding, fighting insects, and probably fertilizing. They must work longer hours than long-fallow farmers. *Annual plowing* requires even more time because animal manure must be used to fertilize and traction is needed for plowing. A much more complex technology is required. In the transition from long-fallow to annual plowing, *more food is produced per acre of land but less food is produced per hour of labor.* It is difficult to see why humans would seek such change unless it was forced upon them, probably by population growth. In the past hundred years, agriculture has experienced another major change with the introduction of fossil fuels in traction, fertilizing, and fighting pests. Recently, the technique has been modified with a *Green Revolution* which is supposed to help agricultural production in the Third World.

Just as our understanding of systems of production has changed greatly so, too, have we reinterpreted systems of distribution. Early anthropologists tended to see only market exchanges as economic; other kinds of exchange were interpreted as ritual or otherwise misunderstood. Karl Polanyi, however, showed how *reciprocity* and *redistribution* were equally valid systems of exchange. The motivation for the flow of goods in reciprocity is personal relationships. These social ties are reinforced by "gift-giving," but the gift is really a way of doing social business. It cements ties between both individuals and groups. Generally, these ties are between equals and the goods will be of equal value. In some cases, one side may regularly give more wealth than it receives. The recipient makes up the difference with prestige which then becomes skewed reciprocity. Skewed reciprocity looks as if it might be a step toward redistribution, but the latter is fundamentally different. Authority, rather than personal ties, motivates the flow of goods, but this authority has the power of tradition, not force. People willingly give up wealth to a hierarchy, usually called a *chiefdom,* in the form of *tribute.* Tribute differs from taxes in that taxes are paid because of coercion. *Taxes* go to a state hierarchy and will be explained further in a later chapter.

These systems of adaptation and economics are generally similar throughout a geographic area. A common environment helps account for the similarities, but anthropologists are more impressed with the forces of diffusion in producing the similarities. *Diffusion* involves the borrowing of traits; where change is much more intensive, it is called *acculturation*. Whatever the reasons, neighboring cultures can be grouped into *culture areas*. The culture area is a classification device for handling the thousands of different cultures that are basic for cross-cultural comparisons. Generally, the cultures selected for comparison are ones that have not experienced great influence from a dominant society so the cultures of a culture area are described in the ethnographic present. The *ethnographic present* is that point in time when a culture has been contacted by another society that records its way of life but has not yet caused much acculturation.

By continuing to examine thousands of cultures in the ethnographic present, anthropologists should eventually determine the extent to which culture is elaboration while also being adaptive. They now are able to compare a multitude of cultures documented in the Human Relations Area Files or they compare in detail a limited number of groups within a culture area.

9

Kinship, Kin Groups, and Social Structure

Comparisons of Human and Nonhuman Social Life

In the past few decades, remarkable findings have been made in *ethology*, the study of animal social behavior. Earlier scientists had assumed that nonhuman social life was almost totally instinctive or fixed by genetics. Much more careful observation has shown that considerable variation occurs among the social ties of most species, showing that learning is a part of social life. That is, the statuses are not solely fixed by the genes.

However, the learning that occurs is often at an early age in a process that is called *imprinting*. Imprinting is clearly not instinctive, but it is not quite like the learning of humans; it is something in between the two. An illustration best clarifies the nature of imprinting. Once, biologists thought that ducklings followed the mother duck because of instincts. Now we know that, shortly after they hatch, ducklings fix on any object about the size of a duck and will henceforth follow it. So ducklings may follow a basketball or a briefcase if these are substituted for the mother duck at the time when imprinting occurs. Thus, social ties can be considerably altered, even ones that have a considerable base fashioned by genetics.

Even among the social insects something like imprinting must influence social behavior. For example, biologists once thought bees communicated with others purely by instinct. But, in examining a "dance" that bees do to indicate the distance and direction of a pollen source, observers found that bees raised in isolation could not communicate effectively. Likewise, sheepherding dogs that are raised in isolation will sometimes attack and kill the sheep they are supposed to protect. At a higher level, the genetic base seems to be much more for an all-purpose learning rather than the more specific responses of imprinting. Chimpanzees, for instance, generally make very good mothers, but Jane Goodall reports that some chimps carry the infant upside down or otherwise fail to nurture the young. She believes that these females were the youngest or the only child of a mother. In such circumstances, they did not have the opportunity to observe how their own mother cared for her young. Certainly adolescent chimps who are still with their mothers when other young are born take much interest in the rearing of their young brother or

FIGURE   25

Although revolutionary change has occurred in Chinese society, respect for the aged remains and a sharp age division has persisted. (Photos by Ernest Schusky)

sister. They have an excellent opportunity to learn, and the social ties that are created between mother and young lead Goodall to describe the social unit as a family. The mother-offspring tie is beyond doubt; there is some evidence to suggest that ties also continue between siblings of the same sex, that is "brother-brother" and sister-sister."

In sum, the primate background is one that suggests learned social ties are important in some species. From fossil evidence, it will be a long time before we discover just how social life required even more learning, because of greater complexity, among hominids. Since the most unique thing about the hominids is their bipedalism, the need for more complex social life may have begun when humans left the forest for the grassland. Even if the initial move was simply to forage on vegetation, they would have had to organize for protection against predators, such as cheetahs or hunting dogs. Just as baboons learn a fairly rigid age and sex division of society in order to protect themselves in the grasslands, the first hominids would have needed comparable organization.

Given some kind of politics to protect against external enemies and to regulate conflict within the group, early hominids would have had the basic ingredients of a social system. As they went from being the hunted to being hunters, it is easy to imagine the need for a growing complexity of social relations. Instead of simply reacting to external threats, the groups would be required to exert the initiative of the chase. The conversion from defense to offense no doubt selected for all kinds of abilities, not the least of which was the ability to establish and maintain social ties.

In the shift from hunted to hunter, demands for effective communication would be high. For defense, communicating about the present suffices. Group hunting requires planning and thought about the future. "If the prey stampedes, we should do this; if it circles, then we should do that." Such communication is facilitated by discussion of the past. Judgments about past mistakes and successes must have been a boon to future hunts. In such communication, people in long-enduring social relations would have considerable advantage. They know much about how others are thinking even before they speak. Siblings and spouses often read each other's minds. Likely, the best hunters were not necessarily the fastest or the strongest; rather, they were the best at cooperating and communicating. Selection would have been for able learners—masters at organizing one's fellows, learning their strengths and weaknesses as well as the circumstances of the natural environment.

Hunting also seems likely to have brought about a more rigid sex division of society. We should be careful to avoid simply projecting the present on the past; because contemporary food-collecting peoples have males who do most of the hunting does not guarantee that Paleolithic hunters were all males. Yet, pregnancy and a long nursing period likely meant that most females spent more time than males in less risky tasks such as gathering vegetation. Such work may not require the same kind of cooperation, but it is certainly lightened by combined effort. Shared knowledge allows for a greater range of plants collected and especially for a variety of technology that remained simple and unchanging for hundreds of thousands of years.

As the importance of group ties increased, one possible strategy was for the members to remain together throughout life. Many baboons follow such a pattern; a baboon born into a group remains with it for a lifetime. Every baboon well knows its place. In contrast, the human group gives up some of its members as they become mature. No one is certain why this break-up should occur, but one possible answer is that bipedalism makes it possible to travel long distances. To use this potential it is useful to have social ties in the many groups dispersed over a wide range. Such ties are steadily created if members of one's original group are somehow transferred into other groups. The issue is: How could such transfers occur where people were likely not to be conscious of the advantages to them?

Incest and Marriage

The unique aspect of human social life is the regulation of sex. Among other primates, the typical pattern is for many males to mate with a female in estrus. No lasting tie is created between a male and female. In contrast, all human groups impose some regulation on sex through the customs of *incest* and *marriage*. In effect, incest says that one must not mate with close members of a group; marriage directs sexual relations to nongroup members. Many theorists have speculated about the origin of incest and marriage, offering a variety of psychological and sociological reasons, none of which is particularly satisfying.

However, it seems most likely that the beginnings of incest and marriage lie in the kind of overall adaptation that humans made to the grasslands. In this environment and with their bipedalism, the human group was small but stable with a very sparse population. Like other social primates, they must have occupied a territory, but unlike other primates the space between territories was great. Diagram 9-1 illustrates the differences.

For example, three baboon troops may have overlapping territories at a waterhole but, for most of their lives, baboons will remain in the territory where they were born. They will mate with a baboon sharing the same area with only occasional gene flow occurring in the overlapping territories. In marked contrast, humans who share a territory will regularly establish mating relations with members of other territories. In effect, members who grow up together will define each other as ineligible for mating. That is, they will define sexual relations with each other as incestuous. They will have numerous sanctions to regulate incest. The most effective of these prohibitions will be the device of making group members brothers and sisters to each other. The creation of brotherhood and sisterhood means that, at the same time, some idea of husband and wife was also created. To have a concept of sister means that one must also have a concept of wife. Husband and brother are, likewise, two sides of the same coin. Or, more generally, one's world is divided between those one can marry and those one must not marry. Everyone becomes a kind of "blood" relative, known as *consanguine,* or an in-law, known as an *affine.* We will see later that in most small societies even today that all people are related to each other, either as a kind of spouse or in-law or as a kind of brother-sister or father-mother.

By creating such wide-ranging ties of kinship, the human group achieved a remarkable kind of adaptation to the savannas. In normal times, it could range over a wide area in largely independent fashion. However, if a critical waterhole were to

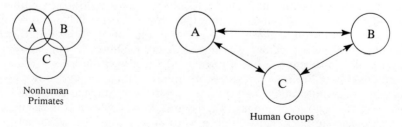

DIAGRAM 9–1   Contrast Between Groupings of Nonhumans and Humans.

dry up or if a game herd moved or a vegetation patch suffered a disease, the group could move out of its territory into another one where it had close ties of kinship. In sum, incest and marriage are the basis of kinship, and kinship ties were a way of establishing close ties with surrounding groups. When ecological conditions were such that a territory could not sustain a group temporarily, kinship allowed the group to move into other territories. As is the case today, all the members of a group did not need to move into one other territory; they could scatter into half a dozen or more adjoining territories.

The ties created among groups by marriage generally become patterned. In part, they are regular or systematic because of the nature of reciprocity. Just as a group feasts each other, taking turns at being host, groups will exchange spouses with each other. Two major patterns occur in this exchange. In small farming societies, the men of a group will often go to live with their wives at the time of marriage. In societies where the norms direct men to live with the wives' groups, the practice is called *matrilocal residence*. A variation on this pattern occurs when a man takes his bride to live with his mother's brother, a practice known as *avunculocal residence*. In a pastoral society or with intensive agriculture, or where warfare is common, women are likely to go to live with their husband's group. This custom is termed *patrilocal residence*. In a variation of this theme, a man often lives a year or two with his wife's group after marriage, but the couple then moves to the groom's group. Anthropologists describe the practice as *matri-patrilocal residence*. People often analyze the custom as a groom's way of paying for the value of the wife, but another important function is that the man makes a niche for himself in a second group.

Westerners are not unique in thinking that it is best for a newly married couple to establish an independent household in a pattern known as *neolocal residence*, but it is comparatively rare because it reduces the close ties between kin groups. One further point is necessary about these patterned relations. When a society is described as matrilocal or patrilocal, it is because most people say that a groom should live with his wife or a wife with her husband. In everyday life, considerable freedom of choice usually exists. A couple may agree that everyone should live with the groom's group when in fact they have lived with the wife's group for five years. When questioned about their practice as a violation of their norms, they may simply assert that their residence is only temporary; they expect to live with the groom's group eventually. Such practice, of course, is common in the West. A married couple may see themselves as "neolocal" because they are planning on their own house, despite having lived with one of their parents for years.

In many other ways, Western marriage is quite different from the traditional form. The neolocal pattern is actually a way of cutting ties with other groups, and marriage is seen as the union of two people, never two groups. In contrast, traditional marriage was a way of uniting groups, not a husband and a wife. Thus, *arranged marriages* are common, even in modern-day India or other parts of Asia. A bride and groom may never have seen each other before the wedding. The union that is important is the one between groups.

A further illustration of marriage as alliance is the custom known as *levirate*. In this practice, a widow is expected to marry the brother of her deceased husband. Westerners may be familiar with the custom since it occurs in the Old Testament. It is a way of ensuring that an alliance made between groups is not broken by the death of a spouse. Instead, the group of the deceased is expected to provide an immediate substitute. Of course, the obverse custom also occurs. When a widower is expected to marry a sister of his deceased wife, the practice is called the *sororate*.

Frequently, the norms of a society call for both the sororate and the levirate but, among some peoples, only one of the practices may be present. Until marriage was recognized as a kind of treaty-making or alliance among groups, practices such as the levirate and sororate were regarded as exotic customs. They made little sense, and they were generally explained by history or diffusion which said nothing about their origin. Of course, practices may have several functions. The sororate, for example, is also a way of providing for older females when husbands are principal sources of income.

Another custom that was regarded as an oddity was a tradition known as *bride-capture*. This marriage ritual captivated earlier anthropologists who wrote about it at length; psychologists have also been engaged in its explanation. Nevertheless, it immediately makes sense when one regards marriage as an alliance. The ritual is something like a feud with groups regularly "attacking" each other to secure wives. The attacks, however, are carefully regulated to reduce physical injury, and the bride's group, but not necessarily the bride, is well aware of what the outcome will be. They are also aware that the capture means that they will eventually have a right to take a bride from among the attackers. In short, many peoples today, and very likely throughout much of the Paleolithic, marry as a form of exchange that served to link widely dispersed groups.

Marriage as Exchange

While incest is a foundation for looking for spouses outside the group, it will not in itself suffice to tie groups together over long distances. Some of the persons present in the local groups may not be consanguines. Thus, human groups have gone beyond the norms of incest regulation. They add a rule of *exogamy*. Exogamy is a norm specifying that marriages must occur outside of the local group or other social groups. It is important to note that incest regulations cover sexual behavior. Sex is prohibited among family members. Exogamy regulates marriage; it requires a marriage with someone outside the group.

A prominent French anthropologist, Claude Lévi-Strauss, has argued that the beginning of human society occurred when the men of a group denied themselves sexual rights to women of their group, that is, the women who were like sisters. By seeking mates elsewhere, they intensified ties of reciprocity that might have been initiated by feasting or exchange of material goods. To some degree, the theory resembles the ideas of Sigmund Freud who also saw the origin of human life in the creation of incest regulation. However, he believed the causes for this step were quite different, as we will see in a later chapter.

The precise steps in the origin of incest and exogamy may never be known, but Lévi-Strauss has captured for us the important symbolic value of exogamy. Almost everywhere it is practiced, the exogamous groups are far more than a unit that exchanges mates. Instead, they have much political and economic importance, and an individual's life is largely fashioned by his or her membership in an exogamic group.

Lévi-Strauss has called kinship organizations, which have rules for the regular exchange of women as wives, *elementary systems* of kinship. Westerners are unfamiliar with such patterns because among them an individual avoids only a few relatives, covered by incest rules, and marries anyone else. Lévi-Strauss has called such practice a *complex system,* but in effect it is not a system at all. There is no pattern or regularity in the marriage choices unless one sees that most marriages do occur within social classes, ethnic groups, or within major religions. If such marriages within a group were prescribed, they would be known as *endogamy.* However, in the West, marriage preferences create no pattern. In contrast, caste endogamy in India does pattern marriage, and caste societies reflect marriage exchange patterns because of endogamous norms.

Curiously, there is evidence that the endogamous caste system of India was preceded by a system of exogamy. Even today, clans of North India are exogamous within an endogamous caste. A clan system is also prevalent in China and most of Asia. These elementary systems are most often symmetrical in nature. The simplest type of symmetrical alliance is to have society divided into two groups. Such *dualism* is called a *moiety* system. That is, two moieties or two halves comprise society. The moieties are exogamous. The men and women in one moiety consider themselves brothers and sisters. All women in the other group are possible wives or sisters-in-law; the men are husbands or brothers-in-law. In societies of a few thousand people or less, everyone is going to be related. How better to organize such relations than in moiety style?

Food collectors and numerous Neolithic-like peoples are organized into exogamic moities today, and historical evidence suggests moieties for parts of ancient India and China. In many respects, each moiety appears to be an almost complete society. Each controls its own economic and religious life in large part but, since each marriage represents a tie between the two groups, they cannot be politically independent. Marriage finally unites them as a single society.

Exchange between moieties is the simplest form of restricted exchange. At another level, restricted exchange occurs among three or more groups. Lévi-Strauss was particularly interested in Australian groups, usually called *sections,* that resemble moieties. Anthropologists have long debated whether Australian aborigines have a kinship system that represents a very basic system or whether they have elaborated systems beyond the comprehension of everyone except aborigines. Lévi-Strauss is convincing in that the systems do represent the restricted exchange of elementary systems. Somewhat simplified, two sections comprise one generation; two other sections comprise the next generation. A person must marry someone of the other sections but of the same generation. Their children will belong to another section of the next generation. These children must marry into the fourth section. The system remains basically one of reciprocity, although not as immediate as the one of moieties.

Considerably more delay occurs in another elementary system known as *asymmetrical alliance.* The societies practicing this indirect exchange are mostly in southwest Asia; most have given up the practice because of acculturation pressures. Still, enough documentation has occurred that the practice caused a great amount of anthropological debate, and asymmetrical alliance well illustrates the nature of social bonds. In effect, asymmetrical alliance was a system in which group A gave women as brides to group B; B gave brides to C; C to D; and D gave its women to A.

In exchanging women, as in other acts of reciprocity, wife-givers receive prestige from wife-takers. Where reciprocity is direct, moieties will remain equal; however, in asymmetrical alliance, one group should always be in an inferior relation to another while being superior to the group to which it gives women. In one of the first of these societies studied, the inequality was notable and the theory well upheld. However, other societies have been found practicing asymmetrical alliance that maintain a kind of marked equality among the exchanging groups because C is superior to D while D is superior to A. The matter has caused one of the major debates among anthropologists and is of central importance in theoretical development. It reveals that humans have devised diverse ways of creating social ties, yet they have shown remarkable similarity in using marriage to create links among widely dispersed groups.

Household and Residence

The actual composition and residence patterns of the groups that align themselves likewise show great diversity but also similarities. It might first be noted that, while all groups have norms for what is a "proper" household, all of them tolerate changes to maximize adaptation. For example, groups living in the Amazon basin often live in a large communal building. It is a large circle with the residences facing a center patio. Husbands and wives with their children occupy segments of the circle. Since these groups are frequently aggressive, the norms call for large residence groups. But, given a large number of men within the circle, internal aggression is inevitable and the circle will splinter. A splinter that leaves must pioneer a new area, and it is likely to find difficulty in farming new land. Thus, a considerable range occurs in size of a residence.

Other groups may change in size according to season. Pastoral nomads may congregate in settlements of a thousand or more in the rainy season in order to live in the highest pastures. Cooperative management of the herds is necessary to protect them from insects and raiders. At the beginning of the dry season, herders will break up into ever smaller groups as they follow disappearing water traces. By the end of the dry season, a handful of cattle may end up being herded by a man, his wives, and their children. A similar pattern occurred on the North American Plains where Indians gathered in a summer camp circle of several thousand people. From this camp, cooperative bison hunts produced large amounts of meat that could be dried for the winter. By the end of fall, the circle had to be broken so people could scatter their pony herds into forests along stream banks where there were winter forage and occasional bison. The trees also gave cover for the winter camp and provided the necessary firewood. The winter residence group was supposedly one of brothers and sisters with their spouses, perhaps some elderly parents, and unmarried children. At least the norms said that brothers, sisters, and spouses should comprise the winter residence group. However, compatibility was likely critical in the winter camp so we suspect that men and women who got along well comprised the winter camp. They may have called each other brother and sister to satisfy normative demands; more likely, they simply felt brotherly and sisterly toward each other.

Even where the settlement is fixed throughout the year, considerable variation occurs among societies in size of the household. Among many New Guinea Highland peoples one large residence is the sleeping quarters for adult men. Their wives and children occupy smaller huts some distance from the large, highly decorated central building where men spend much spare time in addition to sleeping. At the other extreme are many peasants, in all parts of the world, where the *nuclear* family of husband, wife, and children comprise a household. Peasant communities are usually of two types. In the first, households are congregated at the center of fields to make up a village. In the other pattern, the households are scattered around the fields so a family lives next to the field it works. In between the peasant household and the large, communal household is one that is common in Africa but occurs also around the world. A small dwelling is built for each of several wives, and a husband visits them at different times. The two dozen dwellings are surrounded by fencing so goats, sheep, or cattle may be herded within the compound at night. This *kraal* is especially popular among peoples who are *polygamous*, that is, having more than one spouse.

Technically, anthropologists specify where norms call for additional wives or additional husbands. Only a few societies have norms for multiple husbands, or *polyandry*. Tibetans are the best known example. Here, a younger brother may move in with an older, married brother who engages in long-distance trade. The younger cares for the household and acts as husband when the brother is away, possibly for a year at a time. Later, when the younger brother marries he may share his wife with the older brother, in effect an act of reciprocity. The practice creates the idea of a *group marriage* but it is temporary among the Tibetans, rare elsewhere, and not particularly useful as a concept. It is best understood simply as *fraternal polyandry*. In contrast, *polygyny* or multiple wives is far more common; frequently it takes the form of *sororal polygyny* or a man marrying sisters.

Westerners have often believed that polygyny was due to the greater sex drive of men, but there is no evidence for such a sex difference. Curiously, the belief in many societies is that women have a stronger sex drive. Anthropologists see polygyny as more likely connected with an amplification of alliance practices. Men who have created an alliance by one marriage can play upon this tie, if they have wealth, to secure another wife. Wives, in turn, are often the producers of wealth, especially in horticultural societies, so having two wives makes it easier to secure a third. Certainly, a correlation between accumulation of wealth and polygyny is obvious, but the cause and effect of relations are still far from clear.

Whatever the type of household, some decisions must be made when children mature out of their *family of orientation,* the one in which they were reared, and begin their own, a *family of procreation.* Since members cannot marry *siblings,* that is brothers and sisters, a person must move to his or her mate's household or bring a mate home. Earlier, we saw that if brides are brought to the groom's household, the practice is called *patrilocal.* If the couple resides with the wife's group, it is *matrilocal.* Another possibility is *neolocal* residence. Some rare types also occur: A husband and wife might continue to live in their own homes or maintain two households, a practice called *duolocal residence.* Or, they might have a choice of residing with one or the other of the groups, a tradition called *ambilocal residence.*

In any case, anthropologists take a residential census in studying a community, and we would be quite surprised if everyone were living in the household that the norms prescribe. People remain quite flexible and, if it is in a couple's interest to remain with the bride's group, that is where they are likely to be even if the norms "require" patrilocal or neolocal residence. Indeed, residence patterns seem to grow out of many individual choices so that, in effect, "what ought to be" is simply a reflection of "what is." In the case of food collecting peoples, residence patterns are generally quite fluid and, even if there are norms for patrilocality, everyone realizes that numerous exceptions will occur. On the other hand, where a society has some kind of communal property, such as herds of animals or farm fields, residence norms are likely to be fixed. Thus, a herd of cattle needs numerous herdsmen and men must cooperate in guarding and raiding. They will remain with the herds, be they camel, cattle, horses, or yaks, and wives will join them. On the other hand, if farm fields are common property where tools are limited to axes, hoes, and digging sticks, women will be associated with crop production and husbands will come to join their wives. Or, if people are living in confined quarters, such as islands, agriculture may consist of fields, trees, and other resources so that people adjust carefully to their resources. In such a case, they will likely have ambilocal residence. A communal resource must be controlled by a group, but males and females are equally valuable in its management. Such care of property not only affects choice of residence, but the division of labor will also greatly affect how kin feel they are related to each other.

Kinship as Descent

When one sex regularly controls communal property, the feeling of "groupness" develops around that sex. For instance, in southeastern North America the Creek, Cherokee, Chocktaw, and others intensively farmed the creek and river valleys with little conflict before Europeans arrived. In this setting, residence was matrilocal and fields were farmed by women, their daughters, and their daughters' daughters. The brothers of these women were a part of the group but, upon marriage, they moved to live with their wives' groups. The residential core was a line of women or what is called a *matrilineage*. Males were half the matrilineage, but their children were not a part of the group. Only children of the women belonged to the group.

Westerners have difficulty in appreciating the importance of life in such a kin group. It does virtually everything for an individual. The territory one has rights to is a part of the matrilineage. Leadership positions are located in the lineage. Members of the lineage help find a spouse, and will be quite responsible for one's children. A person's memory will be kept alive only by the lineage.

Of course, lineages may be organized around males as well, in which case they are called *patrilineages*. Where men must cooperate, as on a trap-line or with a herd of animals, a grandfather, his sons, and their sons will make up a kin group. On the basis of this patrilineal descent, the care of communal property passes on in perpetuity. That is, a principle of descent allows custodial care or management of property beyond the lifetime of an individual. Indeed, many descent groups trace the origin of human life to the ancestor who started their descent group and they see their descent group as existing in perpetuity.

Casual observation has tended to see the organization of kin groups as based on beliefs about descent. That is, some early observers of the Cherokee thought they had matrilineages because the Cherokee believed a person had closer ties to a mother than to a father. Social scientists now recognize that beliefs are more likely to follow practices. That is, the Cherokee adapted to a particular environment by organizing their relations around women's care of the fields. Only after that organization arose did reasons or a rationale develop to explain why descent was through females.

The flexibility of beliefs or rationalization of behavior is nowhere better illustrated than in parts of Australia close to the Trobriand Islands off the New Guinea coast. In both these areas, there is a curious belief system that males are biologically unrelated to their children. In intercourse, the male simply opens up the birth canal so that a spirit can enter to conceive a child. In Australia, the local group is a patrilineage. Brides are brought to a groom's territory where a hunting area is a major means of production. This area centers on a waterhole where spirits of the patrilineage reside. One of these spirits will enter a woman and reform into human shape. Thus, women are primarily a fertile field for growth; a mother is biologically unrelated to her offspring. In contrast, Trobrianders see dead ancestors entering a woman and joining her in conception. Both male and female are involved in the conception, but the male is a dead member of the woman's matrilineage. As a result, the husband of the woman or father of the child is not considered biologically related. Kin relations, thus, are quite different for children. As part of a matrilineage, they see themselves as related in one way to other matrilineal relatives but in a different way to father and his kin.

Until recently, the tribal world seemed to anthropology to be organized largely into either matrilineages or patrilineages but, in parts of southeast Asia and Oceania, some groups have been found that control various types of property through perpetual kin groups that are neither matrilineal nor patrilineal. If effect, people in these societies have a choice of joining the descent groups of their mother or their father, but never both. Often the choice is made at marriage so a couple can elect to go to the groom's or to the bride's group. Once there, they may have a further option of affiliating with either of the two groups represented by father and mother. In fact, however, the choice has been narrowed by earlier choices. If my mother has chosen to live with my father's group, it is because his group has some comparative advantages. As long as these advantages persist, I will make the same choice. If fortunes change, we may opt for a new household, thus creating a pattern of ambilocal residence.

The descent beliefs that accompany such practices obviously emphasize the importance of both sexes. People do feel similar ties through both sexes. It is the actual, everyday behavior that emphasizes ties with one line more than another. Still, relationships over a wide area have the potential of creating important social ties to most of an area's resources, an important development if the resources should be closely circumscribed.

This type of descent is usually more appreciated by Westerners because of its emphasis upon both sexes, but it is fundamentally different since it insists on selection between one sex or the other; both sexes cannot be a part of one's heritage in any one generation. Anthropologists once described the practice as nonunilineal descent, but it is now usually called *cognatic descent*. Cognatic descent is a way of creating perpetual kin groups, controlling communal property, that are not as fixed as patrilineal or matrilineal descent groups.

In marked contrast to these descent beliefs, the Western world and small simple societies, such as Inuit or Eskimo, have concepts of *bilateral descent* that say one inherits equally from both mother or father who inherited equally from their mother and father. Thus, modern Americans can claim that they share equally one sixty-fourth inheritance from each of their great, great, great grandparents. Yet, it is impossible that any individual has one sixty-fourth inheritance of his or her genes from each ancestor. Of course, descent beliefs are cultural, not biological, so it is possible for us to be equally related to all 64 ancestors through both male and female ancestor. What we believe is what determines our kinship; kinship is not a matter of biology.

Kin Groups

Furthermore, it seems that what we believe is largely a matter of what we do in making our adaptations. Among Inuit, Ute Indians, or modern Western peoples, the small *nuclear family* is the ordinary household. No long-enduring ties survive this unit; it does not go on in perpetuity. Instead, the family breaks up each generation as children mature and each starts a new nuclear family. These units are loosely tied to others like them because of extending ties through the siblings of mother and father. Thus, secondary relatives are recognized as cousins. It is important to note that both sides of the family are treated equally. Father's brother is the same as mother's brother. Father's sister's children are the same kind of relatives as mother's sister's children. All these relatives make up a *kindred*. The kindred is not a particularly effective group because some members are not related to each other. Relatives on your father's side have nothing in common with relatives on your mother's side except shared concern for your family members. Thus, the kindred only congregates when there is a crisis in the family such as births, weddings, illnesses, or deaths. Imagine how difficult it would be to start and maintain a business comprised of kindred members. Among many families, some of the kindred may be strangers to each other.

Another reason that large, enduring kin groups cannot build up among peoples with bilateral descent is that the numbers of relatives will double with each generation. By tracing ancestors through both males and females, we have two parents, four grandparents, and eight great grandparents. This same doubling phenomenon occurs with our children and children's children. Such expansion means that a kin group simply could not be stable or even long enduring. Thus, the nuclear family is the basic, all-important kin unit in societies where large kin groups are unnecessary.

In contrast, where only one sex is selected for descent ties, large kin groups can arise that are stable, yet in addition can change in size in order to perform different tasks. This adaptability is quite unusual to Westerners; additionally, two types of tasks that such kin groups can undertake are remarkable. Once familiar with all the advantages of such kin groups, it is hard to imagine why they are not found everywhere. What we will discover is that in the modern Western world we have had to find substitutes for them.

Descent group flexibility comes from an ability to expand or contract simply by including only a certain number of ancestors. Wherever there are descent groups, a minimal segment consists of three generations. In some simple societies, this segment suffices to organize practically all of daily life. Among food collectors who once were described as patrilineal, three generations of male links may occur. Such a unit occupies a territory and links itself to other similar units through marriage. However, it is the exogamy of the residence groups that makes it distinctive. Otherwise, it is not particularly different from a kindred. This lack of organization is simply a reflection of the fact that the communal property of territory needs little corporate management.

Where agricultural fields are controlled or where large herds must be managed, the descent group includes more distant relatives. If a group is protecting 500 head of cattle during a rainy season, there must be shifts of men to watch over the animals. They must be further organized to protect against raids or to go raiding. With so many families congregated at one spot, there must also be ways of resolving conflicts over accusations of theft, adultery, and witchcraft. Some of these activities require only a dozen or so people; others may require several hundred.

To achieve such tasks, descent groups telescope. Everywhere descent groups are formed into lineages. This line is one in which all members can trace their ancestry through one sex to a common ancestor. The one sex link will be male in a patrilineage, female in a matrilineage. The relatives can be best understood by a diagram where ○ is for females and △ stands for males. A single solid line indicates descent, a broken line alleged descent. Thus, a matrilineage and clan may be pictured as shown in Diagram 9-2.

A lineage may vary in size depending on number of ancestors remembered. For everyday tasks, grandmother or great grandmother suffices as a focal point. For resolving infrequent but serious disputes, reference may be made to a great, great grandmother or perhaps great, great, great mother's brother. Remember that both males and females always comprise a descent group. Or, in organizing large numbers of people, several lineages may claim a mythical ancestor. This organization of two or more lineages is called a *clan*. The mythical ancestor, which is often an animal, is called a *totem*. In effect, the totem is the symbol of a political–economic unit, one bound by ritual and education. Commonly, the clan will include long-dead ancestors so that ancestor veneration is a part of clan ritual. Equally important, the clan acts as if descendants will always be born so the clan will go on in perpetuity.

In this respect, lineages and clans may be described as *corporate groups*. Corporate groups are ones that become much like an individual in terms of the law.

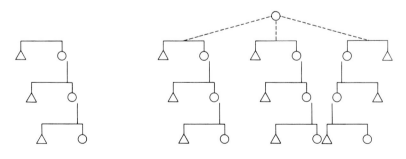

DIAGRAM 9–2   Lineage and Clan Membership.

They may sue each other or engage in a blood feud. They may own property which is kept intact despite the death of individual members. In a way, corporate groups even marry. At least, according to alliance theory, the marriage of a couple really represents a union between two descent groups. In modern societies, the advantages of corporate groups are kept alive by highly specialized corporations. One thinks of General Electric with its well-known totem or trademark, but the Brotherhood of Electrical Workers is equally a corporate group, just as are the Boy Scouts, the Presbyterian Church, Cook County, and the Red Cross. Thus, the modern world has many groups for all kinds of purposes—economic, educational, religious, political, and altruistic. Before this development, the lineage or clan served all these purposes with each descent group being more or less equal to other descent groups in the same society. That is, eight clans made up Seneca Iroquois society. One's education, livelihood, ritual life, political standing, and marriage choice were determined in large part because one was a Deer, Turtle, or a Snipe. The corporate group here was general and all-purpose. It also meant that one was related to nearly everyone else so the social world was a kinship world.

Kinship Terminology

Because kinship was such a prevalent tie, kin were organized quite differently from the modern world, Of course, children learned these systems at a very early age, and they took it as only natural that a person have dozens of brothers and sisters and several mothers and fathers. To have a single father and mother would have been as strange to an Iroquois as it is to a Euro-American to have several.

What the kinship terms of the latter do is to mark off members of the nuclear family as distinct relatives. Other terms simply add the remaining kindred members as relatives, giving us a kinship terminology (Diagram 9-3) that is familiar to Indo-European speakers. It is also one familiar to the Inuit; anthropologists called it an *Eskimo system* before learning that the people prefer to be called Inuit.

A more common system, however, is known as Iroquois. The kinship terms of the Seneca tribe of the Iroquois were described by Morgan, the nineteenth century American anthropologist. When he discovered the same pattern among many other American Indians, he used Iroquois as the prototype. He then submitted questionnaires to missionaries and government agents around the world and found that many different peoples scattered all over the globe organized their kin in the same way as Seneca.

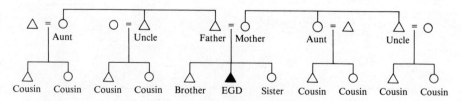

**DIAGRAM 9-3   Eskimo Kinship Terminology, based on terms for cousins.
(Marriages are indicated by parallel lines.)**

What this system does is to divide one's social world into close kin such as brothers and sisters as opposed to spouses and in-laws. Some close relatives that we regard as too close for marriage become the marriageable class. We should remember that, if human society is only several hundred people, everyone is going to be related. Thus, marriage with a relative is inevitable. What is remarkable, however, is the patterning that has arisen from marriage choices. Such patterns can only be explained by seeing marriages as unions between groups, not between two people.

The simplest way of illustrating such regularity is to look at what happens when there are only two groups, or moieties, within a society. Each marriage represents an exchange between groups, or a man seems to exchange his sister—that is, one of the women of his group—with a man of the other group for his sister. Not surprisingly, quite a few peoples around the world have a practice that is described as *sister-exchange marriage.* In order to get a wife, I must be able to trade my sister to a man of the other moiety for his sister. This reciprocity is illustrated by Diagram 9-4.

If the two moieties are unilineal, and moieties usually are, then over generations sister-exchange marriage becomes cross-cousin marriage as well. Note in Diagram 9-5 that all of the men are marrying a woman who is their mother's brother's daughter. She is also their father's sister's daughter. In turn, all the women are marrying someone who is their mother's brother's son or their father's sister's son.

Note that the cousins married are never mother's sister's child or father's brother's child. These relatives are called *parallel cousins* by anthropologists. They will always be in the same moiety as brothers and sisters and will be equated with siblings, that is, brothers and sisters. Cross-cousins, however, will always be in the opposite moiety or among the persons where one finds spouses. Anthropologists see good reasons as to why moieties should be exogamous, and we think it is the marriage between groups that is important. It was only after years of such marriage that a people began to explain their system as based on sister-exchange or cross-cousin marriage. They did indeed marry a cross-cousin or exchange sisters, and that is how they understood what they did. However, such norms make little sense; the pattern can be easily interpreted as reciprocity between groups. Given such exchange, Iroquois Kinship terminology (Diagram 9-6) makes perfect sense; recall, too, that it is the most common type of kinship system outside the modern world.

In this system, parallel cousins are called by the same kinship term as brother and sister. The term for father's sister's daughter or mother's brother's daughter can be translated as "cousin," sometimes it is the same as "wife" for a male ego or "husband" for a female ego. Its best translation is probably "potential wife" or "potential husband." Since this division of cousins is so commonly found, it is well to define them concisely. *Cross-cousins are the children of siblings of opposite sex.* Parallel cousins are children of siblings of the same sex.

DIAGRAM 9-4   Sister-Exchange Marriage, between black moiety and white moiety.

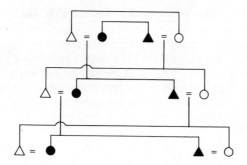

DIAGRAM 9-5   Exogamous, matrilineal moieties over three generations so that sister-exchange becomes cross-cousin marriage.

In many societies there are more than two major groups. Clans range in number from a few to dozens. Cross-cousin marriages may tie together several clans, but marriage ties must usually be supplemented in other ways. *Bride-service* is one means. A man at marriage may live with his wife's group a year or two, working for her lineage. The expectation is that his work compensates the group for the loss of a woman. What is overlooked is that a man establishes close ties with his wife's group who provide training in household and child care. More commonly, the compensation for a wife is in *bride-wealth,* also called *bride-price.* This custom was poorly understood for a long time and even equated with slavery. What occurs is that certain kinds of goods, such as cattle, pigs, iron, or gold bars, are presented by the groom's group to the bride's group. The exchange is typical reciprocity. The gifts are distributed over a long period; the birth of children usually requires further payments, so some anthropologists call it *progeny-price* instead of bride-price. The terms are not important; the point to remember is that the flow of wealth engages two groups in reciprocity, and their social ties will doubtless cause problems. But the ties more often provide channels for resolution of conflict and maintenance of peaceful relations.

Such customs no longer prevail in modern societies because marriage has become a union of only two people. Marriage is not an alliance between groups for us. Interestingly, however, Western marriages reflect their heritage from a time when Germanic tribes exchanged gold among clans. Commonly, the gold was in the form of a ring, and the modern wedding ring can be traced to a time when bride-wealth was a basis for reciprocity between Germanic descent groups.

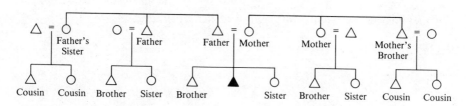

DIAGRAM 9–6   Iroquois Kinship Terminology, Based on Terms for Cousins, Generally Found with Unilineal Descent.

Age-Grades and Associations

Marriage and kinship are the most striking ways that peoples have used to tie together dispersed groups within a single society, but they are not the only means. Everywhere humans have divided along sex and age lines. The division of labor is an essential human characteristic and, as tasks get assigned to a group, other attributes follow. That is, females have to learn a great deal about what it takes to be "woman." Males must learn not only particular work habits, but also whether being a man means being aggressive and domineering or cooperative and equalitarian. At one time, anthropologists thought the *gender roles* of man and woman had to be completely learned; now the interesting question is to determine how biological *sex* may relate to the learning of being man or woman.

The current social revolution in China may eventually reveal much about how fast and how far society can go in changing sex roles. Elderly Chinese women still shuffle along because as children their feet would be broken and bound simply because small feet would please men's eyes. Today, the Chinese government works hard to achieve equity between the sexes, and apparently many Chinese have accepted such a goal. Greater equity is occurring between generations too, although much respect is still shown to elders.

The respect relations show that Chinese society is divided along age lines, but this division is an informal one as it is in the West. In many other societies, the divisions are formalized into what anthropologists call *age-grades.* Age-grades have some specific initiations, generally involving ritual. In Africa, where age-grades are common, the initiation of adolescent boys into the first male age-grade is accompanied by circumcision as well as elaborate ritual. A parallel age-grade initiation for girls involves clitoridectomy.

Age-grading is relatively infrequent for women but, for male groups, the age-grades effectively cut across and unite different descent groups. In East Africa, where age-grading is strikingly developed, it is common for males of about age 10 to 15 to be initiated into a named group. Here they serve in a minor capacity to the one or two age-groups above them. Primarily, the age-grade serves to remove the boys from their mother's care or the world of women and prepare them for manly roles. The creation of this group pushes the 15- to 20-year-old males into a higher grade, one where they learn much about warfare so that in the next two or three age-grades they will be active warriors. The senior warrior grade graduates, in turn, to become respected elders who consult and give advice.

At the same point, the name of the elderly groups may return to the beginning of the cycle in what is known as a *cyclical age-grading system.* A few very elderly men may then be associated with adolescents of the same age-grade. Elsewhere, each new age-grade may receive its own name in what is called a *progressive age-grading system.* In either case, the men of an age-grade are expected to become like brothers to each other, sometimes mixing blood to symbolize their kinship. They may also live together communally, at least before marriage. Although East African societies are more likely to display all these characteristics and more, age-grading is also well developed in West and South Africa, in New Guinea and Australia, and in South America.

Both kinship and age-grades are the result of *ascribed statuses.* Ascribed statuses are ones that are assigned because of birth. One is male or female, son or daughter, an adolescent or youth simply because of genetics. That is, society takes a biological feature and attributes certain behavior to it. In some traditional societies, all statuses are ascribed, but many of them have groups where some membership is voluntary. Such membership is an *achieved status*. Groups comprised of achieved statuses are called *associations* or sometimes *sodalities*. Associations are useful in cross-cutting descent groups; interestingly, some of the best-known associations are the secret societies of West Africa where age-grades are not too important, while in East Africa, with its age-grades, associations are less important.

Associations are also well-known among Plains Indians where one association usually acted something like a police force when all the members of society gathered together in the summer. It was then necessary to regulate large-scale hunting parties or war parties. Other societies served primarily to preserve sacred traditions or practice certain rituals. Still other societies might act as governing bodies. In some instances, men seem to have joined different associations at different times of their lives so the age division of society could parallel association membership. Thus, the associations tended to resemble age-grades.

Like age-grades, male associations were more common and more complex than associations for women. Nevertheless, female associations have wielded considerable power and influence, and women's associations are much more than imitations of men's associations. Among Plains Indians, associations of married couples were important. In the modern world, of course, most associations are no longer based on sex, but sexism has shown a remarkable persistence in determining some group memberships. Although many male associations exist for the ostensible purpose of recreation, contacts made in these groups often carry over into the economic sphere. Thus, females can be put at a disadvantage economically because of male associations even today.

Sociologists as well as anthropologists have studied associations but they remain relatively obscure compared with kin groups. We can say that associations are characterized by test of membership, symbols, and common property, both material and nonmaterial. They are also corporate. Probably one of their most important differences from kin corporate groups is their need to build morale or esprit de corps. Thus, the rituals and tests of membership are often elaborate with kin groups often taken as models. Sorority members become "sisters" and some unions become "brotherhoods." Clearly, associations and kin groups share much in the building of society.

Summary

The study of *ethology* shows that *imprinting* is a modified "instinct" involving learning. Such learning is the basis of much social behavior among nonhumans. Humans depend almost solely on learning, but a genetic base such as imprinting may also be involved. Certainly, the process stems from a primate heritage in which a long infant dependency occurs, creating ties between mother and young, and among the young as siblings. With the human shift to hunting, diverse populations must have settled in scattered bands, such life producing a sexual division of labor.

To tie dispersed groups together, reciprocity is essential. It can start with an exchange of goods. An exchange of spouses is even more binding. To achieve such a step, men and women of one's own group are defined as brothers and sisters, the idea being that intercourse with a sibling is not allowed, or is *incest*. The idea of incest immediately requires the idea of marriage. The concept of sibling means a people must also have the idea of spouse. In traditional society, it is common for everyone to be related. Half the world is close as brothers and sisters are close; the other half of one's relatives are in-laws or potential spouses. The close relatives are called *consanguines*; the others are *affines*.

Patterns in the exchange appear because of *residence rules.* If people manage a resource that requires cooperation, one sex will remain with their group and bring in spouses, while sending out the opposite sex. Where people believe brides should reside with grooms, they practice *patrilocality.* Where grooms live with their bride's groups, they practice *matrilocality.* In *avunculocal residence,* a couple resides with the groom's mother's brother. With the establishment of regular ties between groups, a group that first gave a bride furnishes another one should she die, this second woman being like a sister to the first bride. The practice is called the *sororate.* If a husband dies, his group may be expected to replace him with someone like his brother—that is, a member of his group. Such an expectation is called the *levirate.* Another practice obligating a group to furnish another group with wives is *bride-capture.* Men are exerting their rights in seizing a woman as wife from another group.

Claude Lévi-Strauss pointed out all the implications of marriage as an exchange to form alliances, giving insight into the widespread practice of *exogamy*, a norm requiring marriage out of a group. Where there are only two parts to a society, these parts being known as *moities*, quite precise patterns of kinship arise that are known as *elementary systems* of kinship. *Complex systems* are those lacking patterns. They occur where households are independent and society lacks corporate kin groups.

However, when society is comprised of corporate kin groups, residence units reflect this structure. Seldom will a nuclear family occupy a household. Instead, communal buildings may house the males of a patrilocal group with small dwellings for wives, or a communal building may be marked off from nuclear families. Types of residence will also be affected by *polygamy*, or multiple spouses. If the spouses are female, the practice is *polygyny;* each co-wife may have a separate dwelling for her children and herself, with all such dwellings within a single compound. If the household is *polyandrous,* the dwelling need not be much bigger than one for a nuclear family. Second or third husbands generally move out as they acquire enough wealth to secure a bride for themselves.

Type of household primarily reflects economic adaptations, and control over communal property shows up in beliefs about descent. If a line of males is the core, cooperating group, then fathers, sons, and son's sons will comprise a *patrilineage.* All the sisters of these men will also be in the patrilineage but not their children. Beliefs about descent will focus on a special kind of relationship between male links. Descent may be traced for many generations or only a few; the more links included, the larger the kin group will be. Of course, female links may serve the same purpose. A mother, her daughter, and her daughter's daughters make up a *matrilineage*. This descent group includes the brothers of these women but not the children of the brothers. In some societies, a choice is given to individuals to select either a male link or a female link. That is, a person may opt to join the descent group of mother or of father, but never both. This kin grouping is called a *cognatic descent group*. Cognatic descent exists where people must carefully allocate a resource base.

Bilateral descent contrasts sharply with systems selecting only one sex for tracing descent. Beliefs of bilateral descent consider both male and female links equal. Relatives on the mother's side will be regarded as equals to relatives on the father's side. This treatment is reflected in the generations above so the number of relatives in each ascending generation doubles. This doubling prevents the formation of any permanent, corporate kin groups. Thus, the nuclear or small extended family is typical with bilateral descent, making it differ sharply from unilineal descent.

The effective kin group in bilateral society is the kindred. The *kindred* is composed of the parent's siblings and their children, the group familiar to Westerners. These kin provide emotional support to a person and his or her siblings, but they cannot take permanent cooperative action because relatives on the father's side are not related to relatives on the mother's side. Unilineal societies resolve this problem by designating a particularly close relationship through one of the sexes. In this way, a lineage is made *corporate,* or self-perpetuating, and it remains stable over time. In many societies, lineages are joined for special purposes into a clan. *Clans* are two or more lineages that claim a fictional ancestor or *totem*. Clans serve as large-scale groups for ritual or political purposes requiring large numbers of people. So much is accomplished within clans, that they require *exogamy,* or marriage outside the clan, as a way of maintaining ties with other clans.

The emphasis of descent through one sex in special ways is generally reflected in the treatment of relatives; that is, patrilineal descent creates special ties to relatives traced through male links. This special recognition shows up in kinship terminology; kinship terms serve as an index of behavior. With unilineal descent, one set of parallel cousins will always be of the same lineage as ego and the other parallel cousins may or may not belong. *Parallel cousins* are the children of siblings of the same sex. Cross-cousins will always be in some other lineage. *Cross-cousins* are the children of siblings of the opposite sex. Special terms will be used for the cross-cousins, but parallel cousins will be called by the same terms as siblings. This system of terminology is called *Iroquois*.

Bilateral descent, in contrast, emphasizes the nuclear family. Terms designate its members as special. The terms for brother and sister are limited. Both parallel and cross-cousins are grouped together and separated from siblings. In effect, the terms specify nuclear family membership; the other terms specify kindred membership. Such a system of terminology is called *Eskimo*.

In both cases, marriages provide ties to other groups. Incest regulation seems to be the major way nuclear families have of ensuring marriages outside the group; exogamy is the norm for descent groups. Descent groups are further linked together by *age-grades* and *associations*. Age-grades cross-cut descent groups by joining all males or all females of a common age. Age-grades may be finite so that named groups must cycle. A retiring age-grade next becomes the youngest age-grade, in a system known as *cyclic age-grades*. Or, each new group can be initiated into a newly named grade in which case the system is called *progressive*. Like kin statuses, the position within an age-grade is *ascribed* on the basis of age and sex. The other cross-cutting group is the voluntary association. By being asked to join an association, the individual has *achieved status*.

Associations, age-grades, descent groups, and kindreds are common in traditional societies everywhere. They illustrate how societies are always divided into subgroupings as if it were impossible to exist simply as a total group. We are far from understanding why people are like this, but it is clear that society is always a complex, multifaceted organization.

10

*Political Organization and Social Inequity*_____

The Nature of Political Organization

Early anthropologists debated whether people like the San, (Bushmen of South Africa), or Inuit had any politics or government. The use of the term *government* was particularly misleading because it implies specialized statuses that are only political in nature. In this sense, many peoples do not have governments, but such a view is misleading. A. R. Radcliffe-Brown solved this semantic problem when he focused the issue on the functions of political organization. The two functions are *internal control* and *maintenance of relations with outsiders*. Clearly, all societies must accomplish these two tasks, and whatever ways they have of keeping internal order and establishing foreign relations constitutes their political organization.

This political organization or politics may be defined as *the public process by which structured groups focus power in order to reach public goals*. By noting that politics is a public process, relations within a family are omitted as political, but virtually all other forms of conflict, competition, and cooperation will be included. Structured groups include families vying with other families, or clans against or with other clans, and the relationships between moieties. Associations and age-grades are other structured groups. Structure also characterizes informal or unnamed groups. A major issue may divide a society with two or more groups forming on the basis of proposed solutions. Such groups are termed *factions*. The informal factions may continue as structured groups even after solution of the original issue. Future issues may be judged in terms of factional alignment rather than on the merits of the issue.

Power is likely the most difficult term to define in the definition of politics. In actual cases, power must be determined largely on the basis of process. Whoever it is that achieves their goal possesses power. Clearly, however, power stems from two very different kinds of *authority*. One type of authority consists of force. This authority has access to coercion, whether it consists of positive or negative sanctions. Another kind of authority rests on tradition. We understand this kind of authority when we speak of Webster's dictionary as being "the authority" for spelling a word. Thus, prestige is a kind of power as well as a police force.

Both kinds of authority are regularly used to define and to achieve public goals. All societies have a consensus on many public goals, but the variety of structured groups each have their goals, too. Invariably, achievement of some of these ends will conflict with the means or ends of other groups. For the anthropologist or other outsider, many public goals are not really "public." That is, a group may often proclaim its goal is one thing while its members realize its goals are something quite different. Or, goals may be taken for granted; they are so well known to a membership that no one feels it necessary to state them. In sum, public goals are difficult to define; further, they are not necessarily stable.

Given our definition of *political organization*, two aspects of it are clear. On the one hand, it consists of processes and must be studied as a continuously changing factor. On the other hand, political organization is also the structure of a polity or political body. It is a totality consisting of parts that can be separated for analysis. The structure of a polity is generally far easier to analyze and to compare. Thus, anthropology has largely studied polities or political structures, and much comparative work has been in classifying types of political organization from around the world. These types suggested a kind of social evolution at first, but detailed analysis shows some groups have become simpler while others have become more complex. The present types are not a record of past evolutionary change.

Personalized Equalitarian Polities

Small foraging groups of fewer than a hundred people typically consist of a parent with two or three grown children, their spouses, and children. The adults may not all be siblings but they likely regard each other as brothers and sisters. In short, the group is composed of kin. The relatives that constitute such a polity are not fixed, but everyone in the group regards each other as some kind of relative. Thus, a core of relatives has grown up together. They know each other's capabilities and behavior intimately.

Except for the division of labor between male and female and between young and old, all members are equal. That is, one adult male does what all other adult males do while adult females engage in their activities. Of course, personality differences exist, and these are probably the basis for some members being better able to contact the supernatural, to lead in a hunt, or to negotiate with outsiders. There is no need to elect or otherwise select a leader for any of these activities. Members know each other so well that they all recognize who is best fit for any particular task requiring only one of their number. To ask, "Who is the chief?" is an unanswerable question. Members simply understand that certain situations call forth certain people. When people spend all of their waking contact in close association with each other, how could they not know who is the best to lead in a certain context?

Anthropologists define such a focusing of power according to context as *leadership*. Leaders of a band have only the authority of ability and tradition to back their decisions. Anyone disagreeing with the decision of a leader is free to leave the group and join another one. Ties of reciprocity created through economic exchange and marriage make relocation an easy matter. Kinship ties allow a person to make claims of membership in any of the surrounding groups. Knowledge that leaders cannot impose their will on followers means that leaders know they must lead by example, by claiming they follow tradition, or by making sure their decisions reach public goals. Thus, leaders are typically described as generous, unassuming, and exemplary.

Most internal organization within the small equalitarian polity is nearly automatic, especially in terms of subsistence activity. However, three problems are apparently universal in causing internal conflict: accusations of theft, adultery, and witchcraft or sorcery. (Witchcraft and sorcery will be explained in the next chapter; here witchcraft will be used in its usual sense.) In small polities, the means of production are owned by the group, but individuals have some personal property. They frequently give it away or discard it since property is of little value, but people do seem concerned about their rights to these artifacts. If they feel someone has violated these rights, they make charges of theft. Likewise, spouses may share sexual favors with a friend but if a spouse has not given permission then he or she will make accusations of adultery. The spouse, only the lover, or both may be accused. Finally, most people in small groups believe that illness and other misfortune is due to someone else's envy. This envy leads to witchcraft. When one is ill or loses a close relative, the matter is never explained by chance; death and illness are attributed to witches. Finding the witch is usually the major step; treating the witchcraft is usually quite different and simpler. In sum, problems of social control are minimal and application of sanctions is simple.

The small equalitarian organization is found only among food-collecting peoples, although some food collectors have large populations and less equality. For example, fishing peoples along the Northwest coast of North America were settled in large-size villages and developed complex societies quite distinct from the homogeneity of bands. Yet, Indians up river in the Plateau of North America and its Great Basin were typically organized into small equalitarian polities. The Utes, Shoshoni, and Paiutes are the best-known examples. To the north of them in the coniferous forests of Canada and Alaska, the Dene Indians are also similar, as are the Inuit. In Africa, the San of the Kalahari Desert are probably the best-known small polities, as are the Mbuti-Pygmies of the Congo rain forest. A few other foraging peoples exist in Africa, such as the Hazda, who are little known except to anthropologists. Similar societies of food collectors are found in Southeast Asia, most of them in small, equalitarian polities. The other well-known peoples organized in the same way are the Australian aborigines.

Some foragers existed as polities for part of the year but at other seasons congregated in much larger numbers. At this time, their society became much more complex. Members did not know each other intimately; associations were impersonal in their organization and sometimes acted as a police force. In other words, the authority of coercion was practiced, something that did not happen in the highly personalized group.

Big game hunters and some pastoral peoples illustrate this type of organization that was band-like one season and tribal-like the next season. The Plains Indians of North America are a well-known example. In the winter they lived in groups of 10 to 20. Two or three couples, their children, and perhaps an older relative or two lived in tepees along a wooded stream or river where there was abundant firewood and forage for the horses. Theft or adultery were rare and witchcraft accusations almost unheard of because of close relationships. Moreover, compatible people were the ones who formed the winter camp. In summer these groups came together in a hunting camp that might see a thousand people. Camp leaders had authority over a young man's association that acted as a police force. The equality was of a different kind because authority rested in certain statuses in the associations. Leadership was no longer a part of this larger group's politics.

The large camp circle represents a polity where some relationships have become impersonal but most ties remain based on kinship and equality. Many internally structured groups arise in the larger personalized polity that are mainly responsible for control over their members. They may also be responsible for some foreign relations. Typically, the groups within such societies are descent groups. Within the clan or lineage, most of life is played out. A person's economic, political, religious, and educational life are all within the descent group. Indeed, so much activity is within the clan that it appears to resemble a subsociety. A society of eight clans looked very much like eight societies united by nothing more than common language and religion. Only the rule of exogamy establishes regular links among the descent groups unless associations exist that require multiclan participation.

Emphasizing the lack of political organization except for descent and marriage ties or association membership is not to deny efficient internal controls and effective foreign relations. Large, equalitarian polities have been remarkably adept at adapting to all parts of the world, using diverse kinds of subsistence and spreading rapidly into unoccupied areas. Such adaptation may have arisen in Paleolithic times. Some settled fishing villages have well-developed descent groups with great complexity of organization and, as just noted, some big game hunters spend part of the year as large equalitarian groups.

Yet, the Neolithic must have been an age when small groups began to be replaced by larger ones. Horticultural peoples recognize their land as communal property, and descent groups grow to control this resource. As populations hive off in moving along a river valley in order to farm it, the logical organization is for local control by descent group, most likely the matrilineage. It, or matriclans, remain tied to other parts of society by marriage. Thus, a person could travel the length of the valley and still find relatives everywhere. If he were a male in a matrilocal society, it meant he had brothers scattered along the river along with his sisters-in-law and fathers-in-law. No flag, constitution, or passport provided anyone with society-wide security, but kinship ties were just as effective, and the clan totem had all the symbolic value of a flag or a national anthem. Indeed, the totem carried much ritual power as well as social symbolism.

The situation was much the same where society adapted to pastoral nomadism. Cattle or camels might be concentrated at waterholes or pastures so that one local group had only sporadic contact with other groups. Again, such groups had little in common if there were no outside enemies; otherwise, the only regular tie was provided through marriage. Again, it was enough to allow one to find relatives over a wide area, and served many purposes well. But one can imagine that being in a strange group with the only tie being one of "in-law" does not offer many guarantees in a serious dispute. Nevertheless, large equalitarian political structure sometimes brought together thousands of people with nothing in common beyond language, culture, and ties of kinship and marriage. Even today, in some Third World countries this structure is a significant part of national politics.

In the few instances where anthropologists have been able to observe such groups with little pressure on their boundaries, they have been most impressed with the ways descent ties are used to resolve conflict. Almost always, any disputes will be resolved at the lowest segment of the descent group. That is, conflict between cousins is adjudicated by their grandfather. Following this principle, conflict between any lineage members or any clan members is resolved by the elder who has inherited the position of founder of the lineage or clan.

If societies are patrilineal, much of the conflict is about accusations of adultery or witchcraft. Clan brothers accuse each other of taking sexual favors from their wives, since they are women of other clans. These jealousies may be part of a general struggle among brothers who will succeed to positions of power within the next descent group. They may also be competing for favors from the descent group in helping them accumulate bride-wealth. Thus, brothers are highly competitive and may well be suspected of practicing witchcraft against each other. On the other hand, since property is communally owned, it is almost impossible for one brother to steal from another.

Theft, however, can be directed toward the property of other clans, and it is common among pastoral nomads whether the animals be cattle, camels, or horses. Theft accusations and actual raids are a regular source of conflict, and tribal society can only resort to marital links to resolve such disputes. As a result, much conflict simply is not resolved, but tradition keeps it from escalating or the norms limit extremes such as killing or taking slaves. In semi-arid areas, it may be that conflict is a way of reallocating scarce pasture. In East Africa, where many peoples are cattle herders, age-grades are common and serve as a mechanism to bring together people of different descent groups.

In New Guinea, the remote highlands have presented contemporary anthropologists with numerous polities that appear to reflect two different adaptations. Some peoples seem to have low population densities, and the disputes among descent groups can be resolved through affines—that is, in-laws. Other peoples seem to have reached maximum population size and are exerting ecological pressure on their farmland. In this case, disputes are not resolved; instead, they are settled by one polity driving out the other. Only then does "warfare" appear to be much like "modern warfare," where killing becomes indiscriminate and is no longer meant to be simply revenge or a kind of reciprocity.

New Guinea also offers a political form that contrasts with leadership, but also reflects a kind of equalitarianism. Anthropologists use the Pidgin English term, *Big-Man*, to describe it. The Big-Man is not an elder or leader of a descent group, but rather manages to accumulate power and prestige by giving away wealth. The question immediately arises, "How does he get wealth?" but the answer is not so quick. A typical Big-Man seems to have a wife who produces more than average, and a Big-Man soon acquires other wives. But he, himself, is often hard-working and exerts entrepreneurial skills. By whatever means Big-Men acquire more pigs, shells, feathers, or other wealth, they carefully bestow them upon others who are obligated to follow. Thus, a Big-Man and his lieutenants are often the core group that initiates warfare. To protect borders or to undertake offense, the Big-Man engages in building alliances with neighboring strong tribes and in measuring the weakness of others. By skewed reciprocity and promises of future gifts, the skilled Big-Man is able to expand or defend a territory by continually manipulating his wealth and followers. Yet, despite some remarkable achievements, Big-Men never seem to last long in power. The focus of power among individuals is continually shifting, while the men who succeed to the top of descent groups wield a stable authority within the descent group. Where colonial powers have pressured the large, equalitarian society, Big-Men have come to hold unusual power as people unite behind such individuals to protect themselves from a dominant group.

Ranked Polities and Feudalism

It is tempting to see Big-Man politics as a transitional form leading toward feudalism, but essential differences exist. In *feudalism*, power is focused at the top of a hierarchy where authority is concentrated because it controls wealth. The feudal lord, chief, or king is one who is continually redistributing wealth. The top of the hierarchy receives this wealth because it is the top, and it is the top because it distributes goods to show its power. This circular explanation is frustrating to one wanting to know the origin of feudalism, but it does explain how the system works.

It is critical to distinguish between skewed reciprocity and redistribution in order to appreciate the difference between feudal polities and Big-Man polities. The basic difference appears to lie in the nature of prestige and whether it is obtained by individuals or rests with structured groups. Typically, in New Guinea it was only the individual who was able to acquire unusual prestige through ostentatious gift-giving that could dominate others, and his power was short-lived. In contrast, in the nearby Trobriand Islands, descent groups were *ranked*. Many clans were considered commoner; others were high-ranking and competed with each other for prestige. The head of a commoner clan or village resembled a Big-Man by manipulating wealth to achieve the position. Noble clans, however, were headed by a man who was expected to be polygynous. Such a leader, often with six wives, enjoyed unusual wealth because it was Trobriand custom for a man to provide his sister's family with yams, the prestigious food.

FIGURE   26

Intertribal aggression in New Guinea is common, but numerous cultural traits constrain it. Here, warriors gathered for a fight but eventually dispersed. (Photo by Larry L. Naylor)

Since a noble clan had prestige, the group could use this influence to build alliances. Wives were carefully selected by the chief in order to maximize the flow of tribute or whatever it should be called when people willingly give up a proportion of their wealth in order to continue the system. It is this "willingness" that has been hard to comprehend. If we ask villagers why they contribute to their feudal lords, the answers are, "We have always done so" or "The chief honors us by accepting our yams" or "The chief helps us." Chiefs or lords indeed help when a village or district suffers a food shortage, and when a woman is taken as wife, the chief may give unusually high bride-wealth which honors the bride's group. Yet, such explanations are a far cry from an analysis of the system.

Anthropologists have yet to offer adequate explanation, but we have found that feudal polities operate under certain constraints. The nature of the wealth that circulates, giving the hierarchy power, must be of nondurable goods. For example, among the feudal Bunyoro of East Africa, a "great king" or "chief" ruled over territorial chiefs, some of these men controlling hundreds of villages, others only a few villages. Some of these chiefs had subchiefs under them. At the village level, a chief gathered grain, beer, and cattle and offered them on a regular basis to the hierarchy above him. Each chief in the hierarchy took a share, although the major concentration of wealth went to the feudal lord. But unlimited accumulation of grain, beer, or cattle simply means waste. It was far more prudent to return this wealth on ritual or festive occasion or in time of crisis, thus demonstrating the greatness of the lord.

The Bunyoro explained their hierarchy on the basis of conquest. The very top of the hierarchy was occupied by men and women of the Bito who were supposedly members of a society that had conquered the Bunyoro or commoners. In between was another layer of descent groups, who supposedly had been the next to last conquering society. They occupied positions between the Bito and the commoners. The difficulty with this explanation was that it had some characteristics of mythology, and the supposed conquerers had the same language and culture as the commoners. It seems doubtful that acculturation could have worked so rapidly as alleged, but we must realize that, in their conquests, dominant societies have done much to shape polities in a variety of ways.

Among the best-known examples of polities structured by conquests are the Aztecs, who took over an empire built up by other peoples; in South America, the Incans extended an empire whose building blocks were put in place by several earlier peoples. The Aztec contacted by the Spanish had as many subjects as the Spanish king, but the polity still operated on the basis of redistribution even though an extensive market system had built up in the major cities. This market impressed the Spanish as much as any they had seen in Spain, but they realized that the great network of trade and the major flow of goods was still under direction of a feudal lord. A highly complex hierarchy determined the production and distribution of goods, and this hierarchy was one that operated in large part on the basis of kinship ties. The Incan empire became even more complex, and its political organization resembled a state. Indeed, the Incan dynasty was a model for the later welfare states of Europe. Granaries of the dynasty, located throughout the territory, ensured that no one went hungry, and this food was used for workers who built irrigation and road systems that were comparable to anything built by the Romans. To run such a large, complex system, the Incans had developed a bureaucracy that resembled the Aztec hierarchy but differed fundamentally because it had become impersonal.

In North America, it is possible that a feudal hierarchy arose in prehistoric times at what is now called Cahokia Mounds. A small city here seems to have been a Mexican outpost that became a sophisticated trade center for the area between the Rocky Mountains and the Atlantic coast. This Mexican influence may have been a factor in the fairly rapid conversion of equalitarian polities to ranked polities when North American Indians encountered Euro-Americans. The Iroquois and the Southeastern Indians, such as the Cherokee and Creek, were equalitarian peoples when first contacted by Europeans, but they converted quickly to ranked polities in uniting against the threat. The hierarchies that developed were sometimes headed by councils so an unusual amount of democracy was built into their politics; but, in times of crisis, a single leader often acted to preserve public goals against white encroachment.

The threat from a dominant society has prompted unity in Africa and Asia as well as in the Americas. In some cases, equalitarian groups persist into modern times, but many of them have disappeared after being dominated by state organizations. Even where they persist, they have had to seek accommodation as part of an organized state and, generally, major changes have occurred in political organization. In some cases, quite complex organizations have broken down so that feudal peoples have become equalitarian. No one is certain why the growth of the state is so prevalent and why state organization has so relentlessly spread across the face of the earth, but anthropologists and other social scientists have long been engrossed in the nature of the state.

The Political Organization of States

The shift from feudal organizations to state organization is difficult to follow, but the process of developing into statehood is fairly well understood, even if the factors cannot be quantified. Perhaps the critical point is that somehow the redistributive network ceases to be voluntary but instead becomes compulsory. People are probably constrained within a territory and the tribute of feudalism changes to *taxes*. An important quality of taxes is that they are collected by coercion which means force is vital in the operation of the state. Likewise, the whole operation of the *state* is based on the kind of authority that compels other structured groups to support the public goals of the impersonal hierarchy.

This hierarchy is easily recognized as government; that is, a group with its own particular statuses now has power to determine and reach public goals. It is no longer a part of descent groups or other kin groups. Indeed, the goal of the hierarchy is to operate on the basis of efficiency, and personnel are expected to be experts at a task rather than kin, age-mates, or other personal status relations. Indeed, the hierarchy of the state takes on the major characteristic of *bureaucracy*; it is an impersonal organization in contrast to all other political forms that are highly personalized. And, as states become more complex, they build themselves up by creating levels of bureaucracy, such as county, state, and federal government, and by creating specialized bureaucracies such as administrative, legal, or religious ones. The bureaucracy also assumes spatial form with a center of government, such as Washington, D.C., with ties out to other centers.

Democracies have attempted to give control of the bureaucracies to all the citizens. How far they have succeeded in this attempt is a matter of great debate.

That they have had any degree of success marks them off sharply from typical state organization, as is well-illustrated by the first states. The best known of these first states is in Mesopotamia. Other states arose somewhat later in Egypt, the Indus Valley, and in China to be followed in Peru by the Incan Dynasty.

All these areas suggest that the setting for states occurred in circumscribed environments; that is, populations were hemmed in by natural features. It also seems likely that these regions began using irrigation to increase agricultural production. Once people had learned these techniques and became dependent on them, they could not easily leave the area. Thus, as the power of a feudal lord increased steadily, that polity might convert into the position of head of state because people in the hinterland could be forced into paying taxes rather than giving tribute. Doubtless, some people in the hinterland preferred older methods of agriculture to taxation and did leave the irrigated valley. Many Old Testament stories suggest that the pastoral Hebrews found such a life more attractive than the urbanized valleys, and city life became equated with sin.

The agricultural people within the control of the state were transformed from Neolithic-like farmers into *peasants*. Farmers are relatively independent and equalitarian; they may pay tribute but they feel free to make such a decision. They likewise enjoy considerable freedom in most other decisions. In contrast, peasants come under the domination of the state hierarchy in virtually all aspects of their life. Whereas land was owned communally by kin groups in equalitarian polities, the state typically claims all land or peasants are given individual title as a way of binding them to the land. The state further takes control over religion, with a priestly bureaucracy that claims a religion superior to the "superstitions" of the villagers. The state may even begin some educational programs, which will describe the greatness of the state if nothing else. In short, the state assumes all the functions of kin groups, such as the clan, and the corporate kin group disappears or is restricted in its activities.

The impersonality of the state grows further as warfare expands, and a city-state conquers more territory. The newly incorporated peasants of an area, who may speak a different language and practice a different culture, are treated with even more contempt by the bureaucracy. Conquest increases state power as the labor of more peasants is added to the empire, and the state bureaucracies elaborate their police–paramilitary, priestly, and administrative functions.

The hierarchies enjoy considerable wealth which is provided by increasing numbers of artisans who are supported by a growing peasantry. The first city-states see the beginning of all kinds of sciences because metallurgy makes demands for widespread trade, knowledge of ores, skills in ceramic molds, design techniques, and many related tasks. Thus, the beginnings of chemistry, physics, geology, and geography occur. Monumental architecture is also demanded by the elite so that mathematics, surveying, engineering, and similar sciences likewise arise. In contrast to the village or town, the city is characterized by great heterogeneity or differentiation. While the state sets the stage for all the hallmarks of civilization, it also bears responsibility for the first kings, dictators, pharaohs, and other tyrants. Nor had humans ever before experienced jails, dungeons, and the impersonalized forms of torture that so often accompany statehood.

Throughout history, states have spread and replaced other forms of political

FIGURE 27

A Spanish priest confers with a Mayan priest at Chichicastenango, Guatemala. The peasants have revived an ancient Spanish dance about the Moors to discredit the Conquistadores. Nevertheless, much of their religion is more Catholic based. (Photo by Ernest Schusky)

organization, but the trend has not been straightforward. The city-states of Mesopotamia were dwarfed by some Greek expansion and particularly by the Roman conquest. Then, when the Roman state collapsed, Europe experienced a return to feudalism throughout the Middle Ages. The feudal lord became a redistributor on the estate and the manor was a place of personalized relations. European peasantry was not as free as the commoners among the Bunyoro, perhaps, but they had more rights and freedom than did the people conquered by the Romans. In sum, the change from small equalitarian polity to state organization is not a one-way continuum of evolution.

The Expansion of States

Archaeologists are slowly piecing together the story of what happened when small polities came under domination of the first city-states. For Mesopotamia, the process is glimpsed in the Old Testament which often views the process from the perspective of those being dominated, but the process is best known from modern times, especially in the age of colonialism. Thus, the picture is largely one of what happened when the modern European state collided with equalitarian peoples or feudal polities. It is less well known when Islamic or Chinese states spread.

For Europeans, at least, first contacts were generally friendly and the ensuing trade tended to benefit both sides. This initial period seldom lasted long, and the smaller power generally suffered as diffusion of traits intensified to acculturation, where change occurred in both cultures but primarily in the subordinate one. Population decrease was frequent because of epidemic diseases. While the expeditions of Columbus seem to have brought syphilis back to Spain and the rest of the Old

FIGURE 28

Nearly three thousand years ago an early Chinese state had the ability to organize thousands of craftsmen to produce an army of terra cotta figures to guard the grave of an emperor. The army was recently discovered and excavated near Xian. (Photo by Ernest Schusky)

World, Europeans soon gave smallpox and a score of other diseases to Indians. Deaths from enslavement were also common. Indeed, Indians died so quickly as slaves that Europeans turned to Africa for its source. Millions of blacks were to die, too, because of slavery, but the effects of the practice were better hidden from view than with Indians. Still more deaths were the result of *genocide*, deliberate state policy to exterminate a subordinate population. Some American colonies practiced genocide against some Indians; colonists in Australia nearly wiped out all the Tasmanians in a remarkably short time. Genocide has been rare, but *segregation* of subordinate people has been commonplace. Its effect on a population can be almost as disastrous since the segregated population is usually condemned to poverty, ill health, and early death. Segregation is simply more subtle than genocide.

Aboriginal populations have seldom experienced these policies without some degree of physical resistance as well as political change. Australian aborigines armed only with spears were hardly a match for European guns, but they often fought to the death. North American Indians are well known for their resistance in the face of overwhelming odds. Today, South American Indians are hopelessly resisting agents of the Brazilian government who use airplanes to drop them poisoned candy or to shoot them.

Where the minority has not been in such small numbers, the resistance has often taken a more warlike form. Probably the best-known illustration is the Zulu wars which continually embarrassed the British whose feelings of racial superiority were countered by brilliant Zulu strategy and tactics that prolonged the war for years. The Zulu chief who so well commanded his forces also turned out to be an able negotiator so that the Zulu kingdom persisted even after peace was made.

In contrast, small Spanish forces quickly defeated huge, highly organized armies of the Aztecs and Incans. It is hard to imagine how the Spanish conquistadores ever thought they could win in open combat when they numbered in the hundreds against forces in the tens of thousands. They soon found that their armor was no better than the Aztecs' special cotton quilt armor and their slow-loading muskets were not much of an advantage over Aztec archery. Even the stone swords of the Aztecs were not clearly inferior to Spanish steel; the Aztecs' stone swords could decapitate a horse. No analysis of the Aztec fall is wholly satisfactory, but their defeat seems to have been due largely to their failure to incorporate the peoples they conquered. The Spanish were able to ally numerous Indians with them, and their numbers were probably the most important factor in the Spanish victory. A similar story occurs in Peru where a civil war had just finished when the Conquistadores arrived.

However long the struggle, the state has eventually dominated and made armed resistance futile. Frequently, however, subjugated people have responded by turning to spiritual resistance. They have sought new meanings for their lives in religious movements, usually called *nativistic, revitalistic,* or *messianic.* A major theme of such movements is that, if people only have enough faith in a new ritual, they will be able to restore the glory of the past. Often, then, the movement has a theme that sees the end of the conquerors but, sometimes, coexistence is imagined.

The first messianic movement described in detail by anthropology was the Ghost Dance of the Plains Indians. The Sioux or Dakota and other Plains peoples experienced a series of defeats in the 1870s; by 1880 it was obvious that armed struggle was useless. A Paiute Indian named Wovoka, who worked for a rancher, knew English, and was introduced to Christianity, started a dance that was to bring back the bison. Other Basin and Plateau Indians paid little attention, but Plains Indians began sending missionaries to Wovoka. He also corresponded with Plains people since numerous Indians had been to boarding school by this time. Messengers from Wovoka traveled by train and stagecoach so the Ghost Dance was quickly established throughout the Plains. The dogma of the dance varied but the central theme everywhere was that a ritual dance accompanied by true faith would see the disappearance of whites and the reappearance of bison. The whites misread the hostility in the message and assumed that the Dakota were planning an outbreak. (Custer's defeat was only 14 years earlier.) When a village of Dakota was massacred at Wounded Knee, the Ghost Dance was blamed as the cause of an ''outbreak.'' The massacre ended the Ghost Dance among many groups, but it continued with modifications elsewhere.

Among the Iroquois, Handsome Lake started a movement that incorporated some of his Quaker learning and a prohibition of alcohol. His rituals in the

Longhouse have gradually evolved into an Iroquois religion that now parallels Christian denominations on the reservations. Similar developments could be cited for other tribes. The largest intertribal movement has now been incorporated into the Native American Church, where ritualistic use is made of peyote. Some church members use peyote in Communion, equating it with the body of Christ. Since peyote has been defined as a drug by some states, its use has raised the church-state issue. Anthropologists have aided Indians in their struggle to win government approval of their peyote use. Ritual that once emphasized a return to the past now shows how Indians can adapt to the present. The overall change suggests similarities to the history of Christianity. Jesus, after all, was a member of a group harshly dominated by Romans. Military resistance was not feasible; instead, Jesus preached a resistance to Rome through a spiritual existence. Later, of course, the Greeks and Romans modified this message to make Christianity the religion of the majority.

The process by which a nativistic movement changes into an institution parallel to or part of the dominant society illustrates some of the processes that occur generally under acculturation pressure. The subordinate group can adopt the value system of the dominant society and emulate it. The logical result is *assimilation* or total absorption of the minority by the majority. Government policies are often assimilationist but, in practice, assimilation is rare. Racial or linguistic prejudices often prevent a minority from disappearing; at best, the group simply copies the values and social system of the state peoples. More often, the result of contact is a process of synthesis or *syncretism*. Syncretism is a combination of cultural traits, with the result usually resembling the culture of the state but equalitarian meanings or functions may be combined. For example, European ideas of modesty were picked up by Navajo while in captivity, and women started dressing in the Mother Hubbard dress of frontier times. However, within several generations, Navajo tastes in color and design had changed the Mother Hubbard into the famous squaw dress, which is now eagerly sought by white tourists. Likewise, Indian political organization now appears to follow Western parliamentary procedure, but committees or councils continue to seek unanimous decisions and otherwise continue former customs. Obviously, anthropologists have a lot to learn about such complexity; they have already learned much that is useful in alleviating problems that arise when states dominate other peoples.

The Nation–State and a World Economic System

In contrast, anthropology has spent far less time in studying the nation-state itself and particularly the relations among nation-states. Part of this remiss is due to the work of other social sciences, such as political science, but during World War II anthropology made some valuable studies of national character or personality types, as we shall see in the concluding chapter. Presently, the omission is also being filled in as anthropologists concentrate on the relationship between a growing world economic system in the face of rigid political boundaries erected by the state. This disparity between economic systems and political systems is at the root of many global problems. It is particularly important in the relationship between the Western World and what has become known as the Third World.

The Third World has been variously known as undeveloped, developing, or traditional. The First World, made up of North America and Western European countries plus Japan, is often called *modern* and the process of making the Third World like the West has been called *modernizing*. Modernization theory assumes that the technology and science that developed in the West only need to be transplanted to Third World countries so that they may "catch up" or come to enjoy the same material wealth that is enjoyed by Japanese, Americans, and Europeans.

The difficulty with this assumption became painfully obvious during the energy crisis of 1973. When fossil fuels and electricity became scarce and expensive, it was clear that the modern world is characterized by high energy use. All of the impressive technology ultimately operates on energy, mostly derived from fossil fuel. The limits of this fuel were in sight, and polluting effects of nuclear power showed that humans faced a severe shortage of energy. Westerners were not sure they could continue their own way of life, let alone transport intensive-energy use forms of technology to Africa, Asia, and Latin America.

Furthermore, a growing number of Latin Americans and a few Western social scientists were beginning to realize that industrial capitalism had earlier origins than the Industrial Revolution, and the system had pervaded the world early except where Marxist governments in Eastern Europe and Asia had dissolved it. The system worked in such a way that it prevented capital growth in the Third World and systematically drained wealth away from the poorest countries. These countries were not on a modernization path to become wealthy; instead, international capitalism was making them poorer in a process of *underdevelopment*. The underdeveloped countries were forced quite early into a dependency relationship with the West; *dependency theory* became an explanation for the discrepancy in the wealth among nations and insisted that the difference was caused by the nature of capitalism.

While the theory is flawed in some respects, it has been of much help in perceiving the growth of an economic world order in the past 400 years while growth of nation-states has brought about hundreds of different political units. Until this time, political and economic organization were generally coterminous. Indeed, one cannot imagine an economic order of redistribution in feudalism that is not the same as the political order.

To understand this new economic phenomenon, it is useful to trace the origins of industrial capitalism to Western Europe, where larger towns and denser populations were arising in the mid-fifteenth century. The growth of cities depended on expanding wool mills, later joined by cotton textiles. This growth in industry was aided by an increasing trade with Eastern Europe whereby it provided grain for manufactured products. Later, Spain and Italy would contribute to this trade so that the Western Europe of the Dutch, at times the French, and particularly the English became an industrial core. Southern and Eastern Europe were peripheral.

This process expanded greatly in the 17th century when a policy of mercantilism was formulated. The mercantilists saw that wealth was largely created in manufacturing. Furthermore, they monopolized factories, converted artisans and laborers to industrial workers, and ensured a food supply by founding colonies in the New World, Africa, and Asia. Southern and Eastern Europe were moved closer to the core but never industrialized to the same extent. They became semiperipheral.

North America began as colonies of the periphery but, through revolution, the United States won a right to industrialize, which was probably the basic cause of the 1776 Revolution, and Canada gained similar rights later. Central and South America, however, remained in the periphery, along with Africa and much of Asia. They were to serve as sources of raw materials; equally important, they were a market for the manufactured goods.

It was assumed that the industrialized core might lead in the growth of wealth, but the peripheral countries supposedly would also benefit from the system. Growing numbers of politically independent nations in the 1960s were taken as the evidence for "catching up." However, by the 1970s it was becoming obvious to everyone that the core countries were becoming wealthier at a much faster rate than the peripheral countries, and some peripheral countries were even becoming poorer. The greatest problem was that many Third World countries traditionally had been exporters of food, ensuring at least enough food for themselves, but increasingly Third World nations were becoming net importers of food with famine often striking in Africa and South Asia. Leaders in Third World countries began talking about the necessity for the *New International Economic Order,* or a way of redistributing wealth between the rich and poor nations.

The disappointment that political independence did not bring economic prosperity was not surprising to Latin Americans who had won their independence a century earlier. It had not allowed them to share in the prosperity of the capitalist core, despite a transfer of some technology and manufacturing to their countries. Latin American economists detailed the process. The capital for manufacturing came largely from the core; Latin banks and insurance companies are dominated by Europe and North America. Much of the profit that was made on capitalist investment went back to the core; it did not go into further investment in Latin America. Manipulation of the indigenous profits was in the hands of a very small elite that was so wealthy it used its money in lavish expenditures on consumption, with houses and vacations in Europe or ostentatious displays of wealth at home.

Thus, the capital cities of Latin America presented the paradox of striking wealth in a small downtown area plus the suburbs of the wealthy; but, on the urban fringes were thousands of shanty dwellers driven to the slums by even greater poverty in the countryside. With only a few exceptions, the Third World countries follow a pattern wherein one large city, usually the capital, has a large part of the population and almost all the wealth. It is the dwelling place of the rich and the center of power. Other "cities" are more like overgrown towns; they are neither commercial nor manufacturing centers because all wealth goes directly from the countryside to the capital, where much of it then goes on to the capitalist core outside the nation.

Clearly, the transfer of modern technology is not sufficient to alter this process; indeed, it contributes to it. If the West cannot find some way to change the dependency relationship, it is likely that more and more countries will turn to revolution to end their dependency. As populations become better aware of the great discrepancies in wealth between nations, they are more likely to seek radical means of change, be it the Marxism of the Soviet Union or the messianic-like Islamic movements of Iran and the Shiites. Traditional peoples might well tolerate that a U.S. citizen consumes 50 times more electricity than a citizen of India. However, when the U.S. begins to consume 50 times as much food, much of it going to waste, as an Indian or African who is starving, then such differences are not to be tolerated. Oddly, the intolerance does not come solely from the Third World; many people in the developed world are upset by such differences, and the study of inequity has become an important topic in social science. We still do not know nearly enough about the inequity among nations but an important first step in understanding it is to study what has been learned about stratification and ranking within political systems such as the state and feudal societies.

Inequity in Power and Wealth: Stratification and Ranking

Inequity is so pervasive in modern times that many sociologists have concluded that it is a universal phenomenon and possibly an innate characteristic of humankind. Such thinking is easily dispelled, however, by considering small, equalitarian societies. Some inequity exists between males and females and between young and old, but not in terms of wealth, only in terms of power. Even power, however, is quite limited and no one can go about "building" it. It is simply understood that some individuals in some contexts have more power than others, but are expected to use this strength for the good of the group, not individual gain. Thus, Westerners see San or Inuit as extraordinarily "generous" which is a reading of one's norms onto others. These people cannot be "generous" because they have no way of being "greedy." They simply have to practice reciprocity to be what they are.

In larger groups, equity can be almost as widespread as it is in small groups, or considerable inequity may be found. Where polities are pastoral or horticultural, people are faced with the problem of who should control property or how wealth should be distributed. Control of the means of production is particularly important. Almost all such groups invest ownership of herds or land in the hands of corporate groups, usually descent groups; individual ownership does not occur. Indeed, *ownership* is a misleading term. Typically, a clan has the rights to land which it distributes to its members. If it should cease using the land, other clans could occupy it. That is, land was something that was not "owned;" rather, groups had use rights. Such a concept prevented accumulation of great concentrations of wealth which explains much of the equity; additionally, a variety of customs regularly reallocated wealth from the richer to the poorer. Anthropologists describe these as *leveling* traditions. Witchcraft beliefs are a prime example of a leveling device. Typically, wealthy or powerful people are assumed to be witches; thus, people will give away goods if they have more than average, or they will stop acting powerful if they have any chance to be so. Deaths in the family are also frequent leveling devices. As a sign of mourning, a person gives away all property upon the death of a loved relative. The poor, of course, have little to give, but the wealthy must start over in their accumulation. However, such traditions make wealth accumulation unlikely; that is, there is simply no motivation for it as exists elsewhere.

Yet, inequities do appear among people with leveling traditions and other equalitarian features. It is worth examining Northwest Coast Indians to see stratification in operation among a foraging people. Throughout North America, an institution known as the *give-away* served as a leveling device, but anyone giving away an unusual amount did receive prestige. On the Northwest Coast, individuals and descent groups began competing for such prestige, changing the give-away into the potlatch. A clan or village might work very hard at catching extra fish, carving, weaving blankets, and working copper in order to give all this wealth to a competing clan or village. Recipients were expected to return the gifts, actually even more gifts, at a later date. If they failed to do so, they were shamed and the potlatch givers gained power over them. Individuals competed in the same way, but the potlatch highlighted differences between "nobles" or people who could host a potlatch and those who could not—"commoners." Among the nobility, people remembered who had hosted the best potlatches, the next best, and so on so that the nobility within a village or sometimes a region were graded in terms of their prestige/wealth. Anthropologists describe this system as *ranking*. That is, ranked societies are ones where individuals stand in a first, second, third, fourth order; obviously, people must know each other on a face-to-face basis, and highly personalized relations deemphasize the differences in wealth that occur in impersonalized societies. Poor commoners were some kind of relative to the highest ranking individual.

The system as described by early observers was a highly competitive one that made Northwest Coast people unique among food gatherers. Their striving for wealth equated them with the most ambitious capitalists. We now think that early trade with whites and decimation of populations because of European diseases left unusual amounts of wealth in the hands of a few individuals who greatly upset the original institution. Aboriginal practice more likely resembled the skewed reciprocity of the kula ring or the feasts of a New Guinea Big-Man. However, as reported by the first government agents, the potlatch had gone farther and included destruction of wealth after its ostentatious display as well as gift-giving beyond measure. Almost surely it could not have occurred in such magnitude before the upset of white contact; otherwise, it could not possibly have served to redistribute wealth over a wide area, experiencing microecological change, as described in the chapter on economics.

Another problem in the description is that the society appears to be *stratified* as well as ranked. Social strata are groupings of people who comprise *social classes*. Social classes are characteristic of all modern state societies and seem to have been present in the early city-states. Classes also occur in the redistribution systems of feudalism. Whole groups of people are organized horizontally in contrast to the vertical organization of descent groups. These horizontal layers can become as rigid as descent groups if they insist on endogamy, in which case they are termed *castes*. In other cases, the strata exist largely in tradition and myth; styles of living are not different between groups nor are there gradations of power as occur in socially stratified societies.

Elsewhere, subordination of one group by another is a clear cause of stratification, but such domination did not necessarily have to be in the form of warfare. In the early city-states, for example, the first stratification surely resulted from a gradual accumulation of power and wealth that grew up with the expansion of intensive agriculture. The elite that began to control land and all the complex operations of irrigation systems began to acquire unusual wealth, as reflected in their ornamentation and elaborate burials. Below them arose a widespread grouping of artisans, paramilitary, and lower bureaucrats. At the base of this system were peasants who raised the food necessary for the society to operate.

The number of strata in state societies poses serious problems for social scientists. Karl Marx has logic on his side in arguing that societies must be divided between those who control the means of production, or whatever it is that generates wealth, and those who have to labor to produce the wealth. The two groups obviously differ in their interests and should be in conflict as Marx predicted. Yet, the study of modern societies continually finds three or more classes. Typically, Americans see their communities as organized into upper, middle, and lower classes. Sociologists have often found evidence for more strata than these. The lower and middle classes may be divided in two parts. In one of the best-known studies of a New England town of 50,000, each of the three classes was divided into two parts. The upper-upper class inherited wealth and a tradition of power; the lower-upper class might have more wealth but it was ''new'' money. The upper-middle class received its income from annual salaries while the lower-middle class worked for hourly wages. The lower class received income from sources such as welfare or temporary employment. Those who accepted middle-class values were regarded as an upper-lower class; the lower-lower class had their own values, often rejecting such norms as a neat house and yard.

The importance of this study was determination of the factors for stratification. Amount of income was not very important; instead, source of income was critical. Inherited wealth, for example, carried more prestige than salaries. Occupation was equally important. A plumber might earn as much money as a dentist, but never as much prestige. Where a person lived and type of house were two other essential factors. Given a knowledge of these four factors, the researchers could predict social class quite well. That is, people in the town generally called themselves middle class but then ranked others as above or below themselves. Many upper-class people saw no inconsistency in labeling themselves middle class but were unable to name anyone above themselves.

This multiclass system certainly diffused any concentration of power. People in city government were generally middle class. The middle class also controlled the school board and similar ''centers of power.'' There was no evidence for the kind of class conflict envisioned by Marxists, but focusing on American communities may overlook a large arena where there is a struggle between labor and those who own the means of production.

This arena could be the nation-state instead of the small community. One description of a ''power elite'' in the United States strongly suggests that a small percentage of the population does indeed control most of the wealth and make the important decisions that greatly influence life. Heads of the major business corporations, Pentagon officials, and a few officials in the government form a class that dominates American society. While the middle class may be deciding who to hire as a school superintendent, the power elite decides on the relocations of industries from the North to the South or whether a military contract will go to a Midwest city to save its employment base. Collecting the data to prove how much an elite controls the political-economic life of modern democratic nation-states is exceedingly difficult, but evidence for it has been available even before President Eisenhower warned the United States about the rising power of a ''military-industrial complex'' when he left the White House. Beyond doubt, the study of inequity and stratification must be a basic part of anthropology in any examination of political organizations.

Summary

If politics or political organization is seen as *maintenance of external relations* and *control of internal order,* then all human societies are political. Indeed, even a troop of baboons might be seen as political animals. However, if these processes are further refined into politics, being *a public process by which structured groups focus power to reach public goals,* then nonhumans no longer qualify. The continual focusing of power by differentiated groups is a subtle process requiring thousands of norms and agreed-upon expectations, all characterizing human societies but no others. The best illustration of this subtlety is the nature of *authority.* It can be equated with brute power, as it is in nonhuman groups, but it can also be equated with knowledge. Authority in equalitarian societies is generally that of expertise and tradition. Only in the state is force an integral part of authority.

Among small equalitarian polities, force is never a part of internal control and is quite rare in external relations. Instead, organization is built on highly personalized relations with everyone having learned from childhood a position within the group and all agreeing on public goals. When differences do arise, there is dependence upon *leaders,* the individuals recognized as most capable in a particular context, to decide how to reach goals.

The political process becomes more complex with increasing numbers of structured groups. Yet, these groups are more or less equal, especially if they are corporate descent groups. They are responsible and do indeed resolve most internal conflicts, at least that conflict occurring within the group. When conflict arises between groups, resolution follows marital lines and is difficult to resolve. All the descent groups seldom have mutual public goals until attacked by outsiders. Otherwise, large equalitarian societies have no overarching organization that can be considered governmental; politics is largely a matter of descent and marriage or associations and age-grades.

When large equalitarian societies face domination by states, individuals may focus power outside of structured groups. These people, know as *Big-Men,* manipulate wealth and prestige in such ways as to accumulate power outside the realm of kinship. Big-Men then begin to act like the heads of descent or age-groups, claiming authority and making decisions for a following. Big-Men have concentrated considerable power at some times but it is not long-lasting.

In contrast, where feudalism occurs, the lord or chief inherits power that comes at the apex of a hierarchy. The position of authority is backed by tradition and is enforced by redistribution of wealth. People regularly give *tribute* because of the traditional greatness of the hierarchy. Regularly, the lord, king, or chief gives greater feasts and celebrations than anyone else, and pays more bride-wealth. People are glad to give tribute because they identify with the greatness of the system, and they do share in the wealth of the feudal estate.

Feudalism marks the beginning of social classes, but fully developed stratification is characteristic of the *state* where *social classes* are clear-cut. The state also differs from the feudal polity because of the great impersonality of relations. In feudalism, the hierarchy is expected to be loyal and kinsmen make loyal followers. Thus, kinship is as basic to feudal politics as it is to small groups. But, the state insists upon competence rather than loyalty. The hierarchy of feudalism becomes the *bureaucracy* of the state. The elite at the top become so authoritarian that they may become gods, as happened in Egypt; they always become wealthy and powerful. An important characteristic of the state is that even divine power is backed by naked force as well as tradition in the states. States operate by police force. The demands levied on the populace thus become *taxes* rather than tribute. In the early city-state, the taxes were in the form of goods from the people working at crafts, in the countryside, cultivators paid taxes in the form of food. Because these cultivators became dependent upon state and subjugated to it, they are known as *peasants,* in contrast to farmers who are independent. Peasants are generally the lowest stratum, although peasants in India are an important exception. Various middle strata are made up of skilled and semiskilled urban workers and the lower parts of the bureaucracy. The top of the bureaucracy comprises the upper strata. The transition to such organization saw a radical change in political and social organization, its first occurrence taking place about five thousand years ago.

Since then, most people have come under state organization although, even today, some groups are just now being subjugated by nation-states. The process of subjugation has invariably brought radical or violent change. In many cases, states have practiced *genocide,* a policy of wiping out whole ethnic or racial groups. A more common policy has been *segregation.* The subordinated people are restricted to certain areas; sometimes, parts of their homeland are reserved for them, as happened with American Indians. Or the labor of the minority may be used, as with Black Americans, while they are segregated within a city. States have also followed a policy of *assimilation* wherein the subordinated group is supposed to give up its culture and practice the culture of the state. Most often, the result has been one of *accommodation.* Small polities, after learning that physical resistance is useless, may turn to accommodation and establish a *nativistic,* or *messianic* movement. This step is usually the beginning of *syncretism* which produces a blending of the dominant and subordinate cultures.

Anthropologists have given priority to the study of state-to-small polity relations while largely ignoring state-to-state relations. Neglect of their situation has changed recently as the growth of a world economic system has been recognized. The origin of this growth is now traced to the 15th century in Western Europe, which serves as a *core* for industrial capitalism. Eventually, North America and Japan joined this core as it manufactured most of the world's products. On the *periphery,* nations served to produce raw materials and to consume finished products. Over the past century, the core has grown more wealthy rapidly while the periphery has become poorer.

These poor nations are now known as Third World countries. Modernization theorists maintain that the transfer of Western science and technology will eventually make them develop. Another school of thought maintains that capitalism makes the economies of Third World nations *dependent* upon the core and drains their wealth. The core nations have *underdeveloped* the Third World and will keep them in poverty unless the system is changed. Third World leaders often speak of a changed system as a *New International Economic Order.*

Anthropologists and other social scientists have spent comparatively little time in exploring what might be involved in a new economic order. Radical change would call for a major redistribution of wealth from rich to poor nations. Moderate change could be a slowing of growth rates in the core to allow faster growth in the periphery. What is clear is that anthropology can no longer confine its interest to the politics of small polities, feudalism, or even the state. It must study state-to-state organization and the correspondence of political entities with a global economic system.

11

Religion and Symbolism_____

Religion and Anthropology

Many of the social evolutionists who began the discipline of anthropology were particularly interested in the study of religion. Edward B. Tylor devoted half of his major work, *Primitive Culture,* to an examination of the origin and evolution of religion. Since his time, anthropologists have found that religion is just as pervasive in the cultures of the world as economics, politics, or kinship. Today, of course, states like the Soviet Union and China officially deny any supernatural world, but religious practices by some of their citizens are still common. A notable number of nonbelievers seem to be a part of religious organization everywhere. That is, some skeptics are found in all cultures, and it seems likely that human communities have always experienced a range of belief from the skeptic to the totally devout.

Recognition of such variation was an important step, taken by anthropologists early in the 20th century. Earlier, we had to face a doctrine that said many peoples had no religion. This position stemmed from a theological idea that when humans had "fallen from grace," some people had fallen so far that they lost knowledge of God. Thus, the position justified missionary efforts. In contrast, other theologians felt that when God had revealed himself to the first humans, that knowledge was preserved everywhere and evidence could be found that all peoples had knowledge of a high god. Even this contrasting view could still justify a missionary effort, since many peoples had not had the opportunity to learn of Jesus and his relationship to the high god.

As social science struggled to understand the nature of religion, two viewpoints gradually emerged. The easiest way to explain the universality of any institution is to claim it is part of human nature. Psychologists did not advance such a simplistic notion, but they did argue that religion was a part of the human personality. This view might stress the inquiring nature of humans, their elaboration of the primate play pattern; such an approach concentrated on the explanatory power of religion. Another view, part of the conventional wisdom, is that religion serves humans under stress. When people are in fear for their lives, they turn to the supernatural for aid. It is obvious that religious organization is important for such purposes.

The difficulty with religion as explanatory device is that the puzzles explained by mythology or ritual are quite limited. A myth might well explain the markings of a loon, but dozens of other birds are ignored. One mountain may be thrown up by a god, but other mountains are simply accepted. Westerners assume that all peoples would want answers to how human beings and the earth originated and, while many myths do explain such beginnings, many peoples take the earth and life for granted. Their origin myths explain the beginning of religion or account for some other part of ritual life. Religion as relief of tension is also flawed because, in many difficult situations, no help is sought from the supernatural while others rely on it heavily.

Further, religion itself may become a source of stress. Rigid moral structures are often a source of guilt and anxiety which cannot be relieved through ritual, prayer, or similar practice. And, we find that many persons develop stress as they worry that a prayer will not be spoken properly or a ritual will be flawed. Despite such difficulties with psychological explanation, it is often useful in understanding some parts of religious behavior.

Thus, anthropologists often make use of psychology, but for the most part they have favored sociological explanations—that is, one derived from the nature of social and cultural life. Among the simpler of these explanations is one provided by Karl Marx. He saw religion as an institution built up from the economic system. The individuals who controlled the means of production used religious beliefs to justify their ownership and the fact that others had to work for them. Marxists sometimes see capitalists as deliberately twisting beliefs to further their ends, but Marx himself did not seem to accept a conscious conspiracy. He simply recognized that religion is a conservative force, for the most part, and that it tends to justify the status quo.

Anthropologists understood that Marx had a point in showing the close relationship between religion and the rest of society but, instead of interpreting it as an effect of economics, they stressed the mutual relatedness of institutions. The family, economics, education, politics, and religion were all equal parts of a complex whole. More and more, religion is coming to be understood as a symbolic system that is an expression of other institutions. The roots of such understanding can be traced to the late 19th century when Emile Durkheim recognized that the totems of descent groups were powerful symbolic forms for an expression of the complexity of clan life. He gave impetus to theoretical study of religion, and his thinking, as well as other theories, will be explained later in the chapter. Now, however, it is appropriate to examine some basic aspects of religion that are frequently found among peoples all over the globe. None of these features is found everywhere, but the similarities in religious life are still more impressive than the differences.

Sacred and Secular

Peoples often divide their world into the realms of the sacred and the profane or secular. In Western society, this division is a sharp one and, in the United States, citizens take pride in sharply separating church and state. As a result, governments have refrained from taxing church property, but some church leaders complain that this action is a form of state support of religion. This example illustrates that the various parts of a culture are not easily separated nor are all things and actions strictly sacred or profane. Profanities themselves may be taken lightly on a job; the same utterances in a church could stir religious feelings. The bookkeeping for a church can be entirely secular when done on contract with an auditor; the volunteer church member who keeps accounts must be motivated by religious feelings and likely thinks of his or her duties as part of the religion.

Still, Westerners are notable for sharply segregating their religious buildings from secular ones and even designating one day of the week as sacred, as opposed to six secular ones. In contrast, daily activities of a Mayan Indian are wrapped in religious practices with a continual sliding from secular to sacred practices. In the life cycle, many Mayan families will acquire more and more prestige by first serving in the lowest rung of a political hierarchy that qualifies them to move onto a similar religious ladder. Service in one area is a prerequisite for office in the other. A separation of religion and government, as Americans know it, is simply inconceivable for a Mayan.

Yet, many peoples do recognize that some occasions, places, persons, or times are more sacred than others. The evidence for this sacredness is seen in peoples' actions. They reserve special feelings and awe for the sacred; they talk about it in a measured, respectful way. Feelings guide and motivate behavior toward the sacred. But what is it about the sacred that elicits such a response? In Christianity, there is implicit recognition that the sacred is somehow charged with a supernatural force. Entry into a church brings circumspect behavior, language is more reserved, and one acts as if in the presence of some awesome entity. Elsewhere, this potential force is explicitly recognized and therefore named. In Oceania, the Polynesian word for it is *mana*. Anthropologists have adopted the word as their technical term for the power. Among American Indians, it was called *Manitu* by Algonquin speakers; Siouan speakers called it *Wakan*. This potent force sets things or people out of the ordinary world into what is described as the supernatural. The supernatural is largely the religious world, but it may cover other aspects as well. In the West, for example, werewolves and vampires must be considered part of the supernatural.

Whether or not the potency of mana is explicit recognized, it is often the basis for distinguishing the sacred from the secular. It invests persons, places, or things, giving them the potential for being extraordinary or outside of the natural world. In itself it is not supernatural; neither is it good nor evil. It is simply impersonal power that may be permanent or temporary. It is often compared to electricity because of its inherent danger and the way it can be used.

Mana and Taboo

Because of the potential of mana, it is handled in similar ways throughout the world. Almost always special symbols give warning of it. Buildings, paths, or other places are marked by icons; persons with mana have special dress or ornamentation. Note the use of the cross in Christianity and the collars of many ministers and priests. The people or objects with mana must be treated with special care. The proscriptions or prescriptions of care are what make a thing or person taboo, another term borrowed from Oceania. Taboos are simply the norms that direct circumspect behavior toward mana. Most often, the warning simply calls for avoidance, but it may also dictate elaborate precautions, which are parts of religious practice.

FIGURE 29

A Mayan priest carries a carved horse and Conquistador that are full of mana for a ceremony in Chichicastenango, Guatemala. (Photo by Ernest Schusky)

    In Oceania, where ideas of mana and taboo are most explicit, notable elaborations occur. Persons are often charged with a mana that affects their surroundings. Special footpaths are reserved for them, as well as houses and eating utensils. People with mana can be approached by only a few persons who know how to protect themselves from mana. Individuals with mana control political as well as religious power and, in Hawaii, the man or woman with the most mana had the powers of a king or queen. Indeed, a Hawaiian king was so charged with mana that an ordinary woman could not marry him; he could only marry a woman with similar mana. Logically, this woman had to be a sister. Similar thinking prevailed among the Incas and Egyptians. Although brother-sister marriage did not occur in Africa, except for Egypt, the mana of leading men led to treatment similar to that in Oceania. In fact, some African kings acquired so much mana that they were completely isolated, and their prime ministers became the effective rulers. One suspects that the prime ministers may have been mana manipulators.

    Objects with mana are frequently hidden, to be used only on special occasions or by only a few people. In Australia, the Aborigines paint stones or pieces of wood known as *churingas,* objects central to their religion. Only fully initiated, adult men dare handle or even look upon the churingas. The churinga display occurs only a few times a year; then, a concealed bull-roarer adds to the tension of the occasion for the women and children. Since the uninitiated know they will be struck dead if they see the churingas, the Australians quite pragmatically hide the objects most of the time. Many American Indians have comparable objects that are usually described as *medicine bundles.* Among Plains Indians, the bundles are usually entrusted to one or two persons who only rarely open them for display to a select few. In the Southwest, where life is more sedentary, the bundle is often secreted outside the village. Only a few persons can ever handle the sacred object.

In sum, mana is so powerful that humans must take great precautions. Taboos are the directions for careful use. Most often the taboo simply says, ''keep away;'' with further refinement, the taboos are precise directions about how and when mana is to be handled.

Individuals, Shamans, Priests, and Clergy

Individuals vary widely in their ability to handle or control mana. In some situations, all people may coexist with it, but often the uninitiated are the least able to deal with the power. Where individuals go seeking mana, they often prepare by fasting, going without sleep, or taking other steps that may put them in an extraordinary state. Thus, they may be unusually ready for dreams, visions, or hallucinations—all activities not well understood by science and poorly described as ''trance.'' What we can recognize is that people everywhere take special steps in approaching mana, steps that have psychosomatic results.

It seems likely that some individuals more readily enter such a state than others, or enter the state more deeply as in *trance*. We know little about trance except that the body is able to perform extraordinary feats in such a state; for example, fire may not burn the body and even red-hot rocks may be handled with impunity. Persons in trance also may have uncommon linguistic ability. They will speak what sounds like a foreign tongue, no simple task as anyone knows who has tried doubletalk. Often the person who is speaking in tongues is recognized as having been taken over by a spirit. The supernatural is said to be communicating through the person in trance. In most food-collecting societies, the only specialists in religion are the individuals who control mana to the extent of speaking a spirit language or handling fire. These individuals are called *shamans,* a Siberian word for people who can enter deep trance and speak at length in a strange tongue.

We do not know why some individuals have the abilities for extraordinary states. In their biographies, shamans tell us that they suddenly found the power to control mana. In one case, a woman knew she was unusual when she found an unusual looking stone in the desert. Others have had dramatic experiences such as dying, entering a spirit world, and then being revived. Since the prerequisites for being a shaman seem based on individual ability or experiences, females are as likely as males to be shamans, and some quite young shamans are found. In any case, people are generally skeptical about a person's claim to being a shaman, but the claim is backed by public ritual where the shaman handles fire, speaks in tongues, or otherwise demonstrates unusual ability. In some cases, the unusual ability consists of trickery, and Westerners interpret the behavior as deception. Actually, persons who feel called to be a shaman generally serve as apprentices and take years to learn a variety of techniques.

For example, some Plains Indians had shamans whose feet and hands were elaborately tied; they were further tied into a hide or blanket. They then might be hung upside down from the top of a tepee or log cabin. All light was extinguished. The tepee then shook, objects darted through the air and, when a fire was relit, the shaman was sitting unbound with the blanket and rope neatly stacked. Anyone with such abilities was entrusted with curing, predicting the future, or finding the lost—common tasks for a shaman. Whether trance or tricks were used to demonstrate control of mana mattered little. Clearly, such an individual had unusual power.

Since shamans lived in highly personalized societies, they probably were better than we at predicting what individuals might do in the future or what their health is like. Among ourselves, the person who seeks solutions for such problems from an astrologer likes the results because a good astrologer knows what most people want to hear. A shaman also knows all the personal circumstances of the individuals he or she serves. Thus, shamans probably have a fairly good empirical record as well as building confidence in themselves because of trance or impressive ritual.

Other specialists in handling mana are known as *priests*. In contrast with shamans, priests have long training in religious practice. A common prerequisite for a priest is to be male, and initiations bring a boy into manhood along with priesthood. Female priesthoods, where they exist, often parallel male organizations. In either case, individuality is replaced by group activity. Instead of the drama of trance, priests use the drama of ritual, dance, song, symbol, prayer, and other religious activity.

Priests are found in a few food-collecting societies and most horticultural and pastoral societies where they are not full-time specialists, but they must devote a considerable part of their life to learning and to group organization. Priesthoods may coexist with shamans as occurred on the Great Plains. Among all these tribes, shamans were active year-round but especially during the winter in performing cures. In the summer, when large numbers congregated in the camp circle, associations of priests were responsible for communal rites and worship. The Sundance was the best known communal cult, but a variety of associations and rituals provided a complex religious life for these big game hunters.

Despite very complex rites that may require long, memorized prayers, elaborate costumes and masks, dramatic ritual, or complex songs, priests engage in the same subsistence activities as other persons. If society rewards the priesthoods, it is in goods that are mostly redistributed. Thus, complex ritual is often associated with feasting and the giving of goods. It almost always is an occasion where social ties are intensified through usual, everyday activity on a much larger scale, as well as a highly symbolic activity that includes extraordinary states produced by music, dance, and drama.

Besides using symbols, shamans and priests develop an impressive amount of practical knowledge. In many places, they regularly experiment with herbal medicine and their knowledge has been sought by modern pharmaceutical companies. They have been particularly useful in tropical areas where Western knowledge of plants is slight. Additionally, priesthoods have developed complex ideas of the cosmos, developing calendars in conjunction with their thinking. These calendars usually predict the solstices accurately, and have established the 365-day year. The Mayan priesthood and a few others even determined the year closer to a 365 and one-quarter day period. Indeed, the Mayan are regarded as having been better astronomers than the Spanish at the time of the Conquest. Scientists once thought calendars were probably useful for agricultural peoples, but anthropologists are finding that calendric knowledge is much wider spread than once thought. Furthermore, agriculturists used more refined knowledge in planting, varying times by rainfall, temperatures, and other factors. Strict adherence to a calendar would be disastrous

FIGURE 30

This South Korean shaman is in semi-trance as she makes an offering of food. She practices in a village most often, but occasionally visits Seoul to cure certain illnesses. (Photo by Mary Sue Schusky)

for a farmer. In sum, much of priestly knowledge was accumulated for the sake of knowledge as well as for social control and organization of social activity.

Systematic accumulation of knowledge does not take any impressive leap with the development of a full-time *clergy;* but, with this development, religion does seem to become more specialized as well. That is, the large number of nonspecialists begin to hold a number of beliefs that are not part of the specialists' knowledge. The specialists often develop a hierarchy parallel to hierarchies of the state and, invariably, *clerical cults* are found only in states. Religion became part of the state and some conflict is inevitable between state and clergy because of competition. However, cooperation between clergy and state is more common, and religion tends to explain and justify actions and policy of the state. The relationship between the two is complex, and it can range from a merging of the two, as in a theocracy, to a hostile division as in the contemporary Soviet Union. Whatever the situation, social scientists see close functional ties between the two institutions; yet, clerical activity is much more specialized than that of priests, and the clergy is less involved in everyday activity.

Medicine Men, Witches, and Sorcerers

With a growing complexity of society, it appears that shamans are replaced by priests who are then replaced by clergy in state societies; however, this portrayal is inaccurate. Shamans coexist with priests in many places, and both shamans and priests coexist in the state on occasion. Some fundamentalist Christian ministers suddenly discover they have been "called," they achieve a semitrance state and may speak in tongues or handle rattlesnakes, while using this drama with music in order to cure or promote good fortune. They are clearly shamans even though they may be described as "clergy" in common English usage. In South Korea, shamans practice in the city as well as the countryside side by side with one of the most rapidly growing Christian clergy in the world. Buddhist clergy are also prominent while many Koreans follow Confucian principles in an individualistic approach to the supernatural.

Because shamans vary widely in their practices as well as in their settings, they have been described by many terms. In anthropology, we usually group them all as shamans, but the common English terms are sometimes used. Thus, the shaman who uses herbal cures may be called a *medicine man* or *medicine woman,* but they are likely to use much drama such as prayer, song, and ritual as well as practical knowledge. Doubtless, the drama has psychosomatic value. Shamans may also be described as witches, with some confusion as to whether witches can be good as well as evil. The problem arises because of a chauvinistic analogy of white magic being used by good witches while bad witches employ black magic.

The difficulty in using a good or an evil purpose as a basis for definition is that what is evil for one is usually good for another. When a shaman is working to make enemies sick, his or her purposes are "good" for the community but quite "bad" from the enemies' point of view. Anthropologists refrain from using the terms "black" and "white" magic and do not distinguish witches as either good or evil.

However, the term *witchcraft* has been found useful, especially in conjunction with the term *sorcerer.* As a part of culture, the actual practice of witchcraft is less important than accusations of witchcraft. That is, the threat of being accused of witchcraft is a most significant factor in social control, and who makes accusations is as important to know as whom is being accused. In many places where witchcraft accusations abound, it is likely that no witches exist. Indeed, peoples themselves generally have a belief that implies the witch is unconscious of his or her powers and cannot control them. In effect, witches exert much influence, either good or evil, but they have only slight control over what they do. Sorcerers, on the other hand, deliberately act to harm or to help others. Many of the shamans' practices are characteristic of sorcery. Generally, of course, the sorcerers' deeds are for the public good, but their recognized ability to hurt others generally rewards them with a respect mixed with fear or resentment. Since sorcerers act with deliberate intent, accusations of sorcery will be directed at obvious competitors. A leader suspects an ambitious follower of sorcery, but it would not be in the leader's interest to dissipate his followers with sorcery. However, leaders could be accused of witchcraft because, unknowingly, they might hurt followers.

The wide variation in shamanistic practice has been of long-standing interest to almost everyone. It produced much argument over differences between magic and religion with attempts in the West to define magic, and shamans as magicians, as outside the realm of religion. A major contribution of anthropology was to blur this distinction and to show that so-called magical practices are an approach to the supernatural just as religion is. Still, some of the distinctions made between magic and religion are useful for further understanding the field.

Magic and Religion

Social evolutionists, such as James Frazer, reconstructed an evolution from magic, through religion, and then to science. Sir James' interest centered largely on magic, and he spelled out the differences between types. He found two of these types occurring throughout the world. In *imitative magic,* people obviously were following the principle that similarities must have effects upon each other. An image of a person or a doll resembling a person is manipulated to hurt the actual being. Something like the practice of sticking pins in a doll to harm another is widespread. Likewise, *contagious magic* appears all over the globe. In contagious magic, parts of a person are used to work effects. Cut hair, fingernails, feces, or even shadows of people can be used to bring harm to them; the umbilical cord is particularly valuable and is usually disposed of with great care to reduce a baby's vulnerability.

All of these practices reflect beliefs in deliberate attempts to control events. They well demonstrate how sorcerers might work. Through magic, sorcerers seek to master causes to determine outcomes. In contrast, shamans and priests on many other occasions seem to stand helpless before the supernatural, simply begging for guidance and protection. Feelings of awe appear to dominate the relationship; persons seek only to express their submission to the supernatural or, at best, to placate it. There are no expressions of control. Frazer termed this approach to the supernatural *religion.* Though the distinctions are clear, they are not easily applied to most practices. When a people pray ardently for rain, making certain promises, are they attempting to manipulate the supernatural or are they indicating their helplessness before it? On analysis, prayers are often quite compelling and similar to the formula of a sorcerer. In short, it is often difficult to label a particular practice as magical or religious. The two concepts are useful, however, for indicating the wide range of behavior involved in how humans approach the supernatural. At one end, beliefs and practices are aimed at controlling the supernatural; at the other end, people conceive of themselves as being at the mercy of the supernatural.

Religion and Psychological Processes

Both magical and religious beliefs are frequently regarded as irrational, as either relics from the past or the product of peoples with a prelogical mind. A common question has been, Why do people continue a practice when a desired goal is unfulfilled? Is it not irrational when people continue a rain dance once it has failed to bring rain? The question implies an inferior mentality.

One immediate answer is that religious practices frequently achieve their purposes. Generally, it rains after a Hopi rain dance. Westerners may argue that the dance is always held just before the rainy season: Hopis respond that the dance is what causes the rainy season. Shamans who are asked to track down a thief or murderer, or to predict an outcome, are shrewd judges of their fellows who make better than average guesses, or else they find good reasons not to judge in uncertain cases. Or, even if the shaman has attempted a cure that has failed, there is always the possibility that some other shaman has worked his or her counter power. In short, shamans often do achieve their ends; when they do not, failure is rationalized in terms familiar to anyone. The following case study well illustrates the process.

In a Sioux community where one of the authors worked, a murder had been committed earlier in the year. An FBI investigation had been fruitless. In response, a grandfather of the murdered girl asked a shaman to solve the crime. Although the murderer remained at large, virtually everyone in the community believed the shaman had identified the killer. One rationalization for why the crime remained unsolved was that the murderer was a close relative of the old man, and he did not want to lose another kinsman. This version is realistic since most of the community is closely related and everyone values kinsmen. Another version related that the shaman feared for his own life when he discovered the murderer, so he said nothing. Another story was that the shaman and grandfather took their discovery to the FBI, which was convinced of its accuracy, but no action was taken because such evidence would be unacceptable in a United States court. Clearly, these rationalizations are as reasonable and logical as anyone's; certainly they cannot be judged the product of a prelogical or inferior mind.

Another case provides fuller illustration. While an anthropologist was in the field, a house collapsed on a man, causing his death. Informants assured the anthropologist the death was caused by a witch or sorcerer, and villagers set about to locate the shaman, whom they threatened to kill. The anthropologist argued with the people that the house poles were rotten and termite ridden. He knew the people recognized wood rot and regularly replaced weakened poles, but the people saw little logic in this argument. They posed the question, not in terms of why the poles collapsed but, rather, in terms of why this particular man was sitting under this particular house at the particular time when the poles gave way. The Western answer that these factors were simply a matter of chance or accident can hardly be judged as a more satisfactory explanation than the understanding that a shaman was responsible. Chance or accident is not a very fulfilling answer, even to a Westerner, when the victim is a close relative or oneself. At such times, many Westerners turn to religion for answers. Although statistics on nationwide auto fatalities caused by accidents are easily accepted, chance is an inadequate explanation for personal tragedy.

The Explanatory Value of Religion

While rationalization is characteristic of religion, parts of it are also rational explanations of events. Mythology is particularly noteworthy as an explanation for questions about why, when, and where, but anthropologists have found that mythology is more important as an explanation of why people should behave the way they do. Origin myths, which may explain either the genesis of a people or their religion, seem to be important as guidelines for behavior. As explanations for what is right and wrong, myths codify the norms. Anthropologist Bronislaw Malinowski called mythology "the charter of society." The charter or myth probably follows practice but, once developed, it then influences behavior. In sum, what was being done came to be considered as what ought to be done; once expressed in myth, what "ought to be" then becomes the guideline for practice, and what we have is a self-reinforcing system.

Other students of myth have seen it as explanation of repressed feelings. They interpret myth as a kind of collective dream in which peoples express feelings they cannot otherwise show. Mythology is then useful to reveal covert psychological themes to the social scientists. For the people involved, the myths at least allowed them to play with otherwise unexplained feelings kept at the unconscious level. Other psychological factors may also be a part of mythology.

Most recently, anthropologists have concentrated on an analysis of the structure rather than the content of myth. Claude Lévi-Strauss led this movement, arguing that myths are structured so that certain unresolvable paradoxes, such as life and death, are made analogous to other paradoxes that can be resolved. Resolution of these paradoxes suggests that ones such as life and death may also be resolved. Lévi-Strauss's method for analyzing mythology is subjective and open to argument, but he offers new insight into the explanatory value of mythology.

Lévi-Strauss seems to err in stressing the intellectual part of religious life, even in mythology. For him, the symbols of mythology and ritual are chosen because "they are good to think." Clifford Geertz would agree with Lévi-Strauss, but he would add that the symbols must also be good to feel. Geertz stresses that religion must be as much emotional as it is intellectual, even in explanation. Whatever it does, religion must explain the ultimate nature of reality while providing humans with a code as to how to live in that reality. In turn, this code must be emotionally satisfying according to the terms by which people live in and perceive their world.

Geertz's approach to an understanding of religion is most attractive because of his recognition that much of religious belief must be conscious formulation, while much of it must also be a product of feeling and emotion. That is, the symbols must have intellectual value while at the same time inspiring people to do what is expected of them. Most other theories have stressed one side while neglecting the other.

Social Evolution Theory

The initial anthropological theories of religion began in the late 19th century when interest was concentrated on origin and stages of evolutionary developments, the theorists assuming that primitive peoples worked out rational explanations of phenomena that they could not understand. Edward Tylor proposed the most influential theory, assuming that early humans concluded a dual existence of body and spirit because of their concern with death, dreaming, and trance. For instance, death, with its cessation of breathing and movement, must have suggested that life was something like a "spirit" or "soul." This phantom part of a person could have been assumed to have left the body on occasion, and to have been temporarily absent from it in dreams, trances, or visions. That is, the phantom was thought to be capable of an existence outside of the body. From the accounts of explorers and missionaries, Tylor documented how peoples all around the world held concepts of a soul or a spirit. From this data, he argued that primitive or ancient peoples must have deduced the presence of a phantom soul to account for all the phenomena which suggest a dual nature.

Tylor called this early stage of thinking *animism*, and his explanation became known as a *theory of animism*. The term is still in use to describe the religion of tribal peoples. Although the theory relies too heavily on a rationalistic approach to understanding religious phenomena, it does describe well at least some of the beliefs and practices of peoples around the world. Ghosts or free-ranging spirits, transfigurations of the soul, equation of breath or shadow with soul, and a concept of heavenly residences are widespread and would follow from the animistic thinking described by Tylor.

Sir James Frazer began his explanation of religion with examination of one Western myth. He does not finish until he has described thousands of myths from all over the world. The examination led him to more general problems, such as his explanation of how religion evolved from magic with a projected evolution of religion to science. Frazer also saw how religion was integrated with the rest of culture, and his evolution is one that describes political as well as religious stages. For Frazer, magic was the work of shamans who practiced cause and effect thinking, like scientists, but who often guessed wrong about causation. In *sympathetic magic*, one ate the heart of turtles because it was believed that their strength must give strength to one's own heart. At this stage, the magician wielded political power because of knowledge. However, as people became aware that magic failed to meet their needs, they would revolt against the magician and such beliefs. People then admitted their lack of control over supernatural forces and vested their interests instead in a priest-king who led in the expression of awe before supernatural power. Frazer supported this course of events through references to such incidents in many myths. His arguments have been persuasive for a wide audience, though of lesser concern in anthropology.

The social evolutionists have been criticized at length for their creation of religion from nearly pure intellectualism. Their origins and various stages are backed by neat, logical argument but, in marshalling ethnographic support, the evolutionists conveniently ignored contradictory evidence. As social scientists realized they could never validly demonstrate the proposed origins, they began to ask other questions. Interests now center on what religion does or in what ways is it integrated with other parts of society. Such questions, however, had been suggested by the evolutionists. The approach laid a firm foundation for an anthropological perspective of religion.

Historicism

The opponents of evolutionary theory reacted by searching for particular sequences in specific societies. One school was motivated by the theological belief that God had originally revealed Himself, but most primitive peoples had fallen from grace by developing beliefs in a multitude of gods or by practicing idolatry. Some Roman Catholic scholars pursued ethnography in depth and found societies that still maintained their original knowledge, as reflected by monotheistic beliefs. The most systematic scholar was Father Wilhelm Schmidt, who believed that primeval humans originated in remote Asia. As culture grew, waves of population emanated from this center. Migrants at the outskirts would retain the original culture traits but, according to their degree of isolation, would develop few of the later characteristics. As the earliest and most primitive migrants reached the remote parts of the world, they were followed by peoples with more complex traits but who were relatively simple compared to peoples closer to the center. This pattern of migration led to concentric circles or rings of culture complexity known as *kulturkreise*. Thorough study of trait complexes was meant to reveal which cultures belonged to which of three major circles. Tasmanians and Pygmies, on opposite sides of the world, had many similarities because they supposedly represented one of the earliest circles of migration. This outer circle was supposed to be the best representation of primitive or early humans, and Schmidt was particularly interested in the religion of these peoples. He concluded that they were basically monotheistic, and that animism had been a corrupting influence. Eventually, the bias of Schmidt and his followers flawed his method; moreover, the work of prehistorians illustrated that human origins occurred much earlier than ever imagined and that the place of origin was Africa rather than Asia.

In America, the reaction to social evolution encouraged historical reconstruction. In this case, emphasis was placed on the particulars of an area or a single region. In a study of the Plains Indians' Sundance, Leslie Spier demonstrated how particular traits had spread to form an overall trait complex involving a religious practice. Alfred Kroeber performed similar research on religion among California Indians. Like Franz Boas, the two men were primarily interested in historical reconstruction in areas without written records. Their analysis of religion was interesting because it illustrated the process of the growth and diffusion of thought and practice. However, it did little to explain religion as a phenomenon. Instead, the major theoretical developments came from the sidelines of anthropology; they were outgrowths of social evolution rather than a reaction to it. One theory rested on psychodynamics, the other on function and structure.

Psychological Theory

Some early psychologists accounted for religion as instinctive, attributing it to some kind of primordial dread or to an interest in self-preservation. The biological determinism ideas did not attract much attention until Sigmund Freud developed a comprehensive theory, explaining the elements of what was then regarded as primitive religion. Incest regulations and the Oedipus complex, both major interests of Freud, also were accounted for in this theory.

The theory included work on the problem of religious origins, which Freud described as resulting from an act of patricide, the killing of a father. He conjectured that the protohuman family was composed of mothers, father, and children, much like a baboon troop appears to be. At some point in ancient time, the sons, excluded from any sex relations by the dominant male—their father—conspired to kill him because of sexual jealousy. Only after the killing did the sons experience the horror of their act. Incest regulations arose to prevent any recurrence of patricide because of the sons' remorse. Also, to identify clearly the set of brothers and sisters, humans devised the totem. Thus, the original patricide accounted for human incest rules and the phenomenon of totemism, which was believed to be the basis of the earliest religious form.

The theory attracted anthropologists since it explained so many phenomena, but there was no evidence of an original patricide. Nor was there evidence that humans would react as Freud claimed. Still, Freud dramatized the emotional content of religion. In addition, he noted similarities between obsessive acts and certain types of ritual, so a psychological component must always be recognized in religion. In focusing on the narrow issue of ritual, Freud introduced what was later to develop into concentrated analysis on the components of religion. Emphasis shifted from the origin of an institution to its function, or what it did to satisfy the needs of individuals. In this approach, Freud's work ran parallel to that of a functional, structural view being developed in French sociology at approximately the same time.

Functional Theory

The first functional analysis of religion in anthropology is attributed to Emile Durkheim, who expressed his views in *Elementary Forms of Religious Life*. Durkheim begins with the claim that his intention is to search for the origin of religion by examining the beliefs and practices of Australian aborigines. Such a step parallels much of the work done at the turn of the century. What is unique about Durkheim's is that the concern with origin is secondary to his analysis of the interrelation between religion and the rest of society. This concern with functional relations dominates the book.

Durkheim's theory is often condensed into a statement indicating that he equated God with society. It might be more accurate to say he saw religion as a

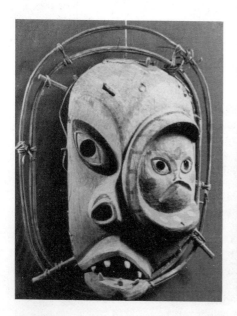

FIGURE 31

Eskimo masks, whether carved of ivory, whale bone, or wood, show feelings of awe and are used in dance, which is also considered sacred. (Photo of mask courtesy of the Skarland Collection, University of Alaska; dancer by Sue Gamache, Anchorage)

system of symbols justifying values of society, the justification making social life possible. In turn, religion had its basis in society. The circularity in reasoning had to be followed because of the nature of the mutual interdependence between social groups, religious practices, and beliefs.

As illustration of the functional relation, Durkheim described in detail how Australian religion centered on the sacredness of the totem, their religion being commonly described as totemism. Much ritual surrounded the totem, and complex taboos defined its sacredness. Durkheim argued that the symbolic value and the feelings of awe for the totem arose from the fact that the totem represents one's clan. Individual aborigines realized that they could not survive except as members of a clan and that the clan was more than the sum of the individual members. Unconsciously or intuitively, humans regarded social organization with veneration directed at its symbol, the totem of the clan. The implicit omnipotence of the clan is made explicit in its symbol, the totem.

This explanation for an origin of religion is intriguing but inconclusive. Durkheim's major contribution was his argument that a group must maintain its solidarity by symbolic identification and by reaffirmation of its norms. Religious practices, symbols, and beliefs are ideally suited for such a task; they function to perpetuate society because, on one hand, they restrict individual whims while, on the other hand, they provide common values and activities.

The initial functional theory suggested two approaches to the study of religion. First, what does religion do for individuals and the society in which they live? Second, what are the functional relations between religion and the rest of society? Two English anthropologists led the attack on these questions, and their answers laid the foundation for most current theory.

Bronislaw Malinowski countered evolutionism by describing Trobriand culture as comprised of magic, religion, and science. The three institutions were analyzed as components rather than stages. Each practice fulfilled different functions for the individuals. The empirical knowledge, or science, provided important control over activities such as gardening. The Trobrianders' extensive knowledge of plants, soils, and tilling practices compared favorably with Western science. However, in years of drought, the elements proved more powerful than human knowledge. Under such stress, people turned to the supernatural. Malinowski's classic example centered on fishing practices. In the calm lagoon waters, Islanders used a simple, reliable method of poisoning; but, on open seas, fishing was dangerous and yields varied widely. In the lagoon, people relied entirely on their empirical knowledge; in the high sea, though using virtually the same technology, the activity was intermeshed with magic, ritual, and numerous prayers. Religion was vital in providing the endurance for dangerous undertakings and in giving people confidence during uncertain times.

Malinowski expanded this functional explanation to account for the use of religion to meet the needs of individuals whenever they were under stress. Everywhere people face such crises as birth, puberty, marriage, illness, and death. Almost everywhere, religions focus on these events and provide rites of passage or ways for transcending the crisis. Malinowski noted that religion accomplished its purposes not simply as a psychological crutch but also by its stress on the positive aspects of social life. He emphasized how religion functioned to strengthen the bonds of social cohesion.

In a similar vein, A. R. Radcliffe-Brown noted the connection between religion and the rest of culture in a theory that owes much to Durkheim. For instance, Radcliffe-Brown describes ritual as the "regulated symbolic expression" of certain collective sentiments. In turn, such sentiments are further generated and consensus is made more certain because of ritual expression. Any orderly social life essentially is dependent upon agreement and consensus among members, a range of agreement that can be achieved only by sharing and continual expression of common sentiments. Thus, the specific function of ritual is to regulate and to transmit between generations the sentiments forming the basis of society.

Malinowski and Radcliffe-Brown contradicted each other on some points but in retrospect their differences were minor. The two made functional explanation a basic ingredient of anthropology. Malinowski stressed what religion did for individuals while Radcliffe-Brown analyzed how society was organized on a foundation of religious thought and practice. Their approach set the framework of analysis for modern theory.

The results of the approach are well-summarized by Raymond Firth. He emphasizes the need to understand religious life within its particular framework. Using new developments from psychology as well as anthropology, Firth made much more explicit the functions of religion for the individual. He shows how the psychological processes of rationalism, projection, and identification constitute much of myth, ritual, and belief, as well as help people to adjust. He concludes that religion provides a referent for the explanation of the main social events that require a meaning, while social life itself provides solutions to the common problems of coping with the natural environment. This essential social life is rife with the disadvantages of rivalry, factionalism, and even violence. While secular social controls reduce some of this conflict, religious controls reduce it even further. For example, religion regulates rivalry by justifying different ranks. Sorcery and witchcraft provide more acceptable explanations of continual social failure rather than recognition of simple human inadequacy. Furthermore, such practices channel aggressive impulses in less disruptive ways than open conflict. Religion provides a unity through its symbolism, supplies principles of order, provides a frame of reference for attitudes toward nature, supports systems of authority, and adds stability to other social relations. It further allows expression of imagination and aesthetic feelings. From the carved masks of hunters and gatherers to the cathedrals of technological society, the finest art is based on religion; likewise, religious thought has promoted much development of the humanities, from poetry to philosophy.

Structural Theory and Symbolic Anthropology

Functional interpretations monopolized anthropological analysis of religion until recently, when Claude Lévi-Strauss provided a new approach generally known as *structuralism*. However, since Lévi Strauss' structure arises from the nature of thought, it is fundamentally different from the that of the structural–functionalists who saw structure arising from the conditions of social life. While Durkheim clearly influenced Lévi-Strauss, as reflected by his continued study of totemism and classification, the latter concentrated on how symbols are expressed and related to each other. Lévi-Strauss found the symbols of myth and ritual especially appropriate for study.

In ritual, and particularly in myth, symbols are organized to encourage speculative thought; Lévi- Strauss expressed it as, "Totems are good to think." By manipulating some kinds of symbols, problems with other kinds of symbols may be resolved. That is, emphasis must be on the structure rather than the content of a myth, as structure is the relationship among symbols. Objects of everyday life, such as animals, become sacred because relations between them are analogous to more problematic relations. For instance, Lévi-Strauss argues that people everywhere are concerned with a contrast between culture and nature and with the position of humans in relation to both. In myth, the opposition between the two may be expressed and then resolved by illustrating how a carrion-eating animal stands between or mediates an opposition between a wild, meat-eating beast and a domestic herbivore. Symbols of myth from all parts of the world express an interest in life and death, maleness and femaleness, incest and marriage, fertility and infertility, nature and culture, good and evil, or even, apparently, mundane issues such as right and left.

The study of symbols in myth coincides with recognition of linguists that sounds are symbols not only for material objects but also for actions and thoughts. In their initial interest in the subject, anthropologists were impressed at the lack of any patterned relationships between a sound and its *referent*—that is, the thing it stood for. The sounds in "hombre" were just as effective as the sounds in "man" to stand for a male human being. thus, anthropologists insisted that *symbols* were arbitrary signs for a referent; they had to have *conventional* meanings. People had to come to agree that a symbol was to mean something; there was nothing in its nature to specify its referent. Thus, few people outside of the Soviet Union ever thought of the bear as a symbol of the U.S.S.R. until that nation became a superpower. Of course, it makes no more sense that the Soviet Union should be symbolized by a bear than it does that the U.S.A. should be represented by an eagle but, once citizens had agreed on these symbols as conventional shorthand signs of a nation, they became filled with meanings. A U.S. citizen can see the eagle as proud, strong, and vigilant; a Latin American may view the eagle as rapacious, threatening, and vicious.

Surely much symbolism must be conventional and arbitrary. It reaches an obvious peak in mathematics where we might let x stand for the sum of two parts and y stand for the quotient of two other factors, and then jump to political science where we can casually say let x stand for North Vietnam and North Korea while y stands for South Vietnam and South Korea. Can there possibly be anything but an arbitrary relation between a symbol and its referent? At the same time that many social scientists and linguists were repeatedly announcing the relationship was arbitrary, psychoanalysts argued that a number of symbols clearly arose from the nature of the referent. In his study of dreams of his Viennese patients, Freud learned that falling symbolized a lack of security in interacting with the opposite sex or that the loss of teeth expressed guilt about masturbation. Symbols like these were sorted out by psychoanalysts with recognition that something in the human brain must turn to some sets of objects as symbols more often than other groups of objects. As anthropologists became aware of Freud's work, they immediately wanted to know if all peoples symbolized in the same way.

The evidence for universal symbolizing is mixed. Cross-cultural dream analysis cannot go very far because not many dreams have been recorded outside the West. However, Freud discovered that some of the symbols occurring in his patients' dreams are also common in mythology. Male and female genital symbols occur in the same way from legends and myths around the world. Myths also symbolize birth, marriage, and death in similar ways. Not just sex but the total relationship between male and female also seems symbolized in similar ways. Likewise, the father-son, mother-daughter, sister-brother relationships are symbolized in patterned ways.

Thus, anthropology has faced the dilemma of most symbols seeming to be totally conventional while, on the other hand, the symbols of myth recur over and over. Could there possibly be something in the psyche that controlled symbol-making? The obvious answer was yes and no. The evidence is overwhelming that some symbols are purely conventional. The fact that the sound "si" can stand for "sea," "see," and also the letter "C" is clear evidence to negate any built-in relationship between symbol and referent. At first glance, we might also assume that the red and white stripes of the American flag, a powerful symbol for many of us, are also completely arbitrary. Surely black and white could serve just as well. But, could pink and orange stripes call forth equally strong patriotic feelings? Doesn't it seem likely that symbols make use of contrast or, more accurately, that the human brain responds differently to contrast than to similarity?

Such a line of questioning led to the modern development of Lévi-Strauss' analysis and to *cognitive* or *symbolic anthropology*. Lévi-Strauss turned from the study of symbols themselves, as Freud had studied symbolism, to the structure of relationships between symbols. His work came at a time when psychologists began pursuing new lines of human perception or cognition, and the combination of psychology and Lévi-Strauss led to cognitive anthropology. This new branch asks how humans form a view of the world and, to get an answer, one has to discover how people organize and classify the world. What is most interesting from this line of investigation is the remarkable similarity that exists in organizing knowledge. Time and again we have been impressed with how nonliterate peoples classify plants and animals, their groupings coming quite close to the taxonomy of modern biology. In short, the branching out from the general to the particular seems to be a part of human thought everywhere. And, as we discover more and more similarity in thought, we will surely see that many symbols are far more than conventions; or, even where symbols may be arbitrary, symbolizing is built into the nature of the brain. Obviously, the field is one that has far more questions than it does answers, but it promises to be a most fruitful area.

Summary

Although early anthropologists were very interested in religion, its understanding has not developed as well as other fields within the discipline. Anthropologists have clarified a number of basic concepts, beginning with the division that many peoples make of the world into sacred and profane. The *profane* is the everyday or ordinary place, person, or time; the sacred is *extraordinary*. It is something that is unusual and dangerous. Many people have found a word for the extraordinary potency of a power that inhabits the sacred. Anthropologists call it *mana*, a word borrowed from Oceania. Events, things, or persons with mana are marked off with warnings. The warnings can be symbols or proscriptions surrounding mana; the proscriptions are *taboos*. A taboo act is a forbidden act. Objects with mana may simply be hidden away from the secular world; even humans with mana are at times isolated.

In most societies, everyone may have mana sometime; that is, individuals may approach the extraordinary or supernatural and experience mana. Often, some individuals are regarded as being especially able to handle mana because of a dream or semitrance experience. These individuals are called *shamans*. The shaman suddenly acquires the ability to use mana and must demonstrate unusual or extraordinary ability. Common demonstrations are speaking in tongues or handling red-hot objects. Trickery may also be used. In other societies priests will be associated with mana. *Priests* undergo a long, systematic training and use organized drama, such as singing, praying, and dancing to illustrate their extraordinary ability. Priesthoods are usually composed of males. Although their knowledge is often quite extensive, priests spend much of their secular time like other males. *Clergy*, however, are fulltime specialists in religion, in everyday English called ministers, priests, or preachers. The clergy are organized into corporate sects with highly complex dogma and systematic codes of morality.

All societies have an individualistic approach to the supernatural; most also have persons like shamans, who may be called *medicine men* or *medicine women* if they have extensive herbal knowledge, or witches if they divine or cause illness and death. *Witches* do not know that they are harming others; *sorcerers* deliberately attempt to harm others. In studying society, anthropologists find little effects of witchcraft and sorcery, but they analyze *accusations* of witchcraft and sorcery. These accusations are significant in many processes, and the accusations reveal much about the divisions and groupings within a society. Both witches and sorcerers may be regarded as shamans and will be found almost everywhere, even in modern societies. Priests are not as widespread and generally occur only where agriculture is developed. They sometimes act much like shamans, or a shaman may direct a priestly activity. Clergy, in contrast, usually belittle priests and shamans. As fulltime workers, they are restricted to state societies, but they seem to have appeared with the early city-states. They added architecture to the dramatic inventory of religious wares, and developed dogma and theologies that justified much of the state's actions, but clergy never became the only religious practitioners. Individualistic, shamanistic, and priestly approaches to the supernatural occur even in contemporary nation-states.

Neither has magic disappeared in the modern world, but its concept has limited use in anthropology. Initially, *magic* was defined as the deliberate attempts to control the supernatural while religion was recognition of an omnipotent supernatural, with one only able to stand in awe of it. Such a distinction was used in proposing social evolutionary stages of magic to religion to science but, in practice, particular events are difficult to categorize. If the President of the United States asked the nation to pray for rain, an observer might conclude Americans were compelling their God to end a drought. Is it useful to analyze such an event as magical rather than religious? Description of magic as *imitative* or *contagious* did, however, focus our thinking on how much alike people are in approaching the supernatural. All over the world, peoples initiate an event they want to happen or they use parts of something in order to affect the whole. Such a discovery led to concentration on psychological processes in religion.

For example, Westerners often puzzle over why people continue to believe in their religion when a shaman fails to cure or predicts wrongly. Of course, most times patients do become well, regardless of treatment, and outcomes can be well guessed or put in ambiguous terms. But, most importantly, there are always *rationalizations*. The shaman was right in diagnosis and gave good treatment, but a stronger shaman wanted the patient dead. Religion is likewise valuable as *explanation*. We do not know why people want the answers they do, but religion clearly provides answers for much of the unknown. It helps resolve problems, sometimes natural but more often created by human failings. Given such importance in human society, it is not surprising that considerable theory has developed to explain why religion exists.

The early theory of anthropology was cast along evolutionary lines, with major emphasis on discovering the origin of religion. Generally, theorists assumed that the most "primitive" people, such as Australian aborigines, had the simplest religions and ones most like the beginning one. Edward Tylor, however, used religious practices from all over the world to devise his theory of *animism*. It stated that experiences such as dreams and hallucinations led early people to conclude that a spirit must inhabit humans and lived on after death of the body. A belief in spirits was Tylor's "minimal definition" of religion and represented its origin. Sir James Frazer presented the case for religion arising from magic, magic being trial-and-error. As the futility of magic was recognized, humans turned to awe of the supernatural world, recognizing that it controlled them instead.

None of this theory particularly satisfied the next generation. Early in the 20th century, an Austrian school of ethnology attempted to recreate the historical growth of religion rather than construct an origin. The recreation was based on an assumption that humanity had started in central Asia and spread out in successive waves, or *kulturkriese*, from there. The wave farthest from the center represented the earliest form of religion. The psychoanalytic theory of Sigmund Freud was contemporary with the kulturkreise method, but radically different in content. It proposed the origin of religion lies in sexual jealousy of sons against their fathers. When some primeval horde killed their father, members suddenly recognized their guilt, made their father a totemic ancestor or supernatural figure, and created religion as a part of social life. Freud had caught the emotional aspect of religion, and his connection between religion and social life became a basic part of functional theory.

Emile Durkheim laid the basis for *functional theory* which concentrates on the mutual relations among the parts of society and culture. Durkheim illustrated this relationship with the totemism of Australian aborigines. Their major religious activity centered on the totem or symbol of the clan. Durkheim argued that the complexity of clan life inspired awe in the aborigines, and their emotional respect was directed toward the symbolic representation of the clan, the totem. Sociologists were influenced by Durkheim in their study of society; in anthropology, Bronislaw Malinowski and A. R. Radcliffe-Brown followed Durkheim in relating religion to all parts of culture while also detailing the relationship between religion and kin groups.

In France, functionalism was reinterpreted by Lévi-Strauss. Most social scientists see society and culture as consisting of patterned relations because of the nature of group life. That is, group life is structured and leads to structuring of its symbols. Lévi-Strauss argued the opposite. He believes that human thought is structured and that the structure of thinking will be imposed on symbols, society, and culture. He has studied symbols ranging from face paintings to totems to mythology. What he sees in all these symbols is a structured opposition. In mythology, this opposition consists of unanswerable questions raised by differences such as between life and death or male and female. To resolve these differences, parallel oppositions are constructed, such as herbivore and carnivore, which are resolved by some mediating symbol, such as a scavenger.

While Lévi-Strauss has been most influential, many anthropologists remain unconvinced that structure originates in the brain. However, he certainly stimulated *symbolic analysis* in anthropology so contemporary work has concentrated on the analysis of symbolism. Early thinking emphasized the arbitrary nature between the symbol and its referent. Linguistic theory and the structuralism of Lévi-Strauss have sought to find patterned or regular relationships between symbols and their referents, a search begun by Sigmund Freud. While Freud concentrated on the symbol itself, Lévi-Strauss analyzed the relationships among symbols, or what is called *structure*.

While some of the most exciting work in anthropology is now in the realm of religion, it remains one of the least understood phenomena in the cultural repertoire. Certainly, it is an area that deserves more attention, and it still raises the intriguing question as to why peoples everywhere, and probably since at least the Neandertals, have practiced religion.

12

*Anthropology and Public Policy*_____

Although anthropologists have studied exotic peoples and pursued problems with no apparent practical value, we have always been concerned about people and their everyday lives. The earliest anthropological societies of Paris and London became embroiled in factional fights over slavery almost as soon as they formed. The abolitionist factions were the ones that remained the core of the professional groups. Those members who wished to remain "purely" scientific, at least in their association, usually found themselves in the minority.

The two individuals frequently considered the discipline's founding fathers also found time to pursue policy issues as well as academic matters. In England, Edward Tylor expressed the need for cultural relativism very well by warning that anthropology must not measure "other people's grain by our own basket"; yet he did not follow this principle to its logical conclusion that anthropology should be value free. Elsewhere, he deplored slavery and stressed his belief in human equality. In the United States, Lewis Henry Morgan, a lawyer and ethnographer of the Iroquois, studied such topics as kinship, house types, and ritual but, in between his interviews to reconstruct the Iroquois past, Morgan found time to defend Indian land claims of the present. The work he did benefitted other Indians by the precedent he set for the Iroquois.

Origins of Applied Anthropology

At the turn of the century, anthropologists found themselves involved in further long-range policy making. In France, Holland, and England, study of the political organization of colonial peoples became well established as a part of anthropology. Professional anthropologists went to the colonies and made detailed studies of indigenous law, economics, and politics. In retrospect, this work has been questioned because it might have been used to continue colonialism and enforce the suppression of native peoples. One defense against this charge is that anthropologists wrote such lengthy and detailed monographs that administrators in the colonies seldom read the reports. However, a better defense is that the anthropologists clearly were concerned about native peoples and did alleviate everyday sufferings of indigenous peoples. While they might have contributed to long-term colonial policy, they achieved short-term goals that helped local people. On a smaller scale, a similar development was happening in the United States at this time. The Bureau of American Ethnology was established to examine and record the cultures and languages of American Indians and peoples in the Philippines. Its interest in Indians was largely confined to such topics as language and folklore. However, in 1890 when a new religion known as the Ghost Dance swept the Plains and was thought to have led to a massacre of Sioux at Wounded Knee, anthropologist James Mooney investigated the social movement in detail. His description of the event led to reform within the Bureau of Indian Affairs, and the report helped Indian agents understand something of the religion and politics on the reservations.

Such work served as a foundation to employ anthropologists in the Bureau of Indian Affairs in the 1930s. Even then, however, Congress resisted funding such work, but Commissioner of Indian Affairs John Collier managed to hire a few anthropologists to investigate Indian political organization in order to help develop self-government. Other anthropologists examined the schools operated by the Bureau of Indian Affairs. The anthropologists investigating politics spent as much as a year in their research, requiring even more time to write their reports. The politics of Washington did not allow such time; eventually, Collier had to depend on lawyers to draft the necessary legislation for self-government. This part of his program is generally judged a failure for anthropology. The anthropologists were at fault for not recognizing the immediate demands upon their employer, but anthropology had learned an important lesson. One must be aware of the culture of the dominant society as well as the subordinate one.

The anthropologists investigating education were not so pressed for time. Their research led to such recommendations as using cooperation in the classroom rather than competition, competition being considered immoral by most Indians because of close, personal relations. Anthropologists also helped produce textbooks so Indian children first learned to read in their own language before having to learn to read English. Also, some of this research called upon teachers to help with interviewing. Their assistance gave the teachers their first opportunity to visit the homes of the school children. The experience led to much better understanding between parents and teachers, an unexpected result of the research.

The outcome of this work is reported in books on the Navajo, Hopi, Papago, and Sioux or Dakota that are popular introductions to contemporary reservation life as well as descriptions of education and personality formation in children. The researchers, most of them women, laid a solid foundation for a Society of Applied Anthropology and made applied work respectable in the field. More importantly, they convinced a number of politicians in Washington that anthropology could contribute important information for the formulation of public policy, although Congress has frequently confused cultural anthropology with archaeology. Thus, it often fails to appreciate proposals that involve anthropologists in programs to improve health, agriculture, or education.

Anthropology and Policy Making in World War II

At the outbreak of World War II, a number of anthropologists were employed by the Federal government to help the war effort. Most of them were placed in the Office of War Information, a bureau that undertook a variety of cross-cultural comparisons. For example, personnel from the Bureau of Indian Affairs were transferred to temporary camps established for Japanese living on the West coast. These people, some of them Japanese citizens but many of them American citizens, were judged to be a security risk. They were forced to relocate into something like Army barracks. Anthropologists served as staff at these camps, helping make decisions ranging from whether to serve food cafeteria-style or allow families to prepare their own meals, to a major issue as to what kind of employment was suitable for these imprisoned citizens.

Eventually, they worked at a variety of tasks ranging from picking cotton to making camouflage netting. Some prisoners were even recruited into the U.S. Army while, in contrast, a group at one camp rioted in protest of conditions. This fascinating range of events and the work of applied anthropologists is well described by Alexander Leighton in *The Governing of Men*. Relocation policy was so controversial that it remains an issue today with Congress regularly attempting to determine a just compensation for the victims.

Other anthropologists undertook the task of analyzing Japanese culture. Always before, anthropologists felt they had to live among the people they studied. Yet Ruth Benedict and Margaret Mead demonstrated how a culture could be studied at a distance. Benedict's book, *The Chrysanthemum and the Sword*, was influential in the Allies' decision to retain the Emperor in post-war Japan. The decision was unpopular at the time, but it seems to have been most effective in providing both stability and a gradual development of democracy. Interestingly, the book had the unintended effect of stimulating post-war Japanese social scientists to examine their own culture more closely. This work has been fundamental in understanding modern Japan. While Mead had assisted Benedict, most of her energy was directed at an analysis of American culture. Her book *And Keep Your Powder Dry* has inspired work in American studies as well as in anthropology. Still other anthropologists reported their findings on the national character of England and of the Soviet Union. This work was probably much more influential in public policy making than the earlier work of applied anthropologists in the British and French colonies.

At the end of World War II, the United States undertook the rebuilding of the European economy through the Marshall Plan. It was a remarkably successful experiment in development, so much so that European countries soon competed with the United States in a number of industries. With the development of Europe accomplished, the Western countries set out to help Third World countries. For these quite different peoples, it seemed logical to employ anthropologists to assist in the process.

Neither the anthropologists nor the West seemed to achieve much success in this work when compared to the war years and European recovery. For anthropology, many of the limitations are now seen to be a result of limited effort. Comparatively few anthropologists were hired and their efforts were widely scattered. They worked to persuade villagers in a few selected communities to adopt new practices in health, agriculture, education, and sometimes politics. As they reported on the great variety of ways in which villagers managed to avoid or disrupt change, the field seemed to be compiling a cookbook of recipes for success, although the recipes were largely based on failures to innovate or to achieve goals. Thus, it was only in retrospect that anthropologists made successful analyses.

Developmental Anthropology

By the 1950s, anthropology had convinced foreign aid administrators that introducing technological change in underdeveloped countries was no simple matter. Even small innovations had many unanticipated effects, not all of them desirable. A new fertilizer, for example, could improve crop yields, but it also might increase land values. Greater land values lead to urban investments and control. Absentee landowners make poor farmers while the local farmer is losing the land. Supposedly, the innovation was to have helped the local farmer. The lesson that the road to hell is paved with good intentions was engraved in anthropological experience.

A still more important lesson emerged during this period: Technological innovations at the village level have important political consequences beyond the village. New technology that raises the living standards of poor people is interpreted as a threat to established elites who have traditionally controlled the peasantry. Wealthy landowners, as well as their immediate underlings, oppose change in distribution of wealth, even when it need not lower their own income. Especially threatening are any changes that have the potential of giving more control over their lives to peasant peoples. Of course, such change is precisely what most anthropologists foresee and want to encourage. Frequently, however, the anthropologist has failed to appreciate the conflict that will be generated with those in power.

The problem is well illustrated by an applied anthropology project in Peru undertaken by Cornell University. Peru had long interested anthropology because of its Incan civilization and long prehistory. Anthropologists also realized that millions of descendants of this civilization were still living in the Andes, most of them in poverty. In the immediate post-war years, the Peruvian Indians existed virtually as serfs. An attempt to change these circumstances began in the Vicos Valley where the *hacienda* of Vicos was leased by Cornell. For a year, the anthropologists did little more than study the situation; in the second year, they introduced a few new techniques such as planting a new variety of potato. In the third and fourth years, they made such changes as allowing the profits from the better harvests to be invested back into the community. The most dramatic change was to bring the adults into a kind of town council meeting and let them discover that they could make decisions for their own community. The investment the Indians most wanted was education for their children, something that the Peruvian government had provided only in token form.

The *Vicoseños* readily took to democratic control of their village. They easily managed the innovations that Cornell anthropologists initiated, and they were soon starting their own changes. The standard of living notably improved, but the changeover to democratic control was an even greater achievement. The final step in the process was for the Indians to purchase the land of their community. Besides education, this had been a major goal for them and they had regularly saved in order to buy the land. However, by this time, the original owner had sold the hacienda to a charitable organization and the directors of the charity asked a greater price. Ironically, the hacienda had increased in value because of the Indians' efforts and their innovations. It is hard to fault the directors for protecting the interests of their charity by raising the price; fortunately, the Vicoseños set about overcoming this obstacle, too. The next year they were able to pay the new price and to become owners of their land.

Alan Holmberg, the anthropologist who directed the Vicos project, could be proud of what he had helped the Vicoseños do, but he also had cause for regrets. As Indians in the valleys next to Vicos learned about the advantages their neighbors were receiving, they came to have similar expectations. The owners of their haciendas, however, had no intention of allowing change, let alone promoting it. The hacienderos called in federal police when their renters, actually serfs, demanded change. Outbreaks between land owners and peasants led to several deaths. Certainly, Holmberg cannot be blamed for the deaths, but the changes he had helped to achieve at Vicos were a part of the regional disruption.

For Holmberg, the incident drove home the point that his success had been limited to one village in one valley. He had changed the lives of perhaps a thousand peasants at Vicos, but millions of other Indians in Peru had not been touched by technological change and social reform. In some countries, it may require a national revolution to bring the fundamental changes to effect the education and democracy that will end serfdom. Clearly, technology cannot be isolated from politics, but making changes in national governments is a complex issue far removed from the experience of anthropology.

Ethics in Anthropology

Soon after the Vicos experiment, anthropologists and other social scientists found themselves in similar, unanticipated political troubles. In parts of Latin America, for instance, the State Department sponsored research that seemed designed simply to measure public opinion and certain attitude changes. As the work progressed, a few researchers suspected that some information could be used by a governing elite to maintain its power. Pursuing their suspicions, the scientists discovered that part of their work was being used by the CIA to advise governments in their policy decisions. They were working to keep certain current governments in power. The situation led to major soul-searching and improved formulation of explicit ethics in applied research among the social sciences.

At about the same time, the U.S. war effort in Vietnam began to expand and to include social science research. Anthropologists were among the early opponents of the war, but they were not unanimous in their opposition. The discipline thus faced the problem: Could some anthropologists dictate what their colleagues could or could not do? The American Anthropological Association debated the issue at length during national meetings. A clear majority opposed U.S. policy in Vietnam, but the association did not move to license anthropologists nor did it sanction anyone supporting the war effort. In retrospect, the anthropologists who had helped gather information for formulating public policy generally regretted the ways in which their research was used. Some individuals felt they had been used by the U.S. government which had misled them in mis-stating the objectives of the research. Other anthropologists believed their work was twisted in order to support policy already ordained by the military or intelligence services. Instead of using research to make policy, research results were rationalized to support policy already decided.

Perhaps the greatest problem to emerge from the Southeast Asian conflict was discovery of the extent to which basic anthropological findings can be used by military or covert organizations. A dramatic illustration of this problem was described by a French ethnologist whose grandmother had been Vietnamese. He had become an expert on the hill peoples of Indochina, tribesmen who later became favorite recruits of the CIA. Since these people often engaged in intertribal warfare, the agents of the dominant society sometimes found themselves fighting mini-wars in order to secure the allegiance of a major hill tribe. Thus, a standard ethnographic description that included such usual topics as political organization and patterns of leadership became useful military information. Even a sketch map of a local village might acquire tactical value over night.

The French ethnologist might never have known how his work had been used except that an American congratulated him for the English publication. (The researcher had had his monograph refused by several English publishers because of lack of demand; even a French publisher had been hard to find.) Surprised to find that the translation had been published by the U.S. Department of Commerce, an American colleague explained that it was likely covert funding by the CIA that had enabled publication, and subsequent use by CIA agents.

For a while, some anthropologists began to wonder if they could be responsible persons and still publish any material on other cultures. No one could have foreseen the kind of use made of the ethnography about the hill peoples of Vietnam. Yet, because of the nature of world politics, any area of the world is a potential battlefield, and what are purely scientific data one day can be tactical facts the next day. Most anthropologists have resolved this paradox by continuing with their research but recognizing that, wherever their finds might reasonably be expected to be of some value in military operations, they have a special obligation to protect the welfare of the people they are studying. This ethical principle is a major one for all applied social scientists. Needless to add, anthropologists must pay particular attention to this obligation because the communities and people they study are often quite unaware of the dangers from the dominant societies of the world.

National and International Issues

More and more, anthropologists also recognized they must not focus entirely on the community level. The Vicos project was a vivid example of this limitation. What good did it do to help change one village if a thousand other villages remained the same? At least it proved such change was possible, and it made clear to us in the 1960s that the source of many problems did not lie within a community or with villagers but with governments or multinational businesses. Anthropologists had to recognize regional and national concerns, and those making public policy would have to learn the social organization of national bureaucracies and international businesses as well as village factions. Success at this level has been infrequent, but at least anthropologists now know to anticipate problems at such levels.

The difficulties are aptly illustrated by a case of applied anthropology among the Sioux Indians of South Dakota. On the Pine Ridge Reservation, near Mount Rushmore, unemployment ranges between 30 and 50 percent. The Bureau of Indian Affairs and the tribal government spend much effort in attracting or creating any kind of industry that will provide jobs. One prospective employer was a sporting goods company manufacturing much of America's fishing equipment. One of their major products is fishhooks, and the company employed many workers simply to tie a nylon leader to the metal fishhook, a simple task requiring only two knots.

The work was ideal for a reservation. Typically, reservations are isolated so that they are far from markets and unattractive to management. They have few or no natural resources, and their workforce is unskilled and under-educated. To overcome these disadvantages, the government and the tribe operate programs to subsidize industry. Through a job training program, beginning salaries of the workers were paid by the Bureau of Indian Affairs while the tribe provided buildings and even some of the utilities for industry. The sporting goods industry could send a station wagon from its Denver center with enough fishhooks and nylon leaders for a week's work, picking up the tied and packaged hooks on its return trip. The work called for the simplest kind of supervision so local people could be trained as managers. While these advantages may seem quite important to some urban dwellers, they should be aware that many rural white towns, suffering high unemployment, are able to make similar offers. Of course, they also suffer from the same problems.

After some preliminary negotiation, industry officials visited the reservation and asked to see Indian volunteers tie fishhooks. An anthropologist in the Bureau of Indian Affairs had selected some skilled craftsmen for the demonstration, individuals who tied deer hair to make a dance costume. These men were quite slow because they took so much pride in their work that they wanted perfect knots. They never thought of time as being important in craft production. The experiment almost brought an end to the industry's interest. However, the problem was finally recognized, new workers were selected, and the Sioux quickly demonstrated they were as able as other workers. Indeed, they were judged as one of the best workforces employed by the company.

When the work first began, problems of absenteeism and worker turnover occurred as workers enjoyed their first, relatively high incomes. Many bought the few material things they had wanted and quit working. This problem is common to poor people everywhere; the company understood it and made accommodations. Within a few months, the Sioux matured into an able, efficient workforce. A second factory was added and employment exceeded the most optimistic early projections. The usual forms of applied anthropology had been both a hindrance and a help. The selection of craftsmen who took pride in their work had been inappropriate in providing a sample. On the other hand, work in social science has made management see that flexible work schedules can accommodate differing work patterns.

Yet, the greatest lesson in policy making came a few years later with circumstances that vividly point up the necessity to understand problems on a global scale. A competing sporting goods company opened fishhook tying factories in Mexico, paying workers well below the minimum wage in the United States. The Mexican government provided further subsidies because the exports brought dollars into the Mexican economy. For a year, the major sporting goods company maintained its factories at Pine Ridge, operating at no profit but figuring the advertising on hundreds of thousands of fishhook packages was to its advantage. However, a third competitor started factories in Asia, where the cost of labor was even lower than in Mexico. The factories at Pine Ridge were forced to close. Nothing in the small community could be changed to accommodate to low wage scales on the other side of the world. United States law determined the minimum wage but, even if Indians could have accepted lower pay, they would have had difficulty living on it. In the American economy, of course, the community was expected to compete by finding some new industry. To some extent this has happened. Electronic assembly plants are now operating on some reservations but with numerous indirect subsidies from the Federal government. It is a situation that requires as much expertise in politics and economics as in anthropology. Above all it requires understanding that even the most remote communities are now part of a global economic system.

Urban Anthropology

The complexity of modern problems is likewise reflected in work being undertaken by anthropologists in the cities. As urban problems multiplied in the 1960s and a variety of solutions were attempted, anthropologists began helping to formulate policy for urban areas. They were well prepared for such tasks as working with street gangs or describing life in an ethnic enclave. They also used their skills as participant-observers to analyze occupations such as those of railroaders or longshoremen. Such work overlapped the interests of sociologists at times, but the two disciplines differed often in their research methods and particularly in their perspective of problems.

Probably the greatest difference between sociology and anthropology occurred in the perspective on human relations. Sociologists regularly contrast the impersonality of the city with the close personal ties of rural life. This perspective developed early in social science with ideas of social evolution. It is reflected in the work of Emile Durkheim. One of his best known concepts, *anomie* or a state of normlessness, is particularly associated with the supposed impersonality of urbanism. Repeatedly, anthropologists have found a remarkable persistence of kinship and similar group ties in the urban setting. For example, in the large modern West African cities, much of urban life is organized around both clan and tribal ties. Similar phenomena are reported for Indonesia and Nationalist China, mainly in Taipei on Taiwan. Often, the functions of a clan may change and the clans take on some of the characteristics of associations. Thus, some Chinese clans have become largely credit cooperatives or the basis for political ties to newly developing parties; yet, the core of these clans remains a unilineal descent group and such traits as veneration of the ancestors show an enduring persistence. This pattern of continuing kin ties or similar organization with an emphasis on personal relations is demonstrated for numerous cities in *Urban Anthropology*, a book edited by Aidan Southall.

Other kinds of research and their implications for urban policy making may be illustrated by a study of skid row in the city of Chicago, where one of the authors learned participant-observation. Urban planners had plotted a new freeway through the heart of skid row located on West Madison Street. Its construction would cause many of the hotels and other facilities used by the men occupying the area to be demolished. Similar projects in other cities had displaced such men; their movement simply caused blight in some other area. Chicago hoped to avoid this problem by building special housing in advance to serve the needs of the skid row population. Thus, the city asked social scientists to determine what kind of housing the men would like; what they could afford; and on what areas they desired to live. To comprehend such problems fully, the survey was extended to determine the general life styles of these men.

One of the most important discoveries of this research was to find that the men differed greatly from the stereotype of them. The drunken bum image was a poor one, indeed. The overwhelming factor that determined residence on West Madison Street was economic; the men who lived there could afford no place else. To be sure, some alcoholics spent all their money on liquor, so they had to live on skid row. However, the large majority of the men were living on the minimum pension paid by social security, or they held jobs that provided work only part of the year, such as railroad employment, or they were handicapped or illiterate. Some men were immigrants who were afraid they had not completed all citizenship requirements and the government might deport them; they sought only temporary employment and maximum mobility in order to keep their anonymity.

Ironically, the men, too, held some of the general stereotypes of the larger community. Madison Street was divided by a major thoroughfare, and the men tended to stay east or west of the thoroughfare even though many of them changed hotels at frequent intervals. In effect, two communities had formed along the street. Inhabitants of each division viewed the other side as living depraved lives. Those "on the other side" were thought to be homosexual, alcoholic, ignorant, mentally handicapped, or lawless. Each community saw the other group as highly impersonal and exhibiting the usual traits of anomie. In fact, both sides could be seen as communities, and many of the men in them had developed a network of personal ties. The retirees, especially, were often stable in their residence and reported that they had a number of friends in the area. Skid row was a home to them.

Men also had regular ties with associations in the area that personalized their lives as community members. A branch of the Chicago public library was quite popular, partly because it provided clean toilet facilities and warmth in the winter, but any visitor could see that its newspapers and journals were popular along with its books. The facilities were used so much that the librarian had to limit the time a man could spend inside, something no other branch ever even imagined. Although rumors abounded of how Chicago police victimized the men, we found that very few of the men ever had an unfavorable experience with the police. In fact, the men usually had stories of how particular police had aided them on some occasion. The only agencies consistently described as unfair were private employment agencies. Workers felt that the agencies kept them on a job only a week or two for fear that an employer might hire the men permanently rather than continue to use the agency.

From the researchers' perspective, the greatest difficulty most of the men experienced was in housing. The interviewing was conducted in January and February because only the bitter cold drove all the men on skid row inside. Yet, even then, some men were seen sleeping under bridges on occasion. The rooms were about eight by five feet, the minimum then prescribed by Chicago housing ordinances. Ventilation was provided by a ceiling that consisted only of chicken coop wiring. Walls were of plaster board or corrugated fiberglass. This kind of construction worked well in former warehouses that had massive space and 12 to 15 foot ceilings; most of the hotels on skid row had once been such buildings.

These warehouses had been built some 50 years earlier when the business core of downtown Chicago was farther away. As the downtown area expanded, the warehousing industry had moved outward to avoid traffic congestion and other problems associated with the core, while the buildings were left behind. They could not be used for modern offices or expensive apartments but, eventually, the land they occupied would be so used. In short, the location had high potential value, but the buildings would have to be torn down. While waiting for the core to expand in order to utilize the land's potential value, a landlord had few options. It was uneconomical to spend money clearing land until a purchaser was ready to build; meanwhile, the building should be used until it was demolished. By using cheap materials, many rooms could be squeezed into the large space; a rental of even a dollar a night would return some profit. Obviously, however, such a system discouraged landlords from reinvesting any earnings in improvements. A premium was placed on keeping costs to the minimum. Thus, furnishings consisted only of a bed; personnel might be a single room clerk, and the original heating and lighting of the warehouse might still be used. Since it had been designed for the open space of a warehouse, it was totally inappropriate for hotel room use.

It is difficult to make the landlords a villain in this case, although they are far from heroes. Like the hacienda owners of Vicos, some of them managed the property for a worthy cause. The obvious conclusion is that when housing is left to the market and individual enterprise is expected to meet the needs of the urban poor, only the poorest type of housing should be expected. It is a vivid illustration of what applied anthropologists learned the hard way. Most of today's problems are enmeshed in political and economic systems; the source of the problem will usually be in the system and not at the individual level.

Fields of Applied Anthropology

While the Society for Applied Anthropology remains the body for organizing anthropological thought on general public issues, specialization has occurred around three issues which have received continual attention since mid-century. These topics are education, health, and agriculture. Each area was important for American Indians, but intensified study of these problems began when anthropologists started working in Latin America, Asia, and Africa in the post-war era. Eventually, the intensive study of these issues led to the creation of specialized organizations.

For example, the Council on Anthropology and Education is composed of educators and anthropologists whose interests are in the problems of cross-cultural education. Such work began within the Bureau of Indian Affairs in the 1930s when it was obvious that Indian children were not receiving an education comparable to non-Indians despite Federal support for schooling that exceeded most state support. School buildings were often first rate and teacher salaries attracted well-qualified personnel. In its examination of the problem, anthropology at first concentrated on such matters as the nature of curriculum or teaching methods. Textbooks were rewritten to put materials into an appropriate setting, and teachers were advised as to how to maximize cooperation among their students to aid in learning.

Similar issues faced us with the end of the war when the United States became responsible for the Micronesian territory. Suddenly, the government was faced with creating a school system for peoples who had never had one. Imagine the questions that needed answering. What should be included in the curriculum? What should be the language of instruction? What was an appropriate school calendar? So many problems arose in Micronesia that anthropologists and educators typically were faced with solving only the short-term problems. They seldom had time even to ask what place education fills within the wider culture. But this issue overrides the others, and anthropologists began to struggle with it in the 1960s.

As one example, Dakota Indians still had high drop-out rates and low achievement scores in upper grades despite considerable research projects and changes in curriculum and methods. Typically, students did very well the first four years, despite some language handicaps, but soon after fourth grade learning seemed to stop. Students erected a wall between themselves and teachers, and only sports seemed to provide any motivation for high school. This puzzle was compounded by parents who continually expressed great interest in education. Yet, research showed that the schools operated in a social vacuum. A Federal school is directed from Washington. The local community has no control over the formal education of its children. No school board elections ever occur; parents have little idea of what happens in the school. While the problem is only partly resolved, attempts to incorporate the schools into the wider community have made students feel that schooling is a relevant part of their lives. Drop-out rates have declined and scores have improved.

Such experience is being incorporated into urban schools where racial or ethnic differences have created similar problems. Because of its cross-cultural comparative approach, anthropology has been particularly useful in the ghetto, whether it is black or Hispanic. Of course, immediate problems are apparent in the appropriateness of teaching materials and methods but, again, it is the long-term problem of how the school is to be functionally related to the community that is all-important. It is clearly an issue that calls for far more research.

Anthropology's interest in health parallels its interest in education. Among its early problems were how to motivate people to use Western medicine. Where cures were almost immediate, as in the use of penicillin, little motivation was necessary. But, where cures were not so obvious, or especially in the area of preventive medicine, innovations were most difficult. Anthropologists found themselves recording cases of failures in how to persuade people to boil water or to drill wells for safe water. They often had the same luck in campaigns to eradicate mosquitoes or to build sanitary sewers.

Gradually, however, as health workers and anthropologists overcame such problems they were able to compile guidelines that have helped with innovations in health care. Notably, these steps are as effective in modern society as in the small, isolated community. Thus, when the Red Cross mounts a blood drive, it knows it must direct its appeal to opinion-leaders or certain types of individuals whose personal contacts will bring in the largest number of donors. Likewise, in the small nonliterate town it is critical to convince a few influential people to get a test for TB or fight flies; their influence will then sway the rest of the people.

Cooperation between health workers and anthropologists in resolving such problems led to creation of the Society for Medical Anthropology whose members have now turned to broader issues. National budgets or distribution of wealth are usually the major determinants of health care. In some countries, applied research may find ways to motivate people to see doctors or even undertake preventive projects; but, if doctors are unavailable or cement cannot be purchased for a sewer, then the applied anthropology is worthless. Thus, anthropologists are finding themselves more and more involved in national politics and economics despite their immediate interest in health.

The overriding effects of national policy have also been felt by anthropologists who organized into a Council on Nutritional Anthropology and another organization, the Anthropological Study Group on Agrarian Societies. In their initial experiences these anthropologists, too, encountered immediate, everyday types of problems involving food use or food production. Nutritionists who were often involved in trying to get people to change their diets began to find that people without scientific knowledge had somehow discovered important principles about nutrition. For example, the protein in corn lacks lysine which detracts from its protein value. However, the addition of beans adds lysine and fully employs the other amino acids of corn. Thus, succotash—even the word is Indian—is a much more nutritious meal than separate dishes of corn and beans. Equally nutritious combinations have been found in the cuisines of peoples in Asia and Africa. In contrast, anthropologists helped focus research on the value of milk in a diet. They aided in the discovery that many peoples cannot digest milk beyond infancy, and that United States aid to many poor countries was ineffective in adding dry milk to new food preparations.

Anthropological study of so-called primitive farming also brought to light that these systems had far more advantages than realized. In the 1960s, many poor farmers were being converted to chemical fertilizer and pesticide use just before oil price increases would make these innovations very expensive. Fortunately, the earlier techniques, independent of fossil fuels, had not been lost, and these organic methods are being remodeled for contemporary farming. Such techniques are proving useful even in North America where chemicals have caused extensive pollution. Thus, composting techniques, use of natural predators on pests, crop rotation, and similar practices are becoming more widely used. While anthropologists and others have been helpful in evaluating such innovations, we have had to face up to greater problems where solutions are yet to be found. For example, tomato production is rapidly growing because of the fast-food market. The largest farmers, often not owning any land, invest in complex machinery that virtually eliminates human labor. By using machines, their production is the most profitable because of low costs; however, their production per acre is less than that of small farmers using labor. In a world where many people are starving, how do we justify farming that is profitable rather than productive? And, of course, we have the further question: How do we justify a part of the world's population eating strawberries and other luxury fruits and vegetables year round while a majority do not get sufficient corn and beans or rice and peas? The question is especially pertinent since more and more peasants, who do not have enough corn or rice, are growing the luxury crops.

Obviously, the major long-term problems that concern anthropologists are equally important to other social scientists and should be of equal concern to all. So long as policy issues were limited to small-scale problems, especially as they affected peasants in far-off lands, the problems and the solutions could be left to experts. However, since we have found that the long-term issues are connected with our own world, we must recognize that we are part of the problem. Although we may not be able to change much as individuals, we must at least become better aware of policy issues and their global nature.

An Emerging World Political Economy

The relationship between economics and politics is nowhere better illustrated than in the growing problems between the West, including Japan, and what are called Third World countries. As we saw in the chapter on politics, this relationship has its roots in the colonialism that began in the 16th century. The emerging capitalists in Europe, especially England, realized they could use the raw materials of Africa, Asia, and North and South America. They brought these resources to the mother countries and manufactured them into end products such as textiles and other consumer goods. The manufacturing greatly increased the value of the resources which were sold back to the colonies as well as domestically. Everyone was supposed to benefit in the process, but clearly the mother countries benefitted far more than the colonies, while the people with capital benefitted far more than the workers in the factories. Since this system caused much of the dissatisfaction in the American colonies leading to the Revolution of 1776, the United States served as a model for the independence that eventually came to India in 1947 and most of the African nations in the early 1960s.

However, economic independence failed to materialize for these new nations as they continued to be primarily exporters of raw materials and consumers of goods produced elsewhere. Increasingly, they engaged in manufacturing processes that called for much unskilled, tedious labor, such as tying fish hooks. While they had political independence, they realized they had even more economic dependence. It is a situation that causes an increasing gap in wealth between countries described as developed and others described as developing. Since developed nations are mostly in the northern hemisphere, and the developing countries are in Latin America, Africa, and Asia, or the southern hemisphere, the fundamental issues are often described as a North-South problem.

Although the Soviet Union and Eastern Europe are in the north, they are generally omitted from consideration because they have remained relatively uninvolved economically. A major exception has been Cuba which has become economically dependent on the Soviet Union; elsewhere, Soviet interaction with the Third World has been largely in terms of military aid or advice. The Eastern bloc countries are known as the Second World. They have remained relatively isolated from the emerging world economic system, although they are a fundamental part of the political system, centered around the threat of warfare between East and West.

Western investments in the arms race have critically limited the economic aid that might be supplied to the Third World. The 1960s were declared a Decade of Development by the United Nations, and optimistic calls were made for developed countries to devote one percent of the Gross National Product to foreign aid. After debate in the United Nations, a compromise of seven-tenths of one percent was reached. However, only a few of the smaller European countries have regularly contributed even this amount. The United States generally spent about half the goal, and in the early 1980s it has contributed barely over two-tenths of a percent.

Nor has the money been used in ways to promote long-term growth. Initially, most aid was directed at industrialization because developers thought the Third World should copy the course of history taken by the West. Modernized factories were supposed to provide the goods being imported, usually things such as refrigerators and similar consumer goods of the well-to-do. This policy of import substitution did little to improve employment and benefitted primarily a small elite group of Western-oriented upper class. Eventually, developers shifted their goals to agriculture where much labor was needed and increases in wealth generally went to the poorer people.

As this shift in policy was occurring, the United States began to experience a growing deficit in its foreign trade. As Japanese cars, TVs, and other goods from many of the developed countries began to penetrate the U.S. market, this country began to rely more and more on agricultural exports. This need for exports became particularly critical when the price of oil soared. Although food prices climbed steadily as well, the United States saw agricultural productivity anywhere as a competitive threat. Nevertheless, Third World agriculture has not prospered, but it has provided more employment than new industry, and the benefits of improved agriculture have been distributed largely among the poor rather than the wealthy. However, there are some striking exceptions in the process that illustrate how a market economy can disrupt the best intended policy. In Colombia and parts of Latin America, food-producing areas have steadily been converted to the growing of flowers and similar luxury crops. A foreign aid project might actually subsidize this process because Third World nations greatly desire to earn foreign exchange. Local landowners are likely to profit more because of an unusually high demand for flowers in Paris or New York; but, less land for corn and beans means higher prices for food and agricultural laborers rarely share in the profits of cash crops.

The Anthropology of Development

Because of its involvement with economic development since World War II, anthropology has been able to understand what has happened to the political economy of the Third World. It has been a costly process; a pessimist would predict that shortages of energy and nonrenewable resources are so critical that the Third World can never expect to reach the living standard enjoyed by the First World. Yet, some exceptions give the optimist hope for the Third World. Before examining these exceptions, it is useful to look at the overall process, one that can be divided roughly into four stages.

The first stage occurred for most countries at the end of World War II. Because of an oppressive colonial power, all people within the colony were united in resisting the oppressor. Various tactics might be used to obtain independence but everyone agreed upon a goal of national independence. Spirit and trust in the future were high; early leaders were heroes nearing mythological greatness. They are regarded much like Americans respect George Washington.

Once independence was won, however, numerous difficulties arose. Expectations of rapid change and growing wealth were frustrated. Daily life remained much the same, except for proclamations about the greatness of the precolonial past and the postcolonial future. But poverty continued. Splinter groups then asserted they had better answers, and the former unity fragmented. The leaders who spoke of equality and made claims to a special morality were tempted to resort to repression and disregard of civil rights. Minorities were often persecuted.

The process leads into a third stage. At independence, the new nations usually had tried to integrate the democracy of the West with the socialism of the East. The nationalization of industry was accomplished by the government going into debt; the necessary borrowing made inflation rampant. Since government salaries usually rise slowly, graft and corruption frequently became commonplace in the bureaucracy, leading to ever more loss of faith in the new government. Factionalism increases.

Most Third World countries remain in something like the third stage, but a few have changed into what might be described as a fourth stage. Enough development occurs that internal dissention diminishes, although governments are likely to continue harsh repressive measures. The dictatorship of a single leader is diffused among a larger group, and there is increasing emphasis on such things as education, science, and management techniques. It was only in the 1970s that a half dozen countries, such as North and South Korea or Taiwan and Cuba, seemed to be moving into this stage of development. They suggest that two quite different paths are open to development, though both have in common a stress on equity in sharing the new wealth.

Interestingly, one model is socialist and the other is capitalist. Cuba and China illustrate the first. They concentrated their resources in education, a minimal but universal health care, and food production and distribution that gave everyone enough to eat. By traditional measurements of development that rely on economic indicators, such as per capita income or growth rates in the GNP, these countries do not stand out. But, another measurement of development is the Physical Quality of Life Index, a statistic composed of literacy rates, infant mortality, and life expectancy at the age of one. Cuba, China, and a few other countries such as Sri Lanka have developed on the basis of this index. South Korea and Taiwan offer a model for capitalistic development. The high amounts of economic aid given them by the United States are doubtless a factor in their development, but their rapid growth started largely after U.S. aid ended. Their method was to concentrate on production for export, and they reinvested almost all profits in further capital development. Once an industrial base was created, they redistributed resources into the countryside. Thus, no major differences between city and countryside grew in the distribution of wealth.

It is true, of course, that some capitalists in Taiwan and Korea have immense wealth while a political elite in China and Cuba have access to creature comforts unimagined by the masses; but, aside from these exceptions, the nations' wealth is fairly reasonably distributed otherwise. Equity, then, seems to be a main key to development. Unfortunately, if it is a vital key, it is lacking throughout most of Latin America, much of Africa, and in some important countries in Asia.

Development and the Arms Race

Equally important in development is the necessity to invest in human and technological capital. Basic education, health, and nutrition needs must be met along with the creation of basic industries and improvements in agriculture. It is now obvious that foreign aid programs are only of minor help in financing these necessities; they must be met largely by each nation itself. It is equally obvious that the Third World countries do not have the resources both to finance this development and to purchase modern arms from the developed countries. Yet, the arms race is just as dramatic in the Third World as it is between the superpowers.

At the time of independence in the early 1960s, Third World countries were spending about $1.5 billion a year on arms purchases from the developed countries. In 1970, the figure had increased to $2.5 billion. Largely because of the wealth generated from oil, Third World spending jumped to $8 billion by 1977, a figure that reflects steady increases in most countries and dramatic increases in the Near East. The effects of the arms purchases were dramatically illustrated in the war between Argentina and England over the Falklands or Maldivas. In a matter of seconds, millions of dollars of destruction occurred, not to mention the number of lives lost. Such consumption of wealth can be stated in less dramatic, but still essential, terms. Adequate education, health, and housing could be provided for the world's poor for about $18 billion a year. Presently it is difficult to see where such a large amount of money could be raised, but it is about what the world spends on arms every two weeks. In just two days, the world spends on weapons what it budgets for the United Nations and its agencies for a year.

Third World nations sometimes defend their military spending by claiming it creates jobs and otherwise helps the economy. Over the long run, however, such spending does not contribute to capital investment because it causes shortages in its use of labor and resources. It demands skilled labor and often depends on rare resources. The result is inflation, and the inflation rates in most Third World countries make U.S. inflation appear insignificant. A 100 percent rate of inflation has occurred in some countries at a fairly regular pace, and frequently rates of 500 to 1,000 percent are recorded. Elsewhere, rates of 20 to 30 percent have become commonplace. One consequence of inflation is to create greater inequity because the poor regularly suffer more than the rich from rapidly rising prices. Such growing inequity makes development even more difficult.

Conclusion

Since the arms race is such a significant factor in development, anthropology has found itself steadily moving farther and farther from its traditional domain of the small community and farther from its traditional concepts. At its onset, applied anthropologists thought they could work within the fairly narrow confines of a community or a region. Their goal was thought to be discovery of principles that could be used to help make acceptable basic innovations in health, education, and agriculture. In less than a decade, they discovered that such principles could never apply separately from policy that was taking place at a national and even international level. It was not enough to study a single community or to limit oneself to customary subjects such as kinship, ritual, or symbolic thought. More and more concepts of economics and international relations have to be incorporated into anthropological thinking if anthropologists are to be effective at public policy making.

Glossary

Acculturation: The process of change that occurs when two or more cultures come into contact (see Chapter 7). Acculturation is a greater degree of diffusion. In the two or more cultures it is, of course, people who exchange ways of doing things. The influence always has effects on all the people involved, though a subordinated people are more likely to be changed, and to a greater extent, than a dominant group.

Acheulean: A tradition of making a fist-ax (see Chapter 5). In the Acheulean tradition a stone is chipped on both sides; this bifacial treatment gives it symmetry and a long cutting edge.

Age Grades: The formal organization of age divisions within a society (see Chapter 9). Age grades are named and usually have totem-like symbols. Organization by age grades is common in East Africa.

Agriculture and Anthropology: A unique view of agriculture that ranges from the Neolithic to contemporary peasants and modern farmers (see Chapter 12). Anthropologists are particularly interested in the cultural setting of agriculture.

Animism: A theory about the origin of religion (see Chapter 11). Edward Tylor proposed that religion arose from human efforts to explain what occurred in dreams or trance. The spiritual part of the body that left it in dreams and death became the basis for a supernatural world animated by spirits.

Associations: Groups with voluntary membership (see Chapter 9). Associations limit their membership by rules and members are not born into such groups, as they are in lineages. Associations are like kin groups in many respects, but they are not based on kinship.

Australopithecines: Fossil hominids from the early Pleistocene (see Chapter 2). The term, Australopithecine, is for the sub-family taxon. Its use avoids the issue of whether there is more than one genus.

Band: A type of society with little division beyond age and sex (see Chapter 10). Relations among band members are equalitarian. Leaders have no power to enforce decisions.

Bilateral: The organization of kin on the basis of tracing descent through both sexes (see Chapter 9). Bilateral descent equates mother's relatives with father's relatives in contrast to unilineal descent, which favors one sex over the other.

Brachiation: A method of locomotion by the forearms, swinging hand by hand from one branch to another (see Chapter 2). The Great Apes have an anatomy that suggests they are brachiators. In fact, they spend most of their time on the ground, except for the gibbon, who is an expert brachiator.

Chromosomes: The material within all cells forming a nucleus (see Chapter 2). In the sex cells the chromosomes serve as a blueprint for the biological development of offspring. In humans the blueprint has evolved to give organisms great potential for learning to behave in nonbiological ways.

Civilization: Large, technologically sophisticated, and highly regulated cultures (see Chapter 6). Anthropologists often equate urbanism with civilization and concentrate on the origins of urban states, especially before writing began.

Clan: A grouping of two or more lineages (see Chapter 9). Clan members claim descent from a common ancestor, but they do not know all the links. The ancestor is often mythical or has superhuman characteristics.

Cognitive Anthropology: A field that determines how people perceive their world (see Chapter 11). To date, emphasis has been upon the kinds of categories other peoples form, especially in kinship.

Communication: The means by which animals convey their feelings to others (see Chapters 3 and 7). Nonhumans communicate by signs, many of which are nonvocal. Human communication is primarily vocal, although nonvocal communication does exist and is more important than we usually recognized. Human vocalization is symbolic; the symbols convey more than feeling and are arbitrary sounds for what is expressed.

Comparative: A major characteristic of anthropology (see Chapter 1; see also, *Cross-cultural comparison*). Much of anthropology consists of comparing one culture to another in order to understand differences. The comparison of differences has led to generalizations about the similarities among all cultures.

Cross-cultural Comparison: The approach of cultural anthropology to understanding a practice by seeing it in a number of cultures (see Chapter 7). A trait selected for analysis can be treated as an independent variable; the importance of dependent variables can be found by looking at their association in a variety of contexts (i.e., cultures).

Cultural Ecology: The perspective that culture must be understood as adaptive (see Chapter 8). This view has emphasized that culture practices must be understood according to their relation to the environment, as well as to each other.

Cultural Lag: The difference between change in material and non-material culture (see Chapter 7). Considerable support exists for the theory that change is inherent in technology or material culture, but not in non-material culture. As a result the latter usually lags behind the former.

Culture: The nongenetic or learned ways in which humans adapt (see Chapters 1 and 7). The learning and sharing involved in culture means that it can be equated with tradition and examined as history as well as adaptation. The interrelatedness or wholeness of culture also means that anthropology may make use of methods from the humanities to illustrate this major concept.

Culture Area: A grouping of similar cultures within a geographic region (see Chapter 8). This taxonomy of cultures makes it possible to catalog the variety of cultures on a continent into fairly simple schemes, but the principles for grouping have been largely subjective.

Dental Arch: The overall pattern of the teeth (see Chapter 2). In hominids the dental arch forms a parabola; in pongids the molars are parallel to each other.

Descent: The belief that there is a special social relationship between parents and offspring (see Chapter 9). It must be stressed that descent is a cultural phenomenon and not the recognition of a biological fact.

Diffusion: The spread or borrowing of culture traits between cultures (see Chapter 7; see also, *Acculturation*). The explanation of why a people have a particular culture trait because it has diffused from elsewhere leads to an historical method.

Dominance: A ranking among many nonhuman primates that results in group stability (see Chapter 3). Dominance seems to arise largely from the play activity of young animals. It is usually striking among males but occurs also among females. Female dominance may affect relations among their young.

Enculturation: The process by which a child learns its culture (see Chapter 7). The learn-

ing of a first culture differs from learning later cultures; therefore, the term acculturation should apply only to this latter situation. Enculturation is what happens as an infant or child is exposed to its first experience with culture.

Endogamy: Marriage within a group (see Chapter 9). Endogamy is most often associated
with castes.

Ethnocentrism: The norms a people hold about their superiority over other peoples (see
Chapter 7). Most norms in a culture are learned very early, so that people take them to
be a part of human nature; thus, other ways of behaving are inhuman.

Ethology: The study of animal behavior (see Chapter 9). Ethology stems largely from biology, but the study of primate behavior has been a joint venture between anthropology
and zoology. Ethology is now often termed sociobiology.

Evolution: A process of change from simple to complex (see Chapter 2). Evolution is seen
in both biology and culture. Biological evolution can be accounted for by natural selection, mutation, and genetic drift. Corresponding explanations for cultural or social
evolution have not yet been found, but a course of cultural evolution is evident.

Exogamy: Marriage outside of a group (see Chapter 9). Exogamy is most often associated
with the rule that members of a descent group marry out of it, but other groups may
also be exogamous. Exogamy is a rule about marriage, not about sex relations.

Extended Family: The inclusion of other relatives with a nuclear family (see Chapter 9).
The nuclear family is most often extended by co-wives or relatives of either the husband or wife.

Form: The physical shape or properties of a cultural trait (see Chapter 7; see also, *Meaning
and Function*). The form of a trait is easily recognized and diffuses readily. Meanings
and functions of a trait are more subtle.

Function: Either what a trait does to satisfy some need or how a trait is tied to other traits
(see Chapter 7). A trait is expected to have many functions both in satisfying needs and
in relating to other traits. The functions of a trait are both manifest—apparent to the
people—and latent—discovered by the social scientist.

Functionalism: A theory stating that societies resemble a biological organism in that the
parts must be understood in relation to the whole (see Chapters 7 and 11). Functional
analysis concentrated on the description of the fit of traits to each other and avoided
explanation in terms of diffusion or history and cause and effect.

Gene Flow: The passage of genes from one population to another (see Chapter 2). The
different populations must be of the same species. When the exchange of genes is on a
major scale, it may be termed hybridization.

Genes: Segments or points on chromosomes (see Chapter 2; see also, *Chromosomes*). The
nature of the gene is understood by an analysis of the properties of deoxyribonucleic
acid.

Holism: A particular characteristic of anthropology (see Chapter 1; see also, *Functionalism*). Anthropology's presentation of communities in their totalities contrasts with
other social sciences in their concentrations on parts, such as economics or political
science. The holism of anthropology has allied it traditionally with the humanities.

Homo erectus: A fossil hominid existing from about 1 million to 250,000 years ago (see
Chapter 3). The largest brained erectus falls within the range of modern hominids.

Homo habilis: A fossil hominid contemporary with the Australopithecines (see Chapter 3).
The larger brain case suggests that the fossil should be in the genus Homo rather than
Australopithecus.

Horticulture: Agricultural systems based on a simple technology (see Chapter 8). The ax,
digging stick, and hoe are usually associated with horticulture, or horticulture may be
thought of as shifting cultivation involving the use of fallow lands. Generally horticulture produces low returns per unit of land but high returns per unit of labor.

Incest: Intercourse between siblings or between parents and children (see Chapter 9). The
regulation of incest indirectly governs marriage; that is, prohibits it. Exogamy is a rule

that directly regulates marriage by requiring members to marry outside of their group.

Involution: Change in culture leading to overelaboration (see Chapter 8). The term was first used for art styles and applies to many developments often called post-classic. Intensity of style leads to a decline in esthetic value. Most recently, the term has been applied to particular kinds of agricultural development, such as those in some colonial empires.

Kindred: A group of close bilateral kin (see Chapter 9). One's siblings and parents, and the parent's siblings and their children comprise the kindred. Since only siblings share the same kindred, the kindred can satisfy only individual needs; it cannot act as a corporate group.

Language: The use of symbols to communicate (see Chapter 7). Symbols are sounds or gestures with arbitrary meaning; a sound often has several meanings. Symbolic use allows conditional thinking–putting events in the past and future, as well as present.

Lineage: The kin group that arises with unilineal descent (see Chapter 9). Lineages can be either matrilineal or patrilineal. Members of a lineage are all descended from a common ancestor with the links being exclusively of one sex.

Magic: Deliberate attempts to control the supernatural (see Chapter 11). The deliberateness of magic is contrasted with the helplessness of religious expression. The distinction is logically sound, but of little use in examining many practices that are a combination of the two.

Mana: A Polynesian word for supernatural force (see Chapter 11). Mana is neither evil nor good; it can be used to express either force. Mana seems often to be the basis for making something sacred.

Market: The exchange of goods based on relative value of the goods (see Chapter 8). Market exchange contrasts with reciprocity. In the former the value of the goods determines their exchange; in reciprocity social relations determine the exchange. Both systems, however, involve decisions about how to allocate valued resources.

Marriage: The union between men and women, which give offspring a legitimate father (see Chapter 9). Marriage practices vary so widely that there is controversy over its definition.

Matrifocal Family: A family in which the father is often absent (see Chapter 9). An adult male status is filled by the wife's brother or father while the biological father is absent, as in migratory work.

Meaning: The way in which a people interpret or see a trait (see Chapter 7; see also, *Form and Function*). The meanings of a trait may vary within a society according to factors such as age, sex, or specialty. Cross-culturally the meanings for a trait are expected to vary greatly.

Method: Anthropological approaches to describing a community (see Chapter 7). The various methods have been divided into: historical, ecological, social-structural, personality and culture, and world view.

Moieties: A dual organization of society (see Chapter 9). Other groupings may comprise a moiety, or a society may simply be organized into two parts. In either case, the moieties show a balanced opposition regardless of relative population.

Morpheme: The unit of sound that has a lexical or dictionary meaning (see Chapter 7). Free morphemes are words. Bound morphemes must be attached to free morphemes, at the beginning, end, or within. They have a meaning, like the "s" in English, which means more than one, or the "a" or "o" in Spanish, which indicate gender.

Mutation: A spontaneous change in a gene, which permanently remains (see Chapter 2). Chemicals, heat, and X-rays cause mutations; other factors may be involved also. Independent invention or discovery is often cited as a cultural evolutionary analogy.

Natural Selection: The process, discovered by Darwin, by which some members of a population pass on greater amounts of their inheritable material than others (see Chapter 2). In simplest terms natural selection is simply differential reproduction. Because of variation in any population, some individuals are more favored than others to reproduce. The favored traits are dependent on particular conditions.

Neanderthal, Neandertal: A fossil hominid first appearing about 200,000 years ago (see Chapter 3). Cranial capacity or brain size is about the same as modern humans. Neanderthals are usually regarded as a subspecies of Homo sapiens. A gracile form is nearly identical to sapiens; a classic or robust form raises questions about a proper species designation.

Neolithic: Literally, the "New Stone Age" (see Chapter 6). Polished stones were characteristic, but the major feature of the period was the change from food collecting to food producing. Domestication of plants and animals is the essential feature of the Neolithic.

Norms: The rules for behavior (see Chapters 7 and 8). Norms are mental guidelines that allow people to expect much of the same behavior from other people. Some agreement on what is "proper" behavior seems essential for human society.

Nuclear Family: Parents and offspring (see Chapter 9). Husband, wife, and children usually, but not always, form a household or domestic group. When other relatives are included in the household the unit is described as an extended family.

Nutritional Anthropology: The cross-cultural study of diets and cuisines to discover the variety of ways that meet nutritional needs (see Chapter 12).

Oldowan: A tradition of making a stone tool associated with Australopithecine (see Chapter 5). A pebble or smoothed stone is broken at one end to produce a cutting edge.

Paleolithic: Literally, the "Old Stone Age" (see Chapter 5). The Paleolithic is divided into Lower, consisting of Oldowan and Acheulean, and associated with Australopithecine and erectus; Middle, consisting of Mousterian, which is associated with Neandertal; and Upper, consisting of many geographically different traditions, associated with Homo sapiens.

Participation-Observation: A basic technique of anthropological research and fieldwork (see Chapter 7). Individuals vary widely in their degree of either participation or observation. The method of technique is dependent in great degree on the personality and training of the researcher.

Phone: The minimal unit of sound (see Chapter 7). Phones are combined into phonemes, which give a kind of meaning. In English, three different phones represented by "P" as in pin, spin, and lamp may combine to make a phoneme.

Phoneme: The minimal unit of sound that carries a meaning (see Chapter 7). The meaning is not a lexical or dictionary meaning, but a set of sounds that are recognized by the ear as one sound. (For an example, see *Phone.*)

Pithecanthropus erectus: An older term for Homo erectus. The name was given to a discovery in Java (see *Homo erectus*).

Pleistocene: The past 2 to 3 million year geological epoch (see Chapter 3). The epoch is known as the age of humans. Possibly the hominids originated earlier, but the most important developments occurred in the Pleistocene.

Polyandry: The practice of a woman marrying two or more men (see Chapter 9). The men are often brothers and the practice may be described as fraternal polyandry. In Tibet one of the best known examples is found. The practice is rare.

Polygyny: The practice of a man marrying several women (see Chapter 9). If the co-wives are sisters, the practice is sororal polygyny. Polygyny is quite common among societies, although it may be rare even when allowed.

Pongid, Pongidae: The family of the Great Apes (see Chapter 3). The present day members are the orangutan, gorilla, and chimpanzee. The gibbon may be included, but is sometimes classified in a separate family.

Prestation: The goods involved in reciprocal exchange (see Chapter 8). Since "gift" or "present" in English connote a free giving with no obligation, at least overtly, anthropologists prefer prestation as the goods that invoke some obligation between donor and receiver.

Priest: Individuals who receive training in order to control mana (see Chapter 11). Priests are enforced by elaborate ritual and group performances of the priesthood. Their activities are usually for community welfare, while shamans are concerned with individuals.

Primate Behavior: Its study among nonhumans provides analogies for what early human behavior may have been (see Chapter 3). The study of nonhuman behavior in the wild has shown the study of behavior in captivity to be misleading.

Primates: The order of animals characterized by a prehensile grip and forearm with great strength and unusual flexibility (see Chapter 3). Most primates also have stereoscopic vision, two breasts, and give birth to single offspring. The suborder Prosimii includes lemurs and tarsiers; the suborder Anthropoidea includes New World Monkeys, Old World Monkeys, Great Apes, and Humans.

Race: A population within a species that differs from corresponding divisions (see Chapter 4). Descriptions of races should take into account the fact that they are populations and cannot be represented by a single physical type.

Ramapithecus: A hominoid fossil of the Miocene (see Chapter 3). The molars are not parallel and the size of the teeth resemble hominids. Ramapithecus may be a candidate for the earliest hominid, although positive verification is dependent upon the discovery of further skeletal remains.

Ranking: Differences in prestige among individuals (see Chapter 10). When inequalities are evident at the individual level, a society is said to be ranked; when the inequality involves groupings of people, a society is stratified.

Reciprocity: Mutual interrelations (see Chapter 8). Status relations are maintained on the basis of reciprocity. The mutual exchange of goods and services is a concrete expression of reciprocal relations.

Redistribution: The exchange of goods or services directed by a central authority (see Chapter 8). A group or person commands the flow of goods, which in turn contributes to the power of those in control.

Residence Rules: Norms specifying where a newly married couple should reside (see Chapter 9). When a couple lives with the groom's group, the rule is patrilocal. If the couple should establish a new residence, the rule is neolocal.

Shaman: An individual who suddenly acquires the ability to control mana (see Chapter 11). Shamans often demonstrate their special qualities by psychosomatic means or other impressive feats.

Sinanthropus: An older term for Homo erectus. The name was given to a fossil discovered near Peking, China (see *Homo erectus*).

Social Evolution: A theory that societies change in a way analogous to biological organisms (see Chapters 6 and 11). The anthropology of the late nineteenth century was developed on the perspective of social evolution; the theory has been revised in the twentieth century. Evolution contrasts with history with the former seeking generalization while the latter emphasizes the particular.

State: A type of society where central authority overrides kinship as a means of organization (see Chapter 10). State societies are characterized also by large size, diversity, and stratification.

Stratification: Differences in prestige among groups within a society (see Chapter 10; see also, *Ranking*). Differences in prestige mean that differences will also occur in control over power or production of goods. The groups that differ are called social classes.

Structuralism: A theory suggesting that societies are patterned because of the way in which the mind perceives reality (see Chapters 7 and 11). The theory of structuralism is largely the product of Claude Lévi-Strauss, who sees the working of the mind particularly in kinship, totemism, and mythology.

Syntax: A combination of morphemes (see Chapter 7). Syntax is often described as the "stringing of morphemes." The study of syntax involves determining how meaning is expressed by the relationship of morphemes within a string.

Taboo: A Polynesian word now used to mean a proscription (see Chapter 11). Taboos are norms implying an avoidance usually associated with strong feelings.

Tribe: A type of society in which unity is provided by common language and culture, but not by any overall political organization (see Chapter 10). Unlike bands, tribes do have some political control vested in the heads of lineages. These power sources may be linked through interlineage marriage or through other means.

Unilineal: The organization of kin on the basis of tracing descent through only one of the sexes (see Chapter 9; see also *Bilateral*). Where descent is determined through females, the lines are matrilineal; where descent is derived through males, the lines are patrilineal.

Urban Anthropology: A division of applied anthropology that focuses on cities, especially in developing countries but also often on life in Western cities (see Chapter 12). Urban anthropology is a rapidly growing field that expands the techniques of study of the small community to segments of the city.

Index